THE LINCOLN NOBODY KNOWS

THE LINCOLN NOBODY KNOWS

RICHARD N. CURRENT

American Century Series

HILL AND WANG · NEW YORK

Standard Book Number (paperback edition) 8090–0059–8

Library of Congress catalog card number 58-12994

Manufactured in the United States of America

FIRST AMERICAN CENTURY SERIES EDITION FEBRUARY 1963

To my mother and my father

ABOUT THE AUTHOR

Born in Colorado City, Colorado, in 1912, Richard N. Current was educated at Oberlin College, Tufts University, and the University of Wisconsin. Among other places, he has taught at the universities of Illinois, North Carolina (the Woman's College), and Wisconsin, where he is Professor of History. He has lectured in Japan, India, and Germany, where he was Fulbright Lecturer at the University of Munich. In 1962-63 he was Harmsworth Professor of American History at Oxford University.

Author of six books, many articles and reviews and co-author of three books, Mr. Current was awarded the Bancroft Prize in 1956 for *Lincoln the President: Last Full Measure,* written in collaboration with the late J. G. Randall. Though best known for his writings on nineteenth-century American history and biography, Mr. Current has also written about the invention of the typewriter (*The Typewriter and the Men Who Made It*) and twentieth-century diplomacy (*Secretary Stimson: A Study in Statecraft*).

FOREWORD

The title for this book is adapted, with thanks and apologies, from Bruce Barton's illuminating work of thirty years ago, *The Man Nobody Knows,* in which he revealed to an amazed world that Jesus was essentially a good advertising man. I fear, however, that I do not possess the confidence in my own interpretations that Mr. Barton has in his. Abraham Lincoln, despite the wealth of words written by him and about him, remains in many ways a mysterious man. There is no formula which will reveal, once and for all, the whole truth about *The Lincoln Nobody Knows.* My purpose is, rather, to set forth several enigmas of his life, several issues which historians and biographers still dispute. On occasion, I advance conclusions of my own, but only on the understanding that they represent fallible opinion rather than incontrovertible fact. For my assumption is that, on issues where competent authorities differ, the questions cannot really be answered, no matter how positive individual experts may be.

These pages do not constitute a biography. They do not pretend to outline Lincoln's character or career as a whole. They concentrate upon selected, controversial phases of the subject. For example, they deal only with a few aspects of Lincoln as family man, Lincoln as politician, Lincoln as war leader, Lincoln as peacemaker. The treatment of such topics may seem as unfair as it is incomplete, unless the reader bears in mind that for every chapter of this book many volumes could be written—and have been.

This, then, is an essay in the uncertain, the undecided, the unknown. I hope it will stimulate the reader to look at many more books on Lincoln and his times, and to look at all of them (this one too) with a heightened sense of healthy caution. I hope also that, by the very process of calling attention to what is not known for sure, the book will add at least a little to the reader's understanding of that enigmatic man, Abraham Lincoln.

R.N.C.

Greensboro, North Carolina

chapter 1

THE MOST SHUT-MOUTHED MAN

His face is as familiar as the penny or the five-dollar bill. Every American has some idea of what he looked like. And yet it is not easy to visualize Abraham Lincoln as he actually was.

There is no lack of records to document his personal appearance. Photographers, among them the famous Mathew B. Brady, focused their cameras on him so often, during the eight years of his national prominence, that he became the most photographed person of his time. Pictures of him in about a hundred different poses are still available. Artists painted him from life, some of them carefully measuring him to get his exact physical dimensions. Sculptors modeled him in clay or stone, and Leonard W. Volk made a plaster cast of his face, a "life mask," and another of his hands. His clothing sizes (he wore a 7⅛ hat) are on record, as is the shape of his feet: he once stood on a piece of paper and drew outlines to send with an order for custom-made boots. Friends and strangers—people who knew him well and people who saw him only once—left detailed word-portraits of him.

And Lincoln described himself. "If any personal description of me is thought desirable," he wrote, in providing material for an 1860 campaign biography, "it may be said I am, in height, six feet four inches, nearly; lean in flesh, weighing on an average one hundred and eighty pounds; dark complexion, with coarse black hair and gray eyes."

That laconic self-description, accurate though it is, fails to suggest the strange and striking effect his appearance had. He was an original. As the London *Times* correspondent William Howard Russell remarked after seeing him for the first time, "It would not be possible for the most indifferent observer to pass him in the street without notice."

His figure (as many an observer saw him) was so proportioned that he seemed taller than he was, especially when he wore his high silk hat. His head, atop a long, scraggy neck with a conspicuous Adam's apple, appeared to be small for the rest of him. His chest was thin and narrow in comparison with the long, bony arms that hung at his side, the giant's hands, the long, bony legs, the oversized feet.

His height was mostly in those legs. When he sat down he was no taller than others sitting with him. His knees projected upward, as if the chair were too low for him. "A marble placed on his knee thus sitting would roll hipward, down an inclined plane," his onetime law partner William H. Herndon noted. "It was only when he stood up that he towered above other men."

He stood with a slight stoop and walked with a firm and even tread. "He steps slowly and deliberately, almost always with his head inclined forward and his hands clasped behind his back," a *Chicago Tribune* reporter wrote. Herndon, who had more opportunities to observe, put the matter more precisely as well as more picturesquely: "... the inner sides of his feet were parallel, if not a little pigeontoed. He did not walk cunningly—Indian like, but cautiously & firmly. In walking, Mr. Lincoln put the whole foot flat down on the ground at once, not landing on the heel. He lifted his foot all at once—not lifting himself from the toes, and hence had no spring or snap . . . to his walk."

He was described as loose-jointed, slow of movement, and creaky, like a piece of machinery in need of oiling. Indeed, he struck many people as clumsy, his elongated arms and legs always getting in his way, though he was athletic enough in some respects. "Physically, he was a very—very powerful man, lifting with ease 400—or 600 pounds," Herndon stated. With one hand he could take the end of the helve, raise a woodsman's heavy ax, and hold it straight out at arm's length. He never quite lost the agility that had served him well as a wrestler in his youth. His body remained lean, sinewy, muscular, hard. "The strongest man I ever looked at," recalled an Illinoisan who had helped him with his bath when he was in Galesburg to debate with Stephen A. Douglas (1858).

However impressive he may have been in the natural state, in clothes he looked (to several observers) like a scarecrow or a dressed-up skeleton. "In matters of dress he is by no means precise," said the *Chicago Tribune* reporter. "Always clean, he is never fashionable; he is careless but not slovenly." But, according to English journalist Edward Dicey, his suit was unfashionably tight, creased in the wrong places, and also soiled. Besides, the pants were too short and the gloves too long—too long even for his bony fingers. Nathaniel Hawthorne commented on the "shabby slippers" and the "rusty black frock coat and pantaloons." Clothes unmade the man.

Until his fifty-first year he was clean-shaven. Then an eleven-year-old girl in Troy, New York, wrote to him, as the Republican presidential candidate, with the suggestion that he wear a beard. In reply he asked (October 19, 1860): "As to the whiskers, never having worn any, do you not think people would call it a piece of silly affectation if I were to begin it now?"

Nevertheless, begin it he did. No President ever had been so adorned, but beards were becoming stylish. Lincoln, while making a concession to style, and to an unknown girl's whim, may have reasoned that a new face would be appropriate to the coming of a new party into power. He might have been glad for an excuse to cover up, as well as he could, a countenance of which he long had been a bit self-conscious.

A couple of years before starting the beard he had referred in public, in his self-deprecating way, to his "poor lean, lank face." His nose was prominent and slightly askew, with "the tip glowing in red," as Herndon noticed. His heavy eyebrows overhung deep eye-caverns in which his eyes—sometimes dreamy, sometimes penetrating—were set. His cheekbones were high, his cheeks rather sunken, his mouth wide, his lips thick, especially the lower one, and his chin upturned. On the right cheek, near his mouth, a solitary mole stood out. His skin was sallow, leathery, wrinkled, dry, giving him a weather-beaten look. He had projecting—some said flapping—ears. His hair was thick and unruly, stray locks falling across his forehead.

The foregoing list of traits hardly adds up to a flattering sum. The physical Lincoln, the external man, was made for caricature, was the delight of cartoonists. But there was more, far more, to Lincoln's appearance than all this. He cannot fairly be depicted by a mere catalogue of his peculiarities. Upon the people he met, he made an impression which no such inventory can convey.

At first glance, some thought him grotesque, even ugly, and almost everyone considered him homely. When preoccupied or in repose he certainly was far from handsome. At times he looked unutterably sad, as if every sorrow were his own, or he looked merely dull, with a vacant gaze. Still, as even the caustic Englishman Dicey observed, there was, for all his grotesqueness, "an air of strength, physical as well as moral, and a strange look of dignity" about him. And when he spoke a miracle occurred. "The dull, listless features dropped like a mask," according to Horace White, an editor of the *Chicago Tribune*.

"The eyes began to sparkle, the mouth to smile, the whole countenance was wreathed in animation, so that a stranger would have said, 'Why, this man, so angular and somber a moment ago, is really handsome.' " He was "the homeliest man I ever saw," said Donn Piatt, and yet there was something about the face that Piatt never forgot. "It brightened, like a lit lantern, when animated."

Here was a Lincoln the camera never caught. When he went to the studio and sat before the lens he invariably relapsed into his sad, dull, abstracted mood. No wonder. He had to sit absolutely still, with his head against the photographer's rack, while the tedious seconds ticked by. It took time to get an image with the slow, wet-plate process of those days. There was then no candid camera, no possibility of taking snapshots which might have recorded Lincoln at his sparkling best. "I have never seen a picture of him that does anything like justice to the original," said Henry Villard, the *New York Herald* reporter. "He is a much better looking man than any of the pictures represent."

The portrait painters were hardly more successful. "Lincoln's features were the despair of every artist who undertook his portrait," his private secretary John G. Nicolay declared. A painter might measure the subject, scrutinize him in sitting after sitting, and eventually produce a likeness of a sort. But "this was not he who smiled, spoke, laughed, charmed," said Nicolay. The poet Walt Whitman commented after getting a close-up view: "None of the artists or pictures have caught the subtle and indirect expression of this man's face." And again, some years after Lincoln's death: "Though hundreds of portraits have been made, by painters and photographers (many to pass on, by copies, to future times), I have never seen one yet that in my opinion deserved to be called a perfectly *good likeness;* nor do I believe there is really such a one in existence."

The word pictures do much to supply what the photographs and paintings missed, yet these descriptions also fail to show the man complete. All who tried to describe him admitted that the phenomenal mobility and expressiveness of his features, the reflections of his complex and wide-ranging personality, were beyond the power of words. "The tones, the gestures, the kindling eye, and the mirth-provoking look defy the reporter's skill," the reporter Noah Brooks confessed after seeing Lincoln deliver the Cooper Union speech (1860).

Beyond a certain point Lincoln's appearance not only defied description; it also baffled interpretation. "There is something in the face which I cannot understand," said Congressman Henry L. Dawes of Massachusetts. And the leader of German-Americans in Illinois, Gustave Koerner, remarked: "Something about the man, the face, is unfathomable."

In his looks there were hints of mysteries within.

2

Some aspects of his inner self he revealed in his voluminous writings. His published words add up to an impressive total. It once was estimated that they numbered 1,078,365 in comparison with 1,025,000 for the complete works of Shakespeare and 926,877 for the entire Bible, including the Apocrypha. That estimate was made before the publication (in 1953) of the eight volumes of Lincoln's *Collected Works,* which contain nearly twice as many items as previously were in print.

These items are amazing in their variety. They range from formal and official communications, which tell nothing about the man himself, to personal correspondence in which he opened his mind and heart, though never all the way. And they range from the most eloquent of his state papers, with haunting strains like those of the Second Inaugural ("with malice toward none, with charity for all"), to such bits of foolery as the one he wrote out for a court bailiff in Springfield. "He said he was riding *bass-ackwards* on a *jass-ack,* through a *patton-cotch,* on a pair of *baddle-sags,* stuffed full of *binger-gred,* when the animal *steered* at a *scump,* and the *lirrup-steather* broke, and throwed him in the *forner* of the *kence* and broke his *pishing-fole,*" this little-known piece of Lincolnian nonsense goes. "He said, about *bray-dake* he came to himself, ran home, seized up a *stick of wood* and split the *axe* to make a light, rushed into the house, and found the *door* sick abed, and his *wife* standing open."

Thus Lincoln could play with words, and he could also use them to convey ideas with the utmost precision, or to stir the spirit with subtle and deathless overtones. He must rank as the most gifted writer among American statesmen of all time. Of the other Presidents, only Thomas Jefferson and Woodrow Wilson could be compared with him in powers of literary self-expression, and surely at his best he surpassed them both.

These powers of his are the more remarkable in view of the fact that he was one of the most poorly educated and least widely read of all public men in American history. While he read comparatively few things, he turned again and again to certain favorites, among them the tragedies and histories of Shakespeare and some of the books of the Bible, especially the Old Testament. These he greatly admired, and they left their marks upon his literary style. Still, the one piece of literature he was fondest of, the one he most wished he had written himself, was neither in the Bible nor in Shakespeare's works. He did not even know the author's name (it was William Knox, a Scottish poet who remains undistinguished and unremembered except as the author of Lincoln's favorite poem). But he knew the lines by heart. The first and last of the twelve stanzas ran:

Oh! why should the spirit of mortal be proud?
Like a swift-flitting meteor, a fast-flying cloud,
A flash of the lightning, a break of the wave,
He passes from life to his rest in the grave.

. . . .

'Tis the wink of an eye, 'tis the draught of a breath—
From the blossom of health to the paleness of death,
From the gilded saloon to the bier and the shroud;
Oh! why should the spirit of mortal be proud?

"I am not the author," Lincoln explained, regretfully, to a friend to whom he had sent a copy of the verses in 1846. "I would give all I am worth, and go in debt, to be able to write so fine a piece as I think that is." A fellow lawyer who had ridden with him on the Illinois circuit recalled his sitting before the dying embers of a fireplace at the day's end and reciting the lines which the lawyer thought were "a reflex in poetic form of the deep melancholy of his soul." Years later, on a windy, rainy night during the war, a congressman and an actor called at the White House and discussed Shakespeare's plays with the President. After four hours the visitors made ready to go—it was eleven-thirty—but Lincoln held them as he talked on about anonymous but genuine poetry. "There is one such poem that is my almost constant companion," he said; "indeed, I may say it is continually present with me, as it crosses my mind whenever I have relief from anxiety." He proceeded to quote several of the stanzas, then asked his guests to be sure to let him know if they ever learned the author's name.

Lincoln tried his own hand at poetry in the same Gothic style. In 1844, after revisiting for the first and only time the Indiana scenes of his boyhood, he composed a long string of quatrains which began as follows:

My childhood's home I see again,
And sadden with the view;
And still, as memory crowds my brain,
There's pleasure in it too.

O Memory! thou midway world
'Twixt earth and paradise,
Where things decayed and loved ones lost
In dreamy shadows rise,

And, freed from all that's earthly vile,
Seem hallowed, pure, and bright,
Like scenes in some enchanted isle
All bathed in liquid light.

With this effort, it might be said, Lincoln achieved his ambition of writing a poem at least as fine as the one he so much admired, though he would not have agreed.

He was something of a frustrated poet. It is one of the lesser ironies of his career that he failed (as he thought) to write as well as an obscure Scottish versifier—and succeeded in writing some of the most poetic prose in the English language.

His best ideas and finest phrases did not occur in impromptu speeches. In public he seldom was ready with words. Once, when asked to address an unexpected crowd of serenaders at the White House, he told Congressman Reuben E. Fenton he did not know what to say, and asked him to make a few remarks first, to give him "a peg to hang on." When Lincoln at last spoke, he made a few commonplace statements, then referred to General William T. Sherman, who was on his way from Atlanta to the sea and had not been heard from. "We all know where Sherman went in," he said, "but none of us know where he will come out." The crowd laughed and cheered, so he decided it was time to quit, and he did. He had talked for about two minutes, and he had nothing more to say.

His long-remembered sayings were written and rewritten with meticulous revisions ahead of time. Some resulted from a slow gestation of thought and phrase through many years. One of his recurring themes—his central theme—was the promise and the problem of self-government. As early as 1838, speaking to the Young Men's Lyceum of Springfield on "The Perpetuation of Our Political Institutions," he recalled the devotion of our Revolutionary forefathers to the cause, then went on to say: "Their ambition aspired to display before an admiring world, a practical demonstration of the truth of the proposition, which had hitherto been considered at best no better than problematical; namely, *the capacity of a people to govern themselves.*" Again and again he returned to this idea, especially after the coming of the Civil War, and he steadily improved his phrasing. In his first message to Congress after the fall of Fort Sumter he declared that the issue between North and

South involved more than the future of the United States. "It presents to the whole family of man, the question whether a constitutional republic, or a democracy—a government of the people, by the same people—can, or cannot, maintain its territorial integrity, against its own domestic foes." And finally at Gettysburg he made the culminating, the supreme, statement, concluding with the words: "that from these honored dead we take increased devotion to that cause for which they gave the last full measure of devotion—that we here highly resolve that these dead shall not have died in vain—that this nation, under God, shall have a new birth of freedom—and that government of the people, by the people, for the people, shall not perish from the earth."

The ideas of the Gettysburg Address were no more original with Lincoln than those of the Declaration of Independence were with Jefferson. The principles of each of these great statements of American democracy were widely held and had been often expressed. But they never had been put so well. Jefferson and Lincoln, each for his time and for all time, crystallized in superb language the ideals and aspirations of millions of men and women. Herein lies the greatness of the two documents.

Of course, Lincoln also spoke for himself, as did Jefferson. For a quarter of a century or more Lincoln had pondered the subject he was devoted to: democracy, the Union, the American experiment. With a poet's insight Walt Whitman wrote of him: "The only thing like passion or infatuation in the man was the passion for the Union of These States." Thus Lincoln in his public statements revealed a good deal of his private self.

Naturally he revealed even more of it in his personal letters. In the words he wrote, and often between the lines, he indicated much of the substance of his days—his hopes, ambitions, dreams, and loves, his disappointments and his sorrows, his shrewdness and practicality, tenderness and faith.

Yet he seldom told it all. Even in the letters he sent to his friend and confidant Joshua Speed, after the breaking of his engagement with Mary Todd in 1841, he refrained from making clear the details. He mentioned his fits of depression, his "hypo" (hypochondria); he referred without using her name to Mary Todd as "*one* still unhappy whom I have contributed to make so;" and he confessed his "peculiar misfortune," his propensity to "dream dreams of Elysium far exceeding all that anything earthly can realize." But he withheld the inside story of the blighted love affair. So it was with many of his doings. Time and again, as we nowadays pry into his personal concerns, we are left wondering.

Though voluminous, the Lincoln papers are much less so than those of some of the other Presidents, notably Jefferson and Theodore Roosevelt. Of the Lincoln items that have been preserved, many survived by chance; many others have been lost, and so the record is neither full nor balanced. And Lincoln kept no personal diary, as did his predecessors John Quincy Adams and James K. Polk. On three occasions he wrote out autobiographical sketches, but none of these amounted to more than a bare factual skeleton.

A full-length autobiography can be put together, and has been, from selections of his writings throughout his life. But any such compilation is bound to leave the reader guessing at certain points. There are subjects on which Lincoln is silent, as he is about Ann Rutledge, who was according to many accounts his one true and unforgettable love. There are also matters on which he appears to be contradictory, among them the question whether, in April 1861, he intended to force the country into war.

So, for all of Lincoln's skill at expressing himself with words, for all the abundance of the writings he left behind, his own record of his life is not complete, nor altogether satisfying.

3

As remarkable as Lincoln's capacity for communicating to others was his capacity for keeping things to himself. He had a gift of reticence as well as eloquence.

"His skill in parrying troublesome questions was wonderful," testified Chauncey M. Depew, who knew him during the war. One of Depew's many Lincoln stories concerned the White House visit of Congressman John Ganson, a War Democrat from Buffalo. Ganson had a bald head, a hairless face, and a forthright, aggressive manner. "We are voting and acting in the dark in Congress," he told Lincoln, "and I demand to know—think I have the right to ask and to know—what is the present situation, and what are the prospects and conditions of the several campaigns and armies." Lincoln looked at him quizzically and then said: "Ganson, how clean you shave!"

Sometimes Lincoln parried troublesome questions with anecdotes of his own. The listeners—his victims—seldom realized the stalling function of his stories. These people supposed that he had, as one of his eccentricities, an uncontrollable urge for storytelling, or that he preferred to talk in parables, or that he resorted to humor as an escape from the ever-present threat of mental depression. Undoubtedly he did find a spiritual prophylaxis in a joke, and he certainly acted as if he enjoyed the stories he told. "When he told a particularly good story, and the time came to laugh," Congressman George W. Julian recalled, "he would sometimes throw his left foot across his right knee, and clenching his foot with both hands and bending forward, his whole frame seemed to be convulsed with the effort to give expression to his sensations." Undoubtedly he also used many an anecdote to make a point. Often, however, the real object was to distract his callers, deflect them from the purpose of their visit, and ease them, laughing, out the door.

His friends were fascinated by his enigmatic silences. Herndon, after sharing a law office with him for more than sixteen years, concluded that he was, when he wanted to be, the most "shut-mouthed" man who ever lived. David Davis, for many seasons a judge on the circuit with him and in 1860 his campaign manager, wrote: "I knew the man so well; he was the most reticent, secretive man I ever saw or expect to see." Leonard Swett, for eleven years a fellow lawyer on the circuit, declared: "He always told only enough of his plans and purposes to induce the belief that he had communicated all; yet he reserved enough to have communicated nothing." Ward Hill Lamon, an Illinois crony who served as Lincoln's volunteer bodyguard during the war, stated that Lincoln "made simplicity and candor a mask of deep feelings carefully concealed, and subtle plans studiously veiled." And, agreeing with these judgments, the Pennsylvania newspaperman Alexander K. McClure, who carried out a number of confidential missions for Lincoln as President, added: "I have seen Lincoln many times when he seemed to speak with the utmost candor, I have seen him many times when he spoke with mingled candor and caution, and I have seen him many times when he spoke but little and with extreme caution."

A man of many secrets—though not necessarily of cunning or deceit—such was Lincoln in the opinion of men who knew him well, or as well as anyone through personal acquaintance was likely to know him. "I am rather inclined to silence," he himself once said (February 14, 1861), "and whether that be wise or not, it is at least more unusual now-a-days to find a man who can hold his tongue than to find one who cannot." At times his silences or noncommittal utterances led his associates to very different conclusions about what he was up to.

4

Even if no scrap of Lincoln's own writings had survived, there nevertheless would exist a huge fund of information (and misinformation) about him. There are the newspapers of his time, and letters, diaries, and reminiscences of the men with whom he had dealings. After his death a cloud of witnesses arose to testify in their memoirs about the great man they had known—or thought they had.

Next to his own written words, the best sources of information available are first-hand accounts by those who heard what he said or saw what he did. And yet, no matter how honest their intentions, the men who thought they knew Lincoln were liable at times to err about him. Like all men, they were inclined to believe what they wanted to. They had their own individual interests and prejudices, and, in the light of these, they tended to record what they considered worth recording and overlook the rest. Thus the diaries of Salmon P. Chase and Gideon Welles, the one man a radical and the other a conservative in Lincoln's cabinet, give two quite different accounts of the same man.

If diaries, newspaper reports, letters, and the like, written down at approximately the time of the events they describe, are likely at certain points to be inaccurate or dubious, the reminiscences put down in after years are even more liable to err. The memoirist is prone to be misled by tricks of his memory. In looking back he is especially tempted to magnify his own part in the events he describes. So it apparently was, for example, with Ulysses S. Grant. When Grant wrote his *Personal Memoirs,* some twenty years after the war's end, he clearly recalled that Lincoln was an ignoramus in military matters and had left every important military decision entirely up to him. If all Lincoln's underlings had done as much as each afterward remembered, there would have been little for Lincoln himself to do.

Among the many who remembered Lincoln, there was one who was sure he had known him more intimately than any of the rest, and who—rightly or wrongly—influenced the world's conception of him more than all the others put together. That one was William H. Herndon.

Billy Herndon, Kentucky-born like Lincoln, and nearly ten years younger than he, was himself something of an original. The two members of the firm of Lincoln & Herndon made an odd yet not ill-assorted pair. Herndon was the more learned, having spent a year at college, and he continued his education throughout his life, reading voraciously. He had the air of both a farmer and a philosopher—a homespun intellectual. Unlike his abstemious senior partner, he smoked regularly and drank occasionally, though not enough to deserve the drunkard's reputation he acquired. On political issues he was inclined to be more rigid, more ideological, and more extreme than Lincoln. Yet their partnership was as nearly perfect as such human arrangements are ever likely to be. In their law business they kept no records, and they split the cash between them whenever either of them was paid. Apparently they had no money quarrels. In politics Herndon was at times a great help to Lincoln, faithfully performing many an election chore and exerting considerable influence among the "wild boys" of Springfield. He admired Lincoln and looked up to him. Still, he apparently had no intimation in advance that Lincoln ever was to win the fame he did after 1860.

When Lincoln died, Herndon began a new career and kept at it as persistently as his impecuniousness would allow throughout the remaining quarter-century of his life. This was a career as Lincoln authority. Herndon could hardly qualify as a true Boswell, for he had neglected to take down the words of the living Lincoln, or keep any contemporary record of his observations. But Herndon did the best he could, afterward, according to his lights. Indefatigably he tracked down the old-timers who had been Lincoln's neighbors in Kentucky, Indiana, and Illinois. Relentlessly he taxed the memories of these people, plying them with question after question, and welcoming any remembered fragment, however trivial. To the stock of reminiscences he thus collected, he added his own store of memories.

Herndon aimed to find and tell the truth, the whole truth, so far as it could be ascertained. Though he thought that Lincoln was in some respects unknowable, he was sure that *he*, if anyone, could see straight into the man's "gizzard." He wrote in 1860: "I know him better than he does himself." Herndon professed to be a psychologist of rare analytical powers: if there were mysteries in Lincoln's life and personality, Herndon had theories to account for them or to explain them away. As he saw it, the main theme was the far more than ordinary rise of a self-made man, a rise from the lowest depths to the greatest heights—"from a stagnant, putrid pool, like the gas which, set on fire by its own energy and self-combustible nature, rises in jets, blazing, clear, and bright." To emphasize this theme, Herndon gave his most eager attention to evidences of the dismal and the sordid in Lincoln's early life, with no awareness that this special interest might deflect his aim to make known the plain and simple truth.

Herndon used his materials to prepare a few startling lectures on such subjects as Lincoln's religion (he called him an unbeliever) and his love life. These lectures he delivered in Springfield and published in pamphlet form. Later he sold the use of his materials to Ward Hill Lamon for a Lincoln biography, which Lamon hired a ghost writer to compose. Finally Herndon found a collaborator in Jesse W. Weik, a graduate of De Pauw University in Greencastle, Indiana. It was Weik who actually drafted the three volumes that eventually (1889) appeared under the title *Herndon's Lincoln: The True Story of a Great Life.*

From first lecture to final opus, Herndon's views on Lincoln provoked a violent and mixed reaction. They horrified those who had come to idealize Lincoln. They highly pleased others who thought of themselves as realists—including a number of Lincoln's former friends. For many years after Herndon's death (in 1891) fact-minded Americans preferred his version to that of other writers whom they considered romantics.

But Herndon was a romantic himself, and not always careful of his facts. His materials are not all of a piece. They may be divided into two general categories: what he got from others, and what he personally observed. Many of the reminiscences he gathered are vague and contradictory, based on rumor or hearsay evidence, imperfectly remembered. But many of his own recollections have the ring of absolute veracity, especially his photographic descriptions of the way Lincoln looked, the way he talked and walked, the way he sat. Others of Herndon's recollections, however, are hard, if not impossible, to believe, including a number of self-revelations which he said Lincoln had confided to him.

True or half-true, improbable or downright false, tales from

Herndon continue to be told and retold. In the minds of many Americans these stories persist as accepted knowledge about Lincoln. His father was a shiftless poor white. His mother was the source of his ambition to learn and get ahead. His one true love was Ann Rutledge, and after her death his never-ending grief shadowed all his remaining years. His wife, Mary Todd, married him to get even with him, then devoted herself to making him miserable. Thus spake Herndon.

Had it not been for Herndon, however, many a colorful incident of Lincoln's early life would have been lost. Had it not been for countless others who recorded their recollections, many phases of Lincoln's later career would have been forgotten or obscured. Much of the testimony about Lincoln is priceless. Much of it is trash. Often it gets in the way of our seeing Lincoln as he actually was. The problem is to know in each case what is counterfeit, and what is the real thing.

5

This problem is the concern of biographers and historians. It is their duty to apply the rules of historical evidence to the vast piles of data on Lincoln and his times. By these methods, it is often possible to work through the contradictions and controversies, and to come out with a fair approximation of the truth. Sometimes the impartiality of hindsight can produce a more accurate version of the facts than any of those directly involved could have possessed.

The rules are fairly simple. When several witnesses agree, and there is no collusion and no dissent, we may be pretty sure they tell us accurately what happened. When they disagree, we should give more credence to those who wrote down their reports while the event was fresh in mind than to those who recorded their impressions later. Among accounts put down at approximately the same date, we should favor those left by witnesses who have a better reputation for accuracy, or who were in more advantageous position for observation, or who seem blessed with greater impartiality regarding the issues.

Unfortunately, there are a number of incidents about Lincoln which have the authority of only one person behind them, and such unsupported testimony is often extremely dubious. There are also instances of conflicting testimony with seemingly equal weight on both sides. Perhaps, in cases of insufficient or indecisive evidence, biographers and historians ought to withhold their judgment. But here, of course, is the crux of the historian's task. If we should content ourselves with a bare presentation of obscure or contradictory evidence, it would be impossible to derive any meaning from it. Understanding requires interpretation, and historians must often trust to their own judgment, based on their knowledge of the sources available. And so where there is neither proof nor disproof they accept those reports, however ill-founded, which fit in with their own conceptions of what is truly "Lincolnian."

For, no matter how expert, informed, and honest the writer may be, he cannot keep his own preconceptions entirely out of his work. Indeed, art has been defined as life viewed through the glass of personality, and in this sense biography is, without question, art. Among the countless writers on Lincoln—vastly more has been published about him, of course, than about any other American—ten or a dozen may be considered artists of note. They have given us books worthy of Lincoln's greatness, and yet none of them shows us the man entire and altogether clear.

Some of the outstanding Lincoln authorities were strongly biased. In their ten-volume history the official biographers, Nicolay and Hay, seemingly said everything there was to say, as they depicted a flawless man and a flawless career. They alone—till 1947—had the use of the voluminous collection of Presidential correspondence which had passed to the custody of Lincoln's son. Yet, with all their advantages, Nicolay and Hay were sorely handicapped. They were bitterly prejudiced against certain of Lincoln's rivals and opponents, notably George B. McClellan, whom they set out deliberately, and none too subtly, to discredit. Also they had to submit their manuscript to Robert Todd Lincoln for his censorship line by line. So the Lincoln of their history turned out to be even less of the man than they, two highly partisan admirers, could see. This Lincoln amounted to no more than his painfully reticent son was willing for the world to know.

Far more disciplined in their judgments than Nicolay and Hay, more recent Lincoln biographers, notably James G. Randall and Benjamin P. Thomas, have searched through original sources and presented their findings in objective spirit and balanced proportions as well as lucid style. Recent biographers have had the advantage of the cumulative work of dozens of other historical scholars, each devoting years to the illumination of this or that event in which Lincoln played an important part. The history of the Civil War, after all, centers so largely upon the career of the wartime President that most of the war studies are also studies of some phase of Lincoln's life and thought.

With all this scholarly effort, it would seem to be a relatively simple matter for someone to condense the findings of the specialists and wrap up these conclusions in a single package, a Lincoln biography to end all Lincoln biographies. The trouble is, the scholars disagree. They differ at many points in their analyses both of events and of personalities. That is one reason why so much is written on this subject. A great deal of the Lincoln literature is controversial, and controversy begets more controversy.

Where more or less impartial experts themselves differ, where there are areas of real doubt, the way is open for the inexpert and the partisan—those who care less about knowing Lincoln as he was than about proving he was one of them, the biosopher, the spiritualist, the high-tariffite, the antitobacconist, the friend of Communism, or what not. A large quantity of books supposedly "explaining" Lincoln consists of this sort of thing.

In some of the controversies there is little to be said on either side. In others there is much to be said on both sides. Where the evidence is tangled in contradictions, and equally fair-minded and well-informed students disagree in their interpretations of it, we may reasonably conclude that we are dealing with a Lincoln nobody really knows.

The question may require a complete analysis of personality, or the assessment of different traits combined in the complex person Lincoln was. The question may be one of motives or intentions. These seldom are entirely clear, even in the case of living persons among our close acquaintances. In the case of men long dead the problem is doubly difficult.

The question may be one of ascertaining not what the man thought or did, but what historical significance his action had. Here views are bound to differ, according to the personal philosophy of the historian or biographer.

Consider the maze of contradictory propositions that have been stated about Lincoln:

He loved only one woman in his life, who was not his wife. He was devoted to his wife. His wife was an angel. His wife was a shrew. He was a born politician. He was completely unable to wield political power in important matters. His deepest convictions were based on a strong foundation of religious belief. He was an agnostic.

When war threatened in 1861, Lincoln did his best to keep the peace. At the same time, he cynically manipulated events in order to precipitate war. He knew nothing about warfare and bungled every time he interfered in military matters. He was a military genius—the master strategist of the Civil War. He was too merciful and tender-hearted to pursue policies as thoroughly as the times demanded. He was a hard, shrewd man whose surface affability and benevolence concealed a hard core of ruthlessness.

His Emancipation Proclamation freed the slaves. It was a piece of calculated propaganda which achieved nothing tangible. At the time of his death he was planning an easy peace for the defeated Confederacy. He was giving way to radical Republican demands that the South be punished for seceding. If he had lived to finish his term of office, he would be remembered with even more admiration than he is now—as a great peacemaker as well as a great war leader. He would have been abandoned by his followers in the embittered aftermath of war, and his reputation would have been ruined by compromises, once the idealistic spirit of the war effort had worn off.

What is truth and what is falsehood? Are these contradictions unanswerable or may they be resolved? With regard to each of them, arguments can be made and have been made both pro and con.

It would be rash to undertake, in the following pages, to settle all such disputes. It would be rash to undertake to say the last word on any of them. But it may be worthwhile to restate some of the controversies, to redefine some of the issues, perhaps even to come to some conclusions, on the assumption that truth may be discovered in the examination of controversy, and understanding in the midst of paradox.

chapter 2

THE SON, LOVER, HUSBAND

"My mother was a bastard," Lincoln once said—according to William H. Herndon. The year he said it Herndon could not remember for sure, though he thought it was about 1850 or 1851. He recalled the occasion with all the detail of verisimilitude. Jouncing along in a one-horse buggy, the partners were just two-and-a-half miles west of Springfield, on their way to court in Menard County. They were talking about the case ahead of them, a suit that involved the question of hereditary traits. "Billy, I'll tell you something, but keep it a secret while I live," Lincoln suddenly put in. "My mother was a bastard, was the daughter of a nobleman so called of Virginia." Lincoln went on to say that, through his mother, he had inherited his qualities of mind from that Virginia gentleman. "God bless my mother," he concluded; "all that I am or ever expect to be I owe to her." Then he sat silent and gloomy as the buggy jolted on.

This was a most unusual disclosure for Lincoln—if indeed he ever made it. He seldom talked about his ancestry on his mother's side. As Herndon observed, "There was something about his origin he never cared to dwell upon."

Lincoln's mother, Nancy Hanks, was a "poor white," according to Herndon's account. She was tall and slender or, as her cousin Dennis Hanks expressed it, "spare made." She looked consumptive, and there were marks of melancholy in her dark-skinned, pointed face and her small gray eyes. "Stoop-shouldered, thin-breasted, sad," she seemed always to be "groping through the perplexities of life."

Yet she possessed certain unexpected spiritual and intellectual resources. Day by day, with quiet heroism, she devoted herself to God and to the duties of this world. She took the best care she could of her husband Thomas, her daughter Sarah, and her son Abraham. According to the recollection of Dennis Hanks, she even taught Abraham to read and write, and she gave her husband such literacy as he ever got, which was barely enough to enable him to sign his name and to pick his way through the Bible a word at a time.

Thomas Lincoln, as Herndon described him, was quite different from Nancy Hanks. Both mentally and physically he was slow, dull, careless, inert. He was heavy-set and strong as an ox. He liked his liquor, though he drank no more than the average Kentuckian of his time, and he was fond of hunting. He also loved to tell a good story, or to laugh at one. Roving and shiftless, he moved about from farm to farm in Kentucky and then migrated to Indiana and finally to Illinois, repeating in each place a tedious pattern of compulsive failure.

Except for his coarse black hair, his leathery skin, and his delight in storytelling, Thomas was also quite different from the bright, ambitious Abraham. Could such a boy really have been the son of such a man? Eventually rumors rose and spread that Abraham was not the son of Thomas Lincoln. According to one report he was sired by Abraham Inlow, a Kentucky miller, who paid Thomas to marry Nancy and assume the paternity of her infant child. On this question whether Nancy, born in bastardy, herself begot a bastard, Herndon had difficulty in making up his mind. Sometimes he was inclined to believe that Thomas had had the mumps or had been "castrated, fixed, cut," hence had become incapable of fatherhood. Still, Herndon wondered about the timing of this (supposed) disaster—whether it had occurred before or after Abraham's birth.

In some ways, it was said, Thomas treated Abraham as if the boy actually were an unwanted stepson. As Dennis Hanks recalled, Thomas occasionally gave Abraham a cuff for neglecting his work for his books. He also punished him for his eagerness to learn about the outside world from strangers who passed by the backwoods farm. He thought him too inquisitive. "His father would sometimes knock him over," Dennis Hanks reported. "When thus punished he never bellowed, but dropped a kind of silent, unwelcome tear as evidence of his sensitiveness or other feelings."

So, as Herndon heard of it, the early years were rather dismal for little Abe. His life was dreariest of all after a plague of "milk sickness" came to Pigeon Creek and took Nancy Hanks away. The ragged nine-year-old saw her buried beneath the snow in the Indiana forest, then with his sister and father returned to the poor shelter of their crude log cabin to face the winter without the warmth and comfort of a mother's love.

This terrible, loveless time was fortunately short. Before the onset of another winter Thomas Lincoln brought home from Kentucky a new wife for himself, a new mother for the children. Sarah Bush Johnston Lincoln, a widow with a brood of two boys and a girl of her own, had energy and affection to spare. Tall, straight, fair, "very handsome, sprightly, talkative, and proud" (as a granddaughter described her), this new stepmother quickly took over and remade the "cheerless cabin," sprucing it up and radiating sunshine "into every neglected corner," as Herndon said. She ran the household with an even hand, treating both sets of children as if she had borne them all, but she became especially fond of Abraham, and he of her.

"Abe was a good boy," she reminisced, as an old woman, when Herndon interviewed her in the fall of 1865. She had not wanted Abe to run for President, she said. She had feared something would happen to him, and it *had* happened, and she sobbed as she thought of it.

She elaborated at some length on Abe's qualifications as a model child. She also told how she had persuaded her husband to let him read and study at home as well as at school, and how her husband was at first reluctant, then reconciled to the idea, and finally willing to add his own encouragement. "As a usual thing Mr. Lincoln never made Abe quit reading to do anything if he could avoid it," she testified. "Mr. Lincoln could read a little and could scarcely write his name; hence he wanted . . . his boy Abraham to learn, and he encouraged him to do it in all ways he could."

This sounds like a different Thomas Lincoln from the one whom Dennis Hanks remembered—the one who cuffed Abraham for reading too much and knocked him down for asking too many questions. The difference is perhaps a measure of the salutary influence that Sarah Lincoln had upon her second husband.

As it was, with his own brand of homespun psychoanalysis, Herndon saw in Lincoln's family background a deep significance for the making of his personality. Throughout his life Lincoln was oppressed by knowledge of his mother's parentage and by doubts about his own. This knowledge, these doubts, cast a sinister shadow upon his inmost consciousness (Herndon thought). They helped to cause those fits of black depression that sometimes seized him—as on that buggy ride in 1850 or 1851 when, for the first and only time in Herndon's hearing, he burst out with the shocking truth about his mother, the unhappy Nancy Hanks.

2

Two or three years after that, Lincoln mentioned his mother again, on another buggy ride. This time he was with Leonard Swett, a fellow lawyer whom he had known on the circuit for four years. It was the fall of 1853, and the two men were on their way from the De Witt County to the Champaign County court. They were crossing a wide stretch of virgin prairie on a perfect Indian-summer day. In the distance a prairie fire filled the air with hazy smoke; near at hand the quail whistled, and occasionally a startled deer ran through the tall grass. To Swett the season and the surroundings seemed ideal for lazy conversation. He turned to his companion and asked him to tell the story of his early life.

Lincoln had no startling revelations to make. "I can remember," he said, "our life in Kentucky; the cabin, the stinted living, the sale of our possessions, and the journey with my father and mother to southern Indiana." He remembered, too, the day his mother died. "It was pretty pinching times at first in Indiana, getting the cabin built, and the clearing for the crops; but presently we got reasonably comfortable, and my father married again."

Of his mother he had only the faintest recollections, but he spoke most kindly of her, as he also did of his stepmother. And he had a good word for his father. "My father," he said, "had suffered greatly for the want of an education, and he determined at an early day that I should be well educated. And what do you think he said his ideas of a good education were? We had an old dog-eared arithmetic in our house, and father determined that somehow, or somehow else, I should cipher clear through that book."

Lincoln, on this buggy ride with Swett, talked of his boyhood as if on the whole it had been a joyous one. He was happy as he talked, and from time to time his hearty laughter rang out over the prairie.

More than thirty years later, recalling that sunny day and

that sunny laugh, Swett could not help thinking that some of Lincoln's biographers had greatly exaggerated the want and misery of his early existence. Swett was sure that Lincoln had enjoyed the kind of childhood that was typical of the frontier farm. The young Lincoln must have been very much like John Greenleaf Whittier's barefoot boy with cheek of tan.

Swett's impressions were so different from Herndon's that we wonder whether both men could have heard and remembered Lincoln aright. What really was his attitude, as a grown man, toward his family background, his upbringing, and his parents? To answer this question, we must appeal to other records, such as they are, and—wherever possible—to Lincoln's own words.

In his authenticated writings there are few references to Nancy Hanks, and these few are brief and matter-of-fact. Once he referred to her, in describing another woman who he said reminded him of her, as having had "withered features" and "wrinkles," a "want of teeth," and in general a "weather-beaten appearance." While campaigning for Henry Clay, in 1844, he revisited the scenes of his Indiana boyhood, and a year and a half afterward he wrote: "I went into the neighborhood in that State in which I was raised, where my mother and only sister were buried." That was all he said about his mother. He may have been thinking of her when, in the poem his Indiana visit inspired, he mentioned the "loved ones lost" who "in dreamy shadows rise." On that visit he may have paused at her grave, but apparently he did nothing, then or later, to see that the grave was properly marked and cared for. When, early in 1865, an artist sought out the site to make sketches for a Lincoln biography, he found no stone or board or marker of any kind.

As for Nancy Hanks's reputed illegitimacy, it has been stoutly denied by genealogically minded members of the Hanks family. Eventually one of them constructed for her a full and respectable family tree. This made her the perfectly legitimate child of Nancy Shipley, who had married Joseph Hanks, the descendant of an honorable line which was traceable all the way back to an ancestor who landed at Plymouth, Massachusetts, in 1699. Unfortunately the evidence regarding the descent of Nancy Hanks is in such a tangle as to baffle the most determined scholars. There are serious doubts as to the genuineness of the genealogy designed to prove her legitimate. Anyhow, it was worked out much too late to be of any reassurance to Lincoln. The probability, though not the certainty, is that his mother was born out of wedlock, and he knew it. What effect the knowledge had on his personality is anybody's guess.

The question of his own legitimacy is quite another matter. Stories arose attributing his paternity not only to Abraham Inlow (or Inloe, or Enlow, or Enloe) but also to Henry Clay, to John C. Calhoun, to an adopted son of John Marshall, to the father of Jefferson Davis, to almost every male in the Carolinas, Virginia, or Kentucky who ever came near any woman named Nancy Hanks, and to many who never did. Some of these stories were brought into politics while Lincoln was yet alive. They were whispered during the presidential campaign of 1860 and put into print during that of 1864, when scurrilous Democratic pamphlets referred to the Republican candidate as "Abe Hanks, likewise named Abe Lincoln," and as "Abraham, the son of Inlow, whose mother was of the Ethiopian tribe of Hanks."

Despite these stories and Herndon's inconclusive speculations, the plain truth is that the parents of Abraham Lincoln were properly married nearly three years before he was born, as the surviving legal record of their marriage shows. And, as an existing letter indicates, Thomas thought of him as his own flesh and blood. There should be, nowadays, no doubt whatever that Abraham was his presumptive father's legitimate child.

There remains, however, the question whether Lincoln ever had occasion to wonder about his parentage. Some inkling of the nasty rumors may possibly have reached him. When he first was nominated for the Presidency, in 1860, the inhabitants of the Kentucky county of his birth, with curiosity and local pride, inquired of one another about his family background. The clerk of the county court looked through the archives and found a record of Thomas Lincoln's second marriage, to Sarah Bush Johnston, but no record of his first marriage, to Nancy Hanks. (This record was not discovered until many years later.) The negative finding, when the news got out, left gossips free to believe whatever rumor they chose. The clerk wrote to Lincoln and asked about his parents.

"In the main you are right about my history," Lincoln replied. "My father was Thomas Lincoln, and Mrs. Sally Johnston was his second wife. You are mistaken about my mother—her maiden name was Nancy Hanks." He did not elaborate about her. And when, at approximately the same time, he wrote an autobiographical sketch for a campaign biography, he said of her only that Thomas Lincoln "married Nancy Hanks—mother of the present subject—in the year 1806." Which is enough to indicate at least this much: he believed, correctly, that Thomas and Nancy had been duly wed well before his own birth, despite the failure in 1860 to locate the official marriage record in Kentucky.

In the few surviving written references to his father, Lincoln is not only brief but also rather apologetic. Responding to one of the Massachusetts Lincolns, who had asked about his ancestry, he wrote (1848): "Owing to my father being left an orphan at the age of six years, in poverty, and in a new country, he became a wholly uneducated man; which I suppose is the reason why I know so little of our family history." In fact (as modern scholarship has proved) the father was by no means the good-for-nothing that Herndon and others considered him. Thomas Lincoln may be viewed as the stalwart scion of a long line of pioneering ancestors—and Abraham Lincoln as a chip off the old block. There is no need for us to look for the genetics of his greatness in an amorous ancestor on the distaff side, and there was no need for Lincoln to do so (despite Herndon's quoting him to the effect that he had inherited his qualities of mind from that Virginia gentleman who seduced his grandmother). Though he never succeeded in pushing hi genealogical inquiries very far, Lincoln came to realize tha his father's relatives included sturdy and reputable men.

Yet there must have been a real estrangement between hin and his father. He did not take the trouble to see the old mar during the latter's last illness, though it was a trip of onl seventy-odd miles from his own home in Springfield to hi father's residence in Coles County. Again and again Thomas' stepson appealed to Abraham, saying in one letter: "I hast to inform you that father is yet a Live & that is all & he Crave to See you all the time & he wants you to Come if you ar abl to git hure. . . ." Abraham did not even bother to answer al the letters. He finally wrote (1851) to explain that both hi own business and his wife's sickness prevented him from visit ing his father. "Say to him," he advised his stepbrother, "tha if we could meet now, it is doubtful whether it would not be more painful than pleasant; but that if it be his lot to go now he will soon have a joyous meeting with many loved ones gone before; and where the rest of us, through the help of God, hope ere long to join them." He did not attend the funeral.

Whatever his feelings toward his mother or his father, he left no doubt of his enduring affection and regard for his step mother. Of her he wrote in the 1860 outline of his life: "She proved a good and kind mother to A. and is still living in Coles Co. Illinois." This is more than he said for Nancy Hanks in that same sketch—more than he ever said for her in any authen ticated utterance. During the years of Sarah Lincoln's second widowhood, after Thomas's death, Lincoln looked after her with a wholehearted devotion which her own son did not share. Her son schemed to sell some of her land and make off with the proceeds; Lincoln insisted that enough property be left to guarantee her support. Between his election and his in auguration as President, he took time off from his busy affairs and made a trip to Coles County for a visit with her—the visit she tearfully recalled in the Herndon interview.

Though Lincoln owed a great deal to his "angel mother"

Sarah, it is doubtful that he owed to her the beginnings of his education or his desire to learn. It is certain that he was not taught his A B C's by his real mother Nancy, despite the inspiring recollections of Dennis Hanks. She could not have taught her son or her husband to read and write—or, if she could, she must have been a wondrous person indeed—for she could not even write her own name, as is shown by existing legal documents which, after the fashion of illiterates, she signed by making her mark. Writing of his Indiana life, Lincoln said (in 1859): "There was absolutely nothing to excite ambition for education. Of course when I came of age I did not know much. Still somehow, I could read, write, and cipher to the rule of three; but that was all." He did not say there was nothing to excite ambition *except* the encouragement of his mother, his stepmother, or his father. He said only that "somehow" he had learned to read and write and cipher. The source of his inspiration remains a mystery.

In looking back he saw more gloom than glamor in his boyhood years. After revisiting southern Indiana he said his home country was "as unpoetical as any spot of the earth" (even though his visit stirred him to compose some melancholy verse). When John L. Scripps, a *Chicago Tribune* reporter, approached him for biographical material, he protested: "Why, Scripps, it is a great piece of folly to attempt to make anything out of me or my early life. It can all be condensed into a single sentence, and that sentence you will find in Gray's Elegy: 'The short and simple annals of the poor.' "

All in all, it would seem that Lincoln in retrospection hardly saw himself as anything like Whittier's carefree, whistling barefoot boy. On the other hand, it is difficult to believe that he thought of himself as having originated in a sort of nineteenth-century Tobacco Road. As a lad he experienced more than his fair share of shocks and sorrows, and yet he appears to have enjoyed a reasonably secure and satisfying home life most of the time. Certainly he did so after the advent of Sarah Bush Johnston Lincoln.

3

As a boy, Lincoln clearly had more affinity for his mother (and much more for his stepmother) than for his father. He did not share many of his father's interests, and certainly not the latter's fondness for hunting. Hence one biographer, Nathaniel W. Stephenson, inferred that Lincoln—"this peculiar boy who chose to remain at home while the men went out to slay"—grew up to be a kind of male equivalent of his mother. For the most part, "the story is that of a man's man, possibly because there was so much of the feminine in his own makeup." Lincoln "lacked the wanton appetites of the average sensual man," Stephenson believed. And another biographer, Edgar Lee Masters, flatly declared: "Lincoln was an undersexed man."

But Herndon took just the opposite view. He was sure that Lincoln possessed far more than the average man's sexual appetite. "Lincoln had terribly strong passions for woman, could hardly keep his hands off them," Herndon explained to his disciple and collaborator Jesse W. Weik, "and yet he had honor and a strong will, and these enabled him to put out the fires of his terrible passion." Herndon quoted David Davis as having said: "Mr. Lincoln's honor saved many a woman." And Herndon swore this was a fact. "I have seen Lincoln tempted," he said, "and I have seen him reject the approach of woman." A man of lust, of powerful libido, yet sternly inhibited and repressed—such was the Lincoln that Herndon thought he had known.

So it would appear that Lincoln was highly sexed—or he was almost sexless. Physically, he was attracted to women in an unusual degree, or he was comparatively indifferent toward them. Perhaps, like many another man, he was both and he was neither, depending on his mood, the occasion, and the woman involved. In any event there is no way of knowing just what his attitudes were toward women as women. The most that can be done is, by a sampling of available evidence, to suggest the range of his feelings and behavior, or at least the range of the reports about them.

He had a reputation for a kind of rough chivalry. He sometimes told dirty stories but none that reflected on the name of any identifiable woman. He never gossiped. With regard to both sexual and political matters he believed in equal rights, repudiating the double standard and (in an early campaign speech) advocating the vote for all white taxpayers, "by no means excluding females."

A couple of anecdotes illustrate his protective way with women. Once in New Salem a man came cursing and swearing into Offutt's store, where Lincoln clerked. He politely asked the man to desist, for there were ladies present. The profane one insisted on his right to say what he damn pleased. After the ladies had left, Lincoln took him outside, threw him down, and rubbed smartweed into his eyes. This deed appealed to New Salem's sense of chivalry and made the store clerk more than ever a local hero. Another time, in Springfield, Lincoln warned a shoemaker to stop getting drunk and beating his wife. When the brute disregarded the warning, Lincoln with a few friends one night tied him up and had his wife switch his bare back. (This tale, though told to show Lincoln as a protector of womankind, also reveals—if it is true—an officiousness that we dislike to think of as characteristic.)

In polite society Lincoln was said to be woefully awkward and embarrassed with the ladies. Henry C. Whitney, who knew him as a lawyer on the circuit, told of his strange and painful performance as a guest one evening at Whitney's Urbana home. Lincoln was left for a while with Mrs. Whitney, her mother, and another woman. When the rest of the men returned they found that Lincoln's earlier ease and good spirits were gone. "Drawn up in his chair and gazing alternately at the floor and ceiling, he would put his arms behind him and then bring them to the front again as if endeavoring in some way to hide them; meanwhile struggling, though in vain, to keep his long legs out of sight." Whitney could think of no explanation for such behavior, except the mere fact that Lincoln had been left to himself in a room with three women. At Springfield social gatherings, Herndon and Weik averred, he treated the ladies with "becoming politeness" but soon got away from them, drawing their husbands off with him, to regale them with his storytelling.

This same Lincoln, however, was one of the managers of a cotillion given at the new state capital in 1839. With his own hand he penned a joint appeal from several young men to Mrs. O. H. Browning, a friend's wife whose company and confidence he enjoyed. "We the undersigned," he wrote, "respectfully represent to your *Honoress,* that we are in great need of your society in this town of Springfield; and therefore humbly pray that your *Honoress* will repair forthwith to the Seat of Government, bringing in your train all ladies in general, who may be at your command; and all Mr. Browning's sisters in particular." This is documented fact, not hearsay. It causes one to suspect that Lincoln's fear of women and his gaucherie with them have been overemphasized.

Some said he was not afraid of women: it was just that he did not particularly like them. "He was not very fond of girls, as he seemed to me," his stepmother commented in regard to his youth. "He didn't go to see the girls much," an acquaintance recalled, referring to his New Salem days. "He didn't appear bashful, but it seemed as if he cared but little for them. Wasn't apt to take liberties with them, but would sometimes. He always liked lively, jovial company, where there was plenty of fun and no drunkenness, and would just as lief the company were all men as to have it a mixture of the sexes."

There are several anecdotes, however, to illustrate the view that Lincoln, especially in his younger days, *was* "apt to take liberties" with girls, and that he had, quite literally, a barnyard interest in sex. One of these stories, as relayed secondhand to Herndon from an old resident of New Salem, concerned Lincoln and Joe Walkins, who used to keep a stallion in the village for breeding purposes. "Lincoln requested him that, whenever a mare came, he would be sure to let him know it as he wanted to *see it*. Walkins did so, and Lincoln always attended, etc."

Another story, which Lincoln supposedly told on himself, and which was retold with varying details, had him stopping for the night at a one-room farmhouse. He was put in a bed the head of which was at the foot of another bed occupied by the farmer's grown daughter. While she was asleep her feet fell restlessly on his pillow. "This put the *devil* into Lincoln at once, thinking that the girl did this of a purpose. Lincoln reached up his hand and put it where it ought not to be." Or, according to another version, the girl was not asleep when Lincoln noticed her feet near his head. He began to tickle them. "As she seemed to enjoy it as much as he did, he then tickled a little higher up, and as he would tickle higher, the girl would shove down lower, and the higher he tickled, the lower she moved." Either way, the story sounds suspiciously like a variation on the old, old traveling-salesman-and-farmer's-daughter theme.

Still another of Herndon's yarns, concerning an alleged visit by Lincoln to a prostitute, seems more comic than pornographic, and equally improbable. Joshua Speed, the story goes, was keeping a pretty woman in Springfield when Lincoln asked him: "Speed, do you know where I can get *some?*" Speed sent him to the woman, and he was in bed with her before he thought to inquire her price. It turned out to be five dollars. He had only three. She offered to trust him for the difference, but he did not want to "go on credit:" he had little money and might never get around to paying her. So he got up and left, his mission unaccomplished. The woman's parting words: "Mr. Lincoln, you are the most conscientious man I ever saw."

Herndon also confided to Weik a far more serious matter, one that Herndon said he never intended the world to know. This was that Lincoln had got, *"when a mere boy,* the syphilis." Said Herndon: "About the year 1835–36 Mr. Lincoln went to Beardstown and during a devilish passion had connection with a girl and caught the disease." Herndon received this confession straight from Lincoln himself, he said. The story makes one wonder whether Herndon ever told the truth about what Lincoln said to him. There is absolutely no reason to believe that Lincoln, a man of rugged health, father of a normal family, ever contracted what was in his time an incurable and devastating malady.

Nevertheless, this is the sort of information with which Herndon plied Weik, so that his disciple and fellow admirer of Lincoln could gain an insight into the great man's heart. To enable Weik further to understand Lincoln's "conduct toward the fair sex," Herndon once sent him to interview a former law client who had been charged with keeping a house of ill fame. What Weik reported perhaps reveals more about that voluble authority, Herndon, than about Lincoln. Weik found the woman, and she readily acknowledged that the firm of Lincoln and Herndon had represented her at her trial. Lincoln had secured a change of venue, then had driven over the prairie to another court, along with the madam and several of the girls.

Having got this much, Weik proceeded to question her closely, hoping to bring out some spicy revelation.

Had Lincoln talked with her?

Yes, a good deal, and with the other ladies also.

Alone?

Yes, at times.

What did he talk about?

Oh, this and that; he was an interesting talker.

How did he conduct himself?

Always a gentleman.

Did he tell stories?

Yes, a great many.

Were any of them suggestive—the sort that would not do for polite society?

No, Lincoln never told stories that would offend ladies anywhere.

The woman paused and Weik waited. Suddenly she exclaimed: "But that is more than I can say for Bill Herndon!"

If Herndon is to be believed, Lincoln the man of "devilish passion" was also capable of divine romance. Indeed, he must have had a weakness for women since (according to Herndon) he proposed to no fewer than three of them, not counting the woman he finally married. But he had only one true love—which ended in tragedy, and shadowed him for the rest of his life.

Here is Herndon's version of the pathetic story. Ann Rutledge was a natural backwoods beauty—a blonde, five feet two, with eyes of blue, as perhaps the heroine of an American pastoral ought to be. She was blessed with every feminine virtue and grace. Quick, bright, industrious, she was unexcelled in housekeeping and needlework. Sweet, and kindly as an angel, she gained and she deserved the adoration of all the villagers in New Salem.

When Ann was seventeen, an enterprising newcomer from New York State, who was known as John McNeil, began to court her. McNeil prospered as a businessman and as a suitor. After a few years, having won a promise from the New Salem belle, he left for the East to bring his parents and his brothers and sisters to Illinois before getting married. On his departure, he confessed to Ann that his real name was not McNeil but McNamar. He explained that he had changed it so as to evade his family and keep them from burdening him until he had made good and was well able to support them. She believed him—at first. As the months and years passed, and his letters became more infrequent and more impersonal, she began to have her doubts.

Not till McNeil-McNamar had been away for some time did Lincoln step forward and try to win the incomparable Miss Rutledge for himself. He already was well acquainted with her, having lived under the same roof while a boarder at her father's tavern. Before long he was wooing her in earnest, escorting her to quilting bees, and even staying with her as she and the other ladies worked at their quilts, though it was not the custom for men to attend such parties. Once, as he sat beside her at a quilting bee, he whispered his love, and her erratic stitches betrayed feelings deeper than respect.

In fact, she felt her affection growing for the ever-present Lincoln, yet she could not forget her promise to the absent McNamar. When Lincoln asked her to marry him, she agreed, on the condition that she first write to her betrothed and get his release from her earlier pledge. She wrote, and waited, but received no answer. So she accepted Lincoln, and they were engaged. Still, she could not dismiss McNamar from her mind; she was torn between her loyalty to him and her love for Lincoln.

This inner conflict having undermined her health, she was put to bed with a raging fever. In her delirium she called for Lincoln again and again. Though her physician had forbidden visitors, the family finally sent for Abe. Alone, he went in to see Ann. It was the last time he saw her alive. She died a few days later, on August 25, 1835.

Lincoln was never the same after that. For weeks he was nearly mad with grief, and he never quite recovered from his sorrow. Ann was in her grave, and he told Herndon long afterward, "My heart lies buried there." As he told another friend, he could not stand the thought of rain and snow falling on that cherished ground. Always afterward his fits of gloom were intensified in dark and stormy weather.

The memory of Ann, remaining forever with him, was the source of much of his melancholy, and it was also the inspiration for most of his greatness. That, at least, is the moral of the romantic tragedy which Herndon put together, and which unnumbered biographers, novelists, and playwrights afterward elaborated upon.

According to Herndon, Lincoln had a second "affair of the heart" which "culminated in a sequel as amusing as the one with Ann Rutledge was sad." The woman in this case, Mary Owens, was very different from Ann. Miss Owens, a year older than Lincoln, was the well-educated daughter of a well-to-do Kentucky family. She was dark-haired, fair-skinned, and handsome, with a figure of matronly but pleasing proportions. She was good-natured, lighthearted, and cheerful.

Lincoln met her in 1833, when she visited a sister in New Salem. Later, after Ann's death, he often thought of Miss Owens, and he was heard to say that if she ever came back to Illinois he would marry her. Her sister, leaving for a visit to Kentucky, promised to bring her back if Lincoln would keep his word. So, in 1836, Mary Owens reappeared in his life, and for the next year he carried on a courtship of sorts.

She had reservations about him. She thought him interesting and kindhearted but not gallant enough. He failed to provide the small attentions that women crave, was "deficient in those little links that make up the chain of woman's happiness." Once, for instance, she and Lincoln, on a horseback ride with several couples, came to a rather difficult ford. While the other men were solicitous to see their ladies safely across, her swain rode on ahead, leaving her to make her way through the water as best she could. When she caught up with him she chided him, and he laughingly replied that he knew she was plenty smart enough to take care of herself. She supposed he meant this as a compliment, and yet she was not satisfied.

Nor was she satisfied with his proposal, when he finally made it. In a letter he sent from Springfield he gave her a number of reasons why she ought not to marry him. He assured her he was willing to keep his bargain and go through life with her if she really wanted to accept him. But he advised her otherwise. "What I have said I will most positively abide by, provided you wish it," he said. "My opinion is you had better not do it." She did not.

Afterward, in a April Fools' Day missive to a friend, he poked fun at himself and, ungallantly, at Miss Owens too. Picturing her as an ugly and oversized old maid, he said that, after much hesitation, he had proposed to her out of a sense of duty, then felt a sense of relief mixed with humility and even regret when, to his immense surprise, she refused to have him. In contrast to the grand passion of Abraham and Ann, so recently cut short, this wooing of Miss Owens was a most unromantic affair.

As Herndon had it, Lincoln was not done with proposing and being turned down. In 1840, only two years after Miss Owens had departed from New Salem and from his life, he sought the hand of a young Springfield girl. Her name was Sarah Rickard, and in his appeal to her he made the most of her name and his. The Sarah of Bible times, he reminded her, had become the wife of Abraham, and so, he urged, Sarah Rickard was destined to become the bride of Abraham Lincoln. She resisted his whimsical logic. Not that she disliked him. He was always thoughtful and attentive to her. But she was sixteen, he thirty-one. Her sister talked her out of marrying a man so old.

Ann Rutledge, Mary Owens and then Sarah Rickard, all within a five-year span. The young Lincoln must have been a star-crossed lover indeed—if Herndon had the record straight. But did he?

As for Sarah Rickard, he got the story directly from her pen. He had received a set of Lincoln letters from Joshua Speed, who requested him to delete the name *Sarah* from them before publication. This request made him suspicious. He had a hunch that the Sarah mentioned was Miss Rickard, and that Lincoln at some time must have been somehow involved with her. He wrote to her (she had been married and was living in the West) and asked about it. In reply she told her story, recalling in some detail the time that Lincoln sought her for a wife. Herndon did not question her narrative, since it only confirmed the hunch he already had.

But the story is not consistent with the contemporary evidence. From the Lincoln-Speed correspondence it is to be inferred that *Speed* and not Lincoln had been romantically interested in Sarah. After Speed married another girl and settled down in Kentucky, he apparently wanted Lincoln to find out for him how Sarah was taking the news. Hence Lincoln's seeming interest in her.

When, more than a quarter of a century later, Herndon presented his leading questions to her, it seems likely she was flattered by the association of her name with that of the man who, since her acquaintance with him, had become the President, the martyr, the national hero. Possibly this man, long ago, had joked with her about marriage, drawing the parallel with Sarah and Abraham of the Scriptures. If so, the joke was lost upon her at the time or was distorted afterward by the haze of her memory.

The affair with Mary Owens stands on an altogether different basis. This story is well documented, better documented even than Lincoln's courtship of Mary Todd, whom he married. Not only did Miss Owens (Mrs. Jesse Vineyard) give Herndon her fairly full and circumstantial account; she also provided three letters that Lincoln himself had written her. Besides, Herndon obtained a copy of Lincoln's version of the events as contained in his letter (April 1, 1838) to Mrs. O. H. Browning. Judged by all the evidence, including his own, Lincoln emerges from the Owens affair as cautious, halfhearted, a little crude, and even self-centered in the role of suitor. But, then, it could be that he never really loved Miss Owens.

The Ann Rutledge romance has far less historical substance than the Owens affair, though possibly somewhat more than the Rickard story. Herndon put together the romance from the more than thirty-year-old recollections of men and women who had been New Salem neighbors of Abraham and Ann. These recollections were confused and contradictory, and many were derived from gossip rather than first-hand knowledge. From them Herndon picked out the statements that gave support to his own romantic imagination, suppressing the rest. He had no contemporary evidence, for there was (and is) none. Nor in the extant writings of Lincoln does the name of Ann Rutledge anywhere appear—unless the inscription in her onetime textbook ("Ann Rutledge is now studying Grammar") is in Lincoln's hand, as it may possibly be.

It is hard to believe that the same Lincoln, who in 1836 began his prosaic courtship of Mary Owens, had lost his reason as well as his heart on account of Ann Rutledge the previous year. It is even harder to believe that his grief for Ann was so great as to darken all his remaining days and prevent him ever afterward from loving another woman. Such imaginings not only lack proof; they also defy common sense.

On Ann Rutledge, the woman Lincoln married deserves the right to speak. Mary Lincoln swore she had never heard of her ghostly rival till Herndon gave his story to the world in his Springfield lecture of 1866. "My husband was *truth* itself," the never-to-be-comforted widow protested, "and as he always assured me he had cared for no one but myself . . . I shall . . . remain firm in my conviction that *Ann Rutledge* is a myth—for in all his confidential communications such a romantic name was never breathed. . . ."

Of course, Ann Rutledge herself is not a myth, though her angelic qualities doubtless have been exaggerated. She actually lived—and died at the time reported. Furthermore, Lincoln was acquainted with her. He was friendly with her. He was saddened, at least temporarily, by her death. The testimony on these points is abundant, and too strong to be disbelieved.

But the question is whether the great love story is a myth, whether there is any reality at all in the "romance of much reality" that Herndon related. The question persists, hauntingly, but it must remain unanswered. This much is believable, though not proved: Abraham was once in love with Ann.

4

Mary Todd, nearly ten years younger than Lincoln, was, as Herndon saw her, the exact opposite of him in physical make-up, in temperament, in background, in almost everything. She was compactly built, had a rounded face and regular features, not beautiful but quite handsome. Gay, quick-witted, talkative, she could be charming when she wanted to be but was likely to be sharp-tongued when offended, as she easily was. One of the aristocratic Kentucky Todds, she was proud of her pedigree. She was educated far above most young women of her time and place. And she was ambitious. Even as a girl, she used to tell her friends she was going to marry a man who would be President of the United States.

Herndon's account of Lincoln's courtship is not only highly dramatic, but significant in light of subsequent political events. In Springfield, where Mary stayed with her sister, Mrs. Ninian Edwards, she moved in a circle far more sophisticated than any society Lincoln had been used to. Nor did she lack eligible admirers. When she accepted Lincoln's attentions her sister thought the match a poor one and did her best to discourage it. Mrs. Edwards was sure that this ill-poised and awkward man, for all his honesty and rugged qualities, would never be able to provide happiness for such a girl as Mary. No matter. Mary said yes when Lincoln proposed to her.

After his engagement, he had to contend for Mary's hand against the dashing lawyer, Stephen A. Douglas. One of her relatives later said, "She loved Douglas, and but for her promise to marry Lincoln would have accepted him." Mary was so distraught that—like the unfortunate Ann before her—she had to take to her bed. Her physician talked Douglas into giving up his pursuit of her, and she recovered.

By this time Lincoln was so hurt and angry because of her flirtations with Douglas that he determined to break the engagement. But when he confessed to her he did not love her she burst into tears, and he took her in his arms and kissed her. Thus, in spite of himself, he reconfirmed the engagement. He and Mary continued to see one another as if nothing had happened. They set a date for their wedding—January 1, 1841.

The day arrived. At the Edwards mansion everything was ready, the guests on hand, the supper hot. In a room next to the parlor Mary in bridal veil and gown sat nervously toying with the flowers that bedecked her hair. The bridegroom was late.

Hours passed. Finally Mary went grieving to her room, the guests departed, and the lights were put out. Lincoln had failed to show up at his own wedding!

At daybreak, after a nightlong search, Speed and a few other of his close friends found him. He was in a desperate state of mental depression. Carefully they removed from his reach all knives, razors, and other possible instruments of suicide. For a long time he was unable to attend to his duties as a member of the State Legislature. Speed took him on a visit to Kentucky for a change of scenery. Slowly Lincoln came to himself.

He was firmly resolved never to renew the engagement. "I must gain confidence in my own ability to keep my resolves when they are made," he wrote to Speed. But he relented when Speed, after many doubts and hesitations of his own, took a wife and discovered that marriage was not only endurable but delightful. Through the intercession of mutual friends in Springfield, Lincoln and Mary were brought together again. On the spur of the moment, in a simple ceremony with almost no advance preparation, they were wed November 4, 1842.

A curious courtship, Herndon thought. He wondered why Lincoln ever had gone through with the marriage. But Herndon readily found explanations, two of them, and it did not bother him that they were inconsistent. One of his explanations is that Lincoln was ambitious, was conscious of his "humble rank," and sought to gain a connection with an influential family so as to further himself in politics. The other explanation is that he was guided by his sense of honor and, once having given his promise, could not bring himself permanently to renege. In either case, he did not marry for love.

Nor did Miss Todd, according to Herndon. If she ever had been in love with Lincoln, she ceased to be in love with him after he "forfeited her affection" by deserting her on her wedding day. Such a humiliation no one so proud and spirited as she could forget or forgive. She got her revenge. She trapped him into marriage and made him miserable ever after. Together, they "reaped the bitter harvest of conjugal infelicity."

Herndon blamed Mary, but he did not blame her alone. "This domestic *hell* of Lincoln's life is not all on one side," he told Weik. Lincoln was "a good husband in his own peculiar way, and in his own way only." He did not know how to make a wife happy, possessed "none of the tender ways that please a woman." Besides, he and Mary were physically mismated. He, after all, was a man of hot passion; she, Herndon supposed, was "as cold as a chunk of ice."

Some of Lincoln's closest friends were reported as saying, and Herndon himself was inclined to believe, that it was a good thing Lincoln got the wife he did—a good thing for the nation and the world. She drove him out of the house and into the path of politics that led at last to the Presidency. "His wife, therefore, was a material though possibly an unintentional aid in his promotion." If he had had at home a well-adjusted, understanding, affectionate woman, he might never have been known outside of Illinois.

Such is the Herndon view of Lincoln's courtship and marriage. In appraising this interpretation—the essentials of which have become a familiar part of Lincoln folklore—it is necessary to bear in mind that Herndon did not get along very well with Mrs. Lincoln, and had absolutely no first-hand knowledge of his partner's home and love life. Mrs. Lincoln never invited him to the house on Eighth Street; not once did he set foot inside the door. Nor did he hear about Lincoln's marital affairs from Lincoln himself; Herndon did not even pretend to base his account on any confidences from Lincoln. Herndon had to rely on a few items of Lincoln's correspondence, on some remembered gossip, and on a great deal of his own intuitive guessing.

Herndon had been acquainted with the spirited Miss Todd, and—despite their mutual dislike—he was, on the whole, fair and accurate in his description of her. He was unjustified, however, in endorsing the rumor of her love for Douglas and in ascribing her attentions to him as the cause of Lincoln's estrangement. And Herndon let his imagination run wild in his narrative of the blighted wedding day, January 1, 1841.

He did not invent that story—at least, not all of it. Mrs. Edwards told him twenty-five years afterward, in 1866: "Every thing was ready & prepared for the marriage—even to the supper &c—. Mr. Lincoln failed to meet his Engagement—Cause insanity." And forty-two years afterward, in 1883, Mrs. Edwards repeated to Weik that "arrangements for wedding had been made—even cakes had been baked—but L. failed to appear." From these few details Herndon and Weik constructed an elaborate scene with waiting guests and grieving bride. These authors, like historical novelists, took a small cue and made the most of it. But it was a false cue to begin with. No wedding had been planned for that January 1; no cakes had been baked, no guests assembled, no bride dressed for the altar. Mrs. Edwards remembered more than actually had happened.

But she was not entirely wrong, nor were Herndon and Weik. *Something* had happened between Lincoln and Mary on January 1. He himself, not long afterward, referred in writing to that "fatal 1st of January, 1841." He also made it clear that the day's events had left him in a mood of terrible depression and despondency which lasted for some time. He did miss more of the meetings of the Legislature than was usual for him, as the legislative records show. He was slow to recover his normal spirits. All this time he seemed to be oppressed by feelings of guilt—but not for leaving a bride in the lurch on her wedding day. What had happened between him and Mary apparently was this: they had broken their engagement, and he had taken the initiative in breaking it.

In the light of the letters he subsequently wrote to Speed, there is no doubt that Lincoln was reluctant to renew the engagement and go through with the marriage. Not that he lacked affection for Mary, but he feared (as did her sister) he could not make her happy. In the case of Mary Owens he had exhibited a similar hesitancy, though his travail then was less wracking, since his attraction to Miss Owens was comparatively weak. At his marriage, when it finally occurred, he certainly suggested devotion to his bride by presenting her with a ring on the inside of which were engraved the words: "Love is eternal."

The married life of the Lincolns lasted about twenty-two-and-a-half years. There is no question that, during the last of those years, Lincoln experienced at times a kind of domestic hell. Mrs. Lincoln, having lost all money sense, ran up embarrassing bills. And she put on some painful scenes of wifely jealousy. Near Richmond, in the spring of 1865, when she with her husband was visiting Grant's army, she flew into a rage when she learned that he had ridden side by side with two officers' wives at a military review. In regard to one of the two women, she demanded: "Do you mean to say that she saw the President alone? Do you know that I never allow the President to see any woman alone?" The other officer's wife she denounced to her face, and when Lincoln tried to calm her, patiently addressing her as "Mother," she turned on him like a tigress, as a witness afterward said.

In those last years, however, Mary was not entirely herself. She had suffered unbearable afflictions in the death of her son Willie, in the ironies of war that made enemies of Kentucky relatives and friends, and in the unfair public criticism of her as mistress of the White House. These experiences aggravated her nervousness, her feelings of insecurity, her lack of self-control. She was beginning to show signs of the insanity which was to engulf her in the lonely years of her widowhood after her husband had been murdered at her side. In that long time of sadness, the thing she treasured most was the memory of her love for him and his love for her.

The question is whether "conjugal infelicity" characterized the Lincolns during their first twenty years or so together. Were they then a typical American couple of the period, with no more than the usual quota of misunderstanding and spats?

Undoubtedly they had in-law trouble (not an unusual problem). "You wish to know if Mrs. Lincoln and the Todd aristocratic family did not scorn and detest the Hanks and the Lincoln family," Herndon once said to Weik, "and in answer to which I yell—yes. Mrs. Lincoln held the Hanks tribe in contempt and the Lincoln family generally, the old folks, Thomas Lincoln and his good old wife." Thomas and Sarah Lincoln never visited their son in Springfield, and Herndon guessed that they never were invited. If they had appeared at the door, he doubted whether Mary Lincoln would have let them in. But, as usual, Herndon probably exaggerated a bit. After all, Mary honored her father-in-law by naming one of her sons for him.

Mary bore her husband four children. The oldest boy, Robert, became somewhat estranged from his father—much as the father had become estranged from his. As a young man of twenty-one, when asked about the earlier career of the newly famous Lincoln, Robert stated: "My Father's life was of a kind which gave me but little opportunity to learn the details of his early career. During my childhood & early youth he was almost constantly away from home, attending courts or making political speeches—" Perhaps Robert was, as Herndon thought, "his mother's 'baby' all through." Still, as is indicated by the letters Mr. and Mrs. Lincoln exchanged in 1848, while he was a congressman in Washington and she was visiting her relatives in Kentucky, the two had a mutual affectionate interest in the doings and the welfare of their boys. Touchingly, she reassured their father that they had not forgotten him.

These long, revealing letters of 1848, three written by Lincoln and one by Mary, show that husband and wife were fond of one another's company and missed each other when apart. Yet these letters, less than six years after the wedding, also suggest that Mary's behavior already was abnormal and that Lincoln occasionally was embarrassed by it. After going with him to Washington she soon found herself bored with the capital routine and distressed by severe, recurring headaches. She began to shut herself up in her room at Mrs. Sprigg's boardinghouse, coming out only for her meals. After three months of this she left for Kentucky with the boys, then wanted to return. In one of his letters to her Lincoln asked: "Will you be a *good girl* in all things, if I consent?"

In Springfield there were tiffs, and worse than tiffs, between Mr. and Mrs. Lincoln. Sometimes he had to resort to devious ways of getting around her. In 1857 he promised, without informing her, to support a Springfield newspaper at least to the extent of paying for a subscription. "When the paper was brought to my house," Lincoln wrote, "my wife said to me, 'Now are you going to take another worthless little paper?' I said to her *evasively,* 'I have not directed the paper to be left.' " Consequently she told the carrier to stop delivering the paper. And Lincoln had to explain it all to the publisher.

A Springfield neighbor of the Lincolns, Stephen Whitehurst, whose back yard adjoined theirs, told (in 1867) of having seen Mrs. Lincoln with a knife in her hand chase her husband down the street (in 1856 or 1857). The fleeing Lincoln saw people coming his way. Thus headed off, he (in Herndon's retelling) "turned suddenly around, caught his wife at the heavy end, her hips, if you please, and quickly hustled her to the back door of his house and forced, pushed, her in, at the same time, as it were, spanking her heavy end, saying to her . . . 'There, d—n it, now stay in the house and don't disgrace us before the eyes of the world.' " Neither Whitehurst nor Herndon explained what happened to the knife.

"Mr. and Mrs. Lincoln were good neighbors," testified James Gourley, who had lived next door to them for nineteen years. Gourley said the Lincolns seemed to get along all right "unless Mrs. L. got the devil in her," and then Lincoln "would pick up one of his children and walk off, would laugh at her, pay no earthly attention to her when in that wild furious condition." But neighbor Gourley felt much sympathy for her. He knew well her daytime loneliness and nighttime terrors during Lincoln's long absences on the lawyers' circuit. "She always said that if her husband had stayed at home as he ought to that she could love him better."

Certainly the fault was not Mary's alone if there was sometimes trouble in the Lincoln household. And certainly the home life of Lincoln was by no means the unmitigated hell that Herndon imagined. Nevertheless, on the basis of such outward signs as may be seen, it appears that the Lincolns must have been blessed with far less than their fair share of domestic happiness.

It is reasonable to suppose that there was a connection between Lincoln's home life and his public career. But Herndon and others probably were wide of the truth in their supposition that unhappiness at home sent Lincoln out to achieve success in law and politics. More likely the true relationship of home and career was the other way around. In the pursuit of success Lincoln had to neglect his family to some extent, and when at last he achieved the highest success, he brought upon his wife the unendurable strains of wartime living in the White House. Thus his strivings as a public man were likely more a cause than a result of his difficulties as a husband.

chapter 3

THE INSTRUMENT OF GOD

No sooner was Lincoln dead than some of his countrymen began to fight about his soul. Preachers claimed him as a heaven-bound member of the Christian flock, one who had died secure in firm, conventional faith. They had the word of Noah Brooks, a journalist and littérateur who had known the President well and was to have been his private secretary during the second term. Brooks gave assurance of "Mr. Lincoln's saving knowledge of Christ" and declared that "he talked always of Christ, his cross, his atonement." The late President, Brooks said again, had expressed himself freely as having "a hope of blessed immortality through Jesus Christ." And yet, among his friends in Springfield, Illinois, Lincoln had gained the reputation of a doubter or even an unbeliever. Bill Herndon gathered the reminiscences of these friends for ammunition. Soon he was at war with the preachers and their pious allies.

When the popular writer Josiah Holland went to Springfield, in search of materials for his projected Lincoln biography, he inquired of Herndon about the great man's religious beliefs. Herndon replied that Lincoln was never a Christian, strictly speaking, and advised that the less said about that, the better. When Holland's *Life of Abraham Lincoln* appeared, before the end of 1865, Herndon was shocked as he began to read one of the 100,000 copies of the best seller. Here was the story of a "true-hearted Christian," with many a tale to adorn the theme of his devoutness. Here was the anecdote of Newton Bateman, superintendent of education in Illinois. Bateman said Lincoln in October, 1860 had confided a belief in the value of prayer and faith—a belief he did not want his friends to hear of! The more Herndon thought about the Holland book, the angrier he became.

He wanted to see the truth told about Lincoln's religion. As the man's long-time law partner, he was sure he knew what the truth was, and he obtained confirmation from (among others) his predecessor, Lincoln's first law partner, John T. Stuart. "Lincoln always denied that Jesus was the Christ of God—denied that Jesus was the son of God as understood and maintained by the Christian Church," Stuart told Herndon, according to the latter's notes. "He was an avowed and open infidel, and sometimes bordered on atheism." Herndon realized that Lincoln had not trumpeted his heterodoxy in stump speeches and state papers. Of course not. Politics was politics, and Lincoln was no fool.

In his startling Ann Rutledge lecture of 1866 Herndon took the opportunity to let the world in on the truth about Lincoln's religion, or lack of it. Newspapers and magazines throughout the country and abroad picked up the news. In Dundee, Scotland, Dr. James Smith read of the Springfield lecture and his temper rose. Dr. Smith, the American consul in Dundee, with an appointment from Lincoln, had been the pastor of the First

Presbyterian Church in Springfield, the church that Mrs. Lincoln and her children had attended, the church that Lincoln himself had rented a pew in. Smith was positive that he, by his own effort, had converted Lincoln to orthodox Christianity. He had given him a copy of the book he had written to lead doubters to the faith by rational argument, and he was sure that Lincoln had read it and had been convinced. So now Smith sent Herndon an indignant letter insisting that Lincoln "did avow his belief in the Divine Authority and Inspiration of the Scriptures." This testimony did not faze Herndon. Impertinently he wrote back to inquire why, if Lincoln was a convert, he never joined Dr. Smith's church.

A new blast against the prim and pious was detonated with the publication (1872) of a Lincoln biography which bore the name of Ward H. Lamon on the title page. Actually, Chauncey Black had written the book and Herndon had provided the materials—the powder for the explosion. This Lamon-Black-Herndon volume proclaimed that Lincoln "was never a member of any church, nor did he believe in the divinity of Christ, or the inspiration of the Scriptures." If in his youth "he went to church at all, he went to mock, and came away to mimic." As a young man in New Salem he composed a manuscript "deriding the gospel history of Jesus." Afterward, as a "wily politician," he regulated "his religious manifestations with reference to his political interests."

Most reviewers of the book were outraged. So were many readers. One, the Reverend James A. Reed, determined to refute once and for all what he considered Herndonian slanders. A stern, unsmiling parson, Reed served in what once had been Dr. James Smith's pulpit at the First Presbyterian Church in Springfield. He had no personal recollections of Lincoln but industriously gathered up the statements of others who did have. This evidence he put into a lecture which he delivered at Springfield and elsewhere, then published in *Scribner's Monthly* (July 1873) under the title of "The Later Life and Religious Sentiments of Abraham Lincoln."

He was defending Lincoln's name, Reed explained, and not trying to get the national hero's endorsement for Christianity, for "the faith and future of the Christian religion in no wise depends upon the sentiments of Abraham Lincoln." He was willing to grant Herndon this much—that in early life Lincoln might have been an infidel or almost one. No matter. As President, he became a believing and a practicing Christian. This was Reed's main point.

Reed supported it in part with new declarations in which some of Herndon's and Lincoln's Springfield acquaintances altered or took back their earlier testimony. John T. Stuart in particular, disclaiming the words Herndon had attributed to him, confessed he had no confidences from Lincoln about the latter's spiritual life.

In Reed's lecture, Dr. Smith repeated his assertion that he had converted Lincoln, and Ninian W. Edwards remembered Lincoln's having said: "I have been reading a work of Dr. Smith on the evidences of Christianity, and have heard him preach and converse on the subject, and I am now convinced of the truth of the Christian religion." Dr. Phineas D. Gurley, pastor of the New York Avenue Presbyterian Church which President Lincoln had attended in Washington, said that (unlike Stuart) he himself had had many conversations with Lincoln about the Bible and Christianity. "I considered him sound not only on the truth of the Christian religion but on all its fundamental doctrines and teaching," Gurley said. More than that. Before the end, Lincoln had told Gurley "it was his intention soon to make a profession of religion."

With such testimony as Gurley's before him, Reed stoutly concluded that Lincoln in his later days "was fast bringing his life into conformity with the Christian standard." He indulged less and less in the "coarse storytelling" of previous times. True, he still went to that godless place, the theater, but only for relaxation and rest. And what was he thinking of, there in Ford's Theater, on the fatal evening of April 14, 1865? Reed had the answer from a Springfield Baptist minister who said he had it from Mrs. Lincoln herself. Lincoln paid little or no attention to the actors on the stage that night. Instead, he talked with his wife about his future plans. He wanted to visit the Holy Land to see the places hallowed by the footprints of the Saviour. "He was saying there was no city he so much desired to see as *Jerusalem;* and with that word half spoken on his tongue, the bullet of the assassin entered his brain. . . ."

Herndon was not going to swallow *that,* or any of the rest of Reed's nonsense. He, too, had a statement from Mrs. Lincoln. In it she admitted that her husband had "had no faith and no hope in the usual acceptation of those words" and was "never a technical Christian." Herndon also had a note from John G. Nicolay, the President's wartime private secretary. In this note, written only six weeks after the assassination, Nicolay averred: "Mr. Lincoln did not to my knowledge in any way change his religious ideas, opinions, or beliefs from the time he left Springfield to the day of his death." Thus armed, Herndon in December 1873 wrote out a lecture in rebuttal to Reed's. The thesis: the young Lincoln was an infidel and the older Lincoln never changed. The conclusion: "He died an unbeliever."

By the time Herndon delivered this lecture, the argument had degenerated into a senseless row. "I don't know anything about Lincoln's religion," David Davis was moved to say, "nor do I think anybody else knows anything about it." Indeed, one could assume that Lincoln had believed anything—or nothing. In the fog of controversy and confusion, sectarians of all kinds could advance their claims upon him and make a case that appeared to be as plausible as any other.

The spiritualists were among the most persistent. They asserted repeatedly that Lincoln had been one of them. In later years a succession of books, pamphlets, and articles told of mysterious goings on at séances at the White House and in private homes, where the President allegedly consorted with mediums. Some of these occasions were reported by more than one supposed witness and in fairly plausible detail.

There was, for example, the case of the waltzing piano. On

February 5, 1863, at the Georgetown home of Cranstoun Laurie, a statistician in the Post Office Department, Lincoln with his wife attended one of the famed Nettie Colburn's séances. After Nettie had communicated with the spirits, Laurie's daughter sat down at a big grand piano, and it began to rise and fall in time with the music. Lincoln, his curiosity aroused, went up to the piano and placed his hands on it but could find nothing amiss. Then, with three other men, he climbed on top and sat there, his long legs dangling. This time the piano rose in the air, remained off the floor for several minutes, and finally began to sway and wobble. Lincoln and his fellow passengers were glad to get off. One of them said, sheepishly, that their friends, if told of this, would accuse them of having been "psychologized." Lincoln replied that any doubter should be brought to one of the séances. "And when the piano *seems* to rise," the President quipped, "let him slip his foot under the leg and be convinced by the *weight* of *evidence* resting upon his understanding."

According to these reports, Lincoln must have been a person of extraordinary psychic powers. He must have been "mediumistic." With his rare sensitivity he must have felt vibrations from the other world. This kinship with the unseen helps to explain that mysterious, elusive quality of his that so many of his contemporaries noticed but could not account for. So it seemed to one spiritualist of a later day, Mrs. Harriet M. Shelton, a New York woman of eighty-odd years. Mrs. Shelton received confirmation from the best possible source—from the ever-living Abraham himself. On the night of January 20, 1952, he materialized himself before her in her New York apartment. Often he communicated with her from afar. Once he told her that, if he had lived longer, he would have written a firsthand narrative of his remarkable psychic experiences while on earth.

And that is not all he has told her. Every morning she sits alone in her room and receives thought messages from him. These she expresses in her own words, aloud. She is talking to the millions of dead souls who wander in a kind of shadowland.

They are strange, sad, gray shapes that she has glimpsed only once or twice. They are earth-bound souls, stranded somewhere between here and heaven. They cannot move on to eternal happiness, because they lack the faith that would give them the desire to go. Among the spirits already in heaven, there is a devoted band engaged in a great Rescue Work to salvage these souls. The leader is Lincoln. He communicates through Mrs. Shelton because the earth-bound dead will listen more readily to an earthling than to a spirit already inhabiting the heaven they do not believe in.

2

There might be a certain element of truth in the spiritualists' conception of Lincoln. There might also be elements of truth in the views of preachers like Smith and Reed and the opposing views of Herndon and his informants. But not all the truth is to be found in any such conception.

Most of these quarrelers were inclined, quite naturally, to discover in Lincoln the beliefs that they themselves espoused. They were prone to exaggerate these particular beliefs and to overlook or deny the rest. But even if preferences and preconceptions had not got in the way, it would have been hard to ascertain the whole truth. After all, the fullness of any man's religion is a secret between himself and God.

Herndon, aggressive freethinker that he was, took extreme positions in his reaction against what he considered the cant of pious moralizers. He did not always mean exactly what he said, and from time to time he contradicted himself. On the one hand he called Lincoln a "theist" (meaning presumably a "deist") and on the other hand an "atheist." The same man could hardly have been both at once. What Herndon apparently intended to convey, and what he said over and over again, was that *Lincoln belonged to no established sect and agreed with none, took the Bible in no literal, fundamentalist sense, and held a rationalistic and mechanistic view of God and His relationship to man.*

In saying this much, Herndon may well have been fairly accurate with regard to the Lincoln he was acquainted with—that is, the Lincoln of the Springfield law office. Except by hearsay, Herdon did not really know the earlier Lincoln, the New Salem youth, nor did he know the later one, the wartime President. Whether he was right about *them* is another question.

According to the recollections of New Salem friends, recorded by Herndon, Lincoln when in his twenties was a skeptic among skeptics. He read books like Thomas Paine's *Age of Reason* and discussed them approvingly in the tavern and the village store. In 1834 he wrote an essay to show that the Bible was not God's inspired word nor Jesus God's divine son. When Lincoln brought this manuscript with him to the store, his employer snatched the pages from him and threw them into the stove.

According to "one of his closest friends," Lincoln still was "enthusiastic in his infidelity" when he first moved to Springfield. In 1838 he carried his enthusiasm with him on his visits to the office of the county clerk. "He would come into the clerk's office where I and some young men were writing and staying," the unnamed friend recalled, "and would bring the Bible with him; would read a chapter and argue against it."

If these reports are true, Lincoln seems at least a bit two-faced in those years of his political apprenticeship, for in public statements he praised the Book which in private arguments he denounced. As a candidate for the State Legislature, he wrote an address to the people of Sangamon County (March 9, 1832) for publication in the *Sangamo Journal,* urging state-supported education. He mentioned the "advantages and satisfactions to be derived from all being able to read the scriptures and other works, both of a religious and moral nature, for themselves." Again, speaking in Cincinnati on September 17, 1839, he declared: "The good old maxims of the Bible are applicable, and truly applicable to human affairs. . . ."

Still, though these references to Holy Writ are respectful enough, what is perhaps most remarkable about them is their restraint. Even in public, the Lincoln of the 1830s by no means implied that the Bible was divinely inspired. He bracketed "the scriptures and other works" as if they were of equal value. He spoke of "the good old maxims of the Bible" as if they were on a par with those of the *Farmer's Almanac.*

And certainly Lincoln in those years was no churchgoing, professing Christian. "I've never been to church yet, nor probably shall not [*sic*] be soon," he wrote to Mary Owens about his new life in Springfield (May 7, 1837). "I stay away because I am conscious I should not know how to behave myself."

Nor is there any question that he became notorious for his unorthodox habits and beliefs. When he lost the congressional nomination in 1843, he explained his defeat as having been due in part to the "strangest combination of church influence" against him. "My wife has some relatives in the Presbyterian and some in the Episcopal Churches, and therefore, whereever [*sic*] it would tell, I was set down as either the one or the other, whilst it was every where contended that no ch[r]istian ought to go for me, because I belonged to no church, was suspected of being a deist, and had talked about fighting a duel."

When Lincoln finally got the nomination and ran for Congress in 1846, he again faced the hostility of the church influence. His opponent, the venerable frontier revivalist Peter Cartwright, was "whispering the charge of infidelity" against him. To clear the air, Lincoln issued a handbill to the voters of the Seventh Congressional District, July 31, 1846. He began this apologia by referring to the charge being circulated that he was "an open scoffer at Christianity." He continued:

"That I am not a member of any Christian Church, is true; but I have never denied the truth of the Scriptures; and I have never spoken with intentional disrespect of religion in general, or of any denomination of Christians in particular. It is true that in early life I was inclined to believe in what I understand is called the 'Doctrine of Necessity'—that is, that the human mind is impelled to action, or held in rest by some power, over which the mind itself has no control; and I have sometimes (with one, two or three, but never publicly) tried to maintain this position in argument. The habit of arguing thus however, I have, entirely left off for more than five years."

Herndon apparently did not remember this handbill, nor did he have a copy of it. None of those who took part in the controversy after Lincoln's death seemed to be aware of the paper's existence. Even if all of them had been aware of it, the issue would not have been put to rest.

On one important point the handbill corroborates Herndon perfectly. Herndon reported Lincoln as saying: "There are no accidents in my philosophy. Every effect must have its cause. The past is the cause of the present, and the present will be the cause of the future. All these are links in the endless chain stretching from the finite to the infinite." Lincoln, in short, did not believe in freedom of the will, said Herndon, who disagreed and often argued the question with him. Sometimes Lincoln changed the expression and said there was no freedom of the mind. In his apologia of 1846 he does not state that he has abandoned his fatalistic belief. He only says he has ceased to argue it.

On another point, however, the handbill appears to give the lie to the Herndon story. "I have never denied the truth of the Scriptures," Lincoln says. Still, this is not a very clear or inclusive disavowal. It does not necessarily imply that he never denied the *literal* truth of any Scriptural passage. Anyhow, the handbill is a campaign document, not a disinterested testament of faith.

In subsequent political speeches Lincoln talked like something other than an orthodox, believing Christian, though he occasionally quoted the Bible and referred to God. Speaking in Chicago (July 10, 1858) he said: " 'As your Father in Heaven is perfect, be ye also perfect.' The Saviour, I suppose, did not expect that any human creature could be perfect as the Father in Heaven. . . . He set that up as a standard, and he who did most towards reaching that standard, attained the highest degree of moral perfection." Moral perfection—not salvation! Lincoln was talking more as a humanist than as a Christian.

In those pre-Presidential years Lincoln was rather sarcastic about politicians who called upon God to support their worldly causes. Stumping for the Whig presidential candidate Zachary Taylor (at Worcester, Massachusetts, September 12, 1848) he criticized the Free Soil men for mixing theology and politics. "In declaring that they would 'do their duty and leave the consequences to God,'" he remarked, "[they] merely gave an excuse for taking a course that they were not able to maintain by a fair and full argument." He was equally critical of pro-slavery people who enlisted God on their side. Regarding the book *Slavery Ordained by God,* written by a Reverend Frederick A. Ross, Lincoln noted (in 1858): "Certainly there is no contending against the Will of God; but there is some difficulty in ascertaining, and applying it." *Was* slavery so ordained? "The Almighty gives no audable [*sic*] answer to the question, and his revelation—the Bible—gives none—or, at most, none but such as admits of a squabble, as to its meaning."

After 1860 Lincoln himself was to refer with growing frequency to the will of God in human affairs.

3

Though Herndon was, on the whole, correct in describing Lincoln the Illinois lawyer as a man of doubt and disbelief, it does not necessarily follow that Lincoln the President was exactly the same. Herndon had little evidence for arguing thus, and the evidence he had is far from convincing.

There is a statement he obtained (September 22, 1870) from Jesse W. Fell, the friend to whom Lincoln had given information for his first biographical sketch. "True," Fell wrote, after referring to Lincoln's skeptical inclinations, "he may have changed or modified these sentiments after his removal from among us, though this is hardly reconcilable with the history of the man, and his entire devotion to public matters during his four years' residence at the national capital." This, obviously, is nothing but inference, and rather illogical inference at that.

There is also Herndon's letter from John G. Nicolay testifying that, in the White House, Lincoln did not change his religious beliefs. "I do not know just what they were, never having heard him explain them in detail," Nicolay admitted; "but I am very sure he gave no outward indication of his mind having undergone any change in that regard while here." Such a confession of ignorance is enough to throw Nicolay's testimony out of court.

Whether Nicolay could see them or not, there are plenty of signs that Lincoln changed his mind and grew in faith after going to Washington in 1861. And, for that matter, there are indications that he was changing before he left Springfield, though Herndon could not see them. In fact, Lincoln passed through several crises of the spirit, and they had a cumulative effect upon him.

The first occurred in 1841, the year that opened with a "fatal first of January" when Lincoln broke his engagement with Mary Todd and was depressed almost to the point of a mental breakdown. While seeking forgetfulness on a visit to Josh Speed's Kentucky home, he received a copy of the Oxford Bible as a gift from Speed's mother-in-law. Afterward he wrote to Mary Speed and asked her to tell her mother that he intended to read it regularly. He added: "I doubt not that it is really, as she says, the best cure for the 'Blues' could one but take it according to the truth." As this qualifying clause suggests, he remained too skeptical to get the full benefit of the Bible's therapeutic charm. Yet he was willing to try the remedy. He was taking a step, short and hesitant though it might be, toward faith.

A second spiritual crisis came in 1850 with the death of the younger of the two Lincoln boys, little Eddie, not yet four. Again Lincoln sank into the depths of melancholy, but this time he had to care for Mary, even more shaken than he, and their son Robert. In their hour of grief they had an unexpected visitor, the Reverend Dr. James Smith, pastor of the First Presbyterian Church, who volunteered his sympathy, though they were not worshipers at his church. Apparently the Lincolns liked Dr. Smith and found some consolation in his words. At Eddie's funeral he preached the sermon. Before long, Mrs. Lincoln joined his church and Mr. Lincoln began to sit with her on Sunday mornings, in a pew for which he paid the rent.

"Mr. Lincoln became a member of my congregation, at my request," Dr. Smith stated some seventeen years later, in the controversy over Lincoln's religion. At the same time Dr. Smith made the claim that he had converted Lincoln to the Christian faith. But in the heat of argument the doctor apparently overdid it. That he gave Lincoln a copy of his book, *The Christian's Defense,* and that Lincoln read it, is probably true. That Lincoln found winning arguments in it is very possible. That he was completely won over is as incredible as Herndon thought it was. For Lincoln became a member of Dr. Smith's congregation only in the sense that he attended services. He did not join the church.

Nevertheless, in going as far as to occupy a pew, he had advanced well beyond his isolated position of the past. And when, less than a year after his son's death, his father lay dying, Lincoln sent the old man the consolations of Christian faith, telling him "to remember to call upon, and confide in, our great, and good, and merciful Maker; who will not turn away from him in any extremity. He notes the fall of a sparrow, and numbers the hairs of our heads; and He will not forget the dying man, who puts his trust in Him."

Later Lincoln underwent a four-year ordeal that began with his inauguration as President and did not end until the last night of his life. Anyone must have been remarkably imperceptive to suppose, as Jesse W. Fell did, that "his entire devotion to public matters" kept the President from giving new and deeper thought to matters of religion. The war—"this great trouble," as Lincoln called it—brought wearying responsibilities he could not escape for a single day. From time to time he took a poor excuse for a vacation by visiting the Army of the Potomac in the field. On one visit, in the spring of 1863, he seemed to be somewhat revived and rested after riding horseback in the open air. One of his companions said as much "Well, yes," Lincoln replied, "I do feel some better, I think but, somehow, it don't appear to touch the tired spot, which can't be got at." To ease that tired spot, he might have been expected to turn more and more toward the solace of religion.

In the midst of the unrelenting torment of his official duties Lincoln had to undergo still another trial of the soul, a personal one, when a second son was taken from him. Willie eleven, died on February 20, 1862. Of all the four boys, Willie had been the most nearly like his father, and between these two there had grown a rare bond of understanding. Now Lincoln grieved as never before—as deeply as the boy's mother though not so openly. Again and again he shut himself in a room to weep alone. Nights he dreamed happy dreams of Willie, then wakened to the joyless reality of day. Eagerly he listened to the assurances of clergymen who came to tell him and his wife that the boy was not dead, that he still lived, in heaven.

These great troubles transfigured Lincoln in the White House, as more than one close acquaintance has testified. Mrs Lincoln said, regarding her husband and religion, "He first seemed to think about the subject when our boy Willie died, and then more than ever about the time he went to Gettysburg." Francis B. Carpenter, the artist who spent six months at the White House, quoted Lincoln as saying he had felt a "*change*" which amounted to a "true religious experience." Gurley, who preached to the President on Sundays, recalled his declaring once with tears in his eyes that he believed his "heart was changed." Noah Brooks reported Lincoln's having referred to a "change of heart" and a "change of mind." Lincoln did not remember having had this experience all at once, but supposed a "process of crystallization" had begun after his election and the start of the war. In the White House he prayed every day, and if no more than ten words occurred to him, he said those ten. And he read the Bible regularly, according to Brooks.

"When I knew him in early life he was a skeptic," Joshua

Speed reminisced about his lifelong friend. "The only evidence I have of any change was in the summer before he was assassinated. I was invited out to the Soldiers' Home to spend the night. As I entered the room, near night, he was sitting near a window intensely reading his Bible. Approaching him, I said: 'I am glad to see you profitably engaged.' 'Yes,' said he, 'I am profitably engaged.' 'Well,' said I, 'if you have recovered from your skepticism, I am sorry to say that I have not!' Looking me earnestly in the face, and placing his hand on my shoulder, he said: 'You are wrong, Speed; take all of this book upon reason that you can, and the balance on faith, and you will live and die a happier and better man.' "

Lincoln read the Bible and prayed, but still belonged to no church. According to Carpenter, a member of Congress asked him why he did not join any of the Christian communions, and Lincoln explained: "Because I have found difficulty, without mental reservation, in giving my assent to their long and complicated confessions of faith. When any church will inscribe over its altar the Saviour's condensed statement of law and gospel: 'Thou shalt love the Lord thy God with all thy heart and with all thy soul and with all thy mind, and love thy neighbor as thyself,' that church will I join with all my heart."

There remains the question whether Lincoln finally, before the end, committed himself to any conventional creed, or ever reached the point of doing it, as the preachers afterward maintained he had. His widow did not seem to think so, but the question is unanswerable.

No matter. His "principles and practices and the spirit of his whole life were of the very kind we universally agree to call Christian," as Jesse W. Fell said. Even Herndon was moved to write: "Do you not see Lincoln's Christ like charity—liberality—toleration loom up & blossom above all?" And Mrs. Lincoln put the point most beautifully when she said her husband had been a truly religious man but his religion was "a kind of poetry in his nature."

4

As for Lincoln and spiritualism, he could hardly have avoided the subject, since spiritualists kept after him almost from the beginning of his presidency. Before the end of 1861 one of them forwarded him from the spirit world a letter written backward, in "mirror writing," which said: "I, like millions of other disembodied spirits, feel a desire to convey expressions of gratitude and hope . . . for the Union." The ghostly writer offered to communicate personally with the President. Soon a message from a "Congress of Spirits" came to Nettie Colburn, with instructions for her to take it to Lincoln. Still another medium was sent by "Spiritual influence" to confer with him "pertaining to the interests of the Nation." The spirits and the spiritualists appeared to be most patriotic, but there is no evidence that Lincoln responded to any offer of supernatural aid until his beloved Willie died.

Then, like so many other bereaved parents before and since, both of the Lincolns became susceptible to almost any assurance that the dead yet lived and could be heard and spoken to. "Your son is alive in paradise," a consoling minister told Lincoln, according to Carpenter's report. "Do you not remember the passage in the Gospels? 'God is not the God of the dead, but of the living, for all live unto Him.' " Hearing this, Lincoln sat for a while with his head bowed. Suddenly he sprang to his feet, his face shining. He exclaimed: "He's alive! He is not dead! He *is* alive!" Soon after that, Lincoln was in a conversation with his Secretary of the Treasury, Salmon P. Chase. "Do you ever find yourself talking with the dead?" Lincoln asked. Without giving Chase time to reply, the President continued: "I do. Ever since Willie's death I catch myself involuntarily talking to him as if he were with me—*and I feel that he is!*" Whether or not Lincoln actually spoke these precise words, he unquestionably was ripe at that time for suggestions of spirit communication, and Mrs. Lincoln was even more so.

At her instance, he welcomed professional mediums to the

White House. There and elsewhere, he attended several séances. He obtained books on spiritualism (for instance, a volume entitled *Further Communications from the World of Spirits . . . Given through a Lady*) which he probably read. And among his political enemies he gained a certain notoriety as a practicing spiritualist. A nameless "Citizen of Ohio" wrote a tract with the subtitle, *The Nation Demoralized and Its President a Spirit Rapper.* Hostile newspapers described him as a gullible man who ran the government on the advice of clever charlatans.

According to accounts by spiritualists, Lincoln was indeed guided in important decisions by words that came through entranced, unconscious mediums. At one séance, in December 1862, as Nettie Colburn later told the story, he sat looking intently at her while she lapsed into a kind of coma and then delivered, involuntarily and in another voice than her own, a strong plea that the Emancipation Proclamation be not changed, nor delayed beyond the first of the new year. When the medium had finished, Lincoln sat spellbound till someone asked him if he had noticed anything unusual in the deep, vibrant voice that had been issuing from her lips. He glanced up at a portrait of Daniel Webster which hung on the wall. "Yes!" he said. "And it is very singular—very!" He had been listening to the godlike Daniel! He obeyed him. The Emancipation Proclamation, unchanged, *was* issued on January 1, 1863!

According to other accounts, however, Lincoln did not always take seriously the messages that were relayed from the departed great. At one séance, which some members of the Cabinet attended with the President, a communication in writing came from Henry Knox, who had been George Washington's Secretary of War. Knox advised: "Less policy talk. More action!" Lincoln turned to his own war secretary and said: "That message is for you, Stanton. It's from your predecessor." Then Lincoln asked Knox if he could tell when the rebellion finally would be put down. This time a written message appeared with contributions by George Washington, Benjamin Franklin, the Marquis de Lafayette, William Wilberforce, and

Napoleon Bonaparte. But the views of these distinguished ghosts were vague and contradictory. Lincoln dryly remarked that opinions must differ among the spirits. "Their talk and advice sound a good deal like the talk of my Cabinet," he said.

While none of these reported details need be taken as literal facts, it seems likely that Lincoln was capable of joking at the mummery of the mediums. And, without credulity, he was capable of treating it as something other than a laughing matter. He is said to have asked the head of the Smithsonian Institution, Dr. Joseph Henry, to find out how one well-known medium, Colchester, produced his sound effects. Inviting Colchester to put on a show at the Smithsonian, Dr. Henry discovered that the man had a device strapped to his arm; by expanding or contracting his muscles, he could cause rappings at a distance even while holding hands with people on both sides of him. Noah Brooks reported that he and a friend also investigated a Colchester sitting and found that a mysterious drum-thumping was not so mysterious after all: it was the work of a human hand in the dark, and the hand was Colchester's. Brooks conveyed to Mrs. Lincoln the disillusioning news.

From such revelations as this, Mrs. Lincoln eventually lost her hope for balm in spiritualism. In 1869 she wrote emphatically: "I am not EITHER a spiritualist, but I sincerely believe —our loved ones, who have only 'gone before,' are permitted to watch over those who were dearer to them than life." And Lincoln, too, lost whatever hope he had had. Most likely, he had attended séances partly to humor his wife and to protect her. But, most likely also, he wanted to satisfy his own spiritual need—and his own intellectual curiosity. His mind was open, to start with, but he could not accept the hocus-pocus: the fraudulent rappings and drummings, the childish mirror-writing, the talking in riddles, the jejune and juvenile messages that came through. He did not become a spiritualist, either.

That is, he cannot properly be called a spiritualist in the usual but restricted sense of one who communicates with departed spirits through the rigmarole of séances, mediums, controls, levitations, trances, strange lights and noises, and the like. But the word *spiritualist* also has a more general meaning. It refers to any person who has a sensitivity to the unseen and incorporeal, who looks for influences from other than rational sources, who is guided by the vision and the dream. In this sense, Lincoln *was* a spiritualist.

He did not need intermediaries or paraphernalia for getting in touch with the invisible and all but unknowable essence that surrounded him. Something of a mystic, he could commune directly with the unseen. "I always did have a strong tendency to mysticism," he once avowed to Speed. Though never quite a Quaker (he assumed that some of his ancestors had been), Lincoln had a strong affinity for the beliefs of the Friends. He could see considerable sense in the idea of the Inner Light, of the spark of universal spirit glowing within each human heart.

"I always was superstitious," he confessed to Speed in another letter (in 1842). "I am superstitious," he wrote to a fellow politician (in 1856). As a young man he thought himself "peculiar" for the strength and frequency of his "forebodings." To the last of his life he never shook off his susceptibility to mysterious signs and portents.

Shortly before his first election to the Presidency he had an odd experience which he never forgot. Thoroughly tired from political excitement, he went home and lay down on a lounge to rest. Opposite him was a bureau with a mirror tilted so that he could see his reflection from where he lay. He was astonished at what he saw. There, in the glass, he beheld a double image of his face, and one of the two faces was very pale, like a dead man's. A few days afterward he tried the lounge again, and the same pair of images appeared.

More than four years later, after his reelection in 1864, he remembered this vision and told Noah Brooks about it. For some time, he said, it had bothered him and he could not keep it off his mind. "For the thing would come up once in a while and give me a little pang, as though something uncomfortable had happened." He said he mentioned it to his wife, and she thought it was a sign he would be elected a second time and (the dead face) that he would die during his second term. Lincoln himself, Brooks gathered, took the double image to be nothing more than an optical illusion, though he seemed superstitious enough to wish he never had seen it.

For this omen of the looking glass, we have to take the word of Brooks, but there is positive proof that Lincoln believed in portents. He paid attention to dream warnings. On June 9, 1863, he sent a telegram from the White House to Mrs. Lincoln, who had gone to Philadelphia and had taken with her their ten-year-old Tad, a boy more precious than ever since the death of his brother Willie. "Think you had better put Tad's pistol away," Lincoln said in the telegram. "I had an ugly dream about him."

Though not so well documented, there is a story of a dream of death that Lincoln supposedly related not long before the assassination. He dreamed he woke, in the middle of the night, to find the White House silent, then began to hear muffled sobs that sounded like the weeping of a number of people. He got up and wandered around until he came to the East Room, and there he saw a catafalque with a body in funeral wrappings on top of it and a crowd of mourners around it. Turning to a soldier-guard, he asked who was dead. "The President," the soldier said. "He was killed by an assassin."

If that story has a pat, made-up quality, it is at least in keeping with Lincoln's well-known propensity to dream and talk about his dreaming. There are a number of similar anecdotes, one of the most credible having behind it the authority of Gideon Welles, Lincoln's diary-keeping Secretary of the Navy. Welles wrote down his account three days after the incident.

It occurred on April 14, 1865. That morning Lincoln held a Cabinet meeting, and the occasion was especially dignified by the presence of General Grant, fresh from his victory at Appomattox. The President was hoping for news from General Sherman in North Carolina, where a Confederate army still was in the field. To the Cabinet conferees Lincoln remarked that he had no doubt news soon would come and would be good. For, he said, he had had a dream the previous night. It was a dream he had in advance of almost every important event of the war—always the same dream. In it he "seemed to be in some singular, indescribable vessel," and he "was moving with great rapidity towards an indefinite shore."

5

In Lincoln's belief, however, there was a power that did far more than prophesy the future in dreams and enigmatic signs. There was a power that determined events. It might be called Necessity, or Fate, or God, and Lincoln referred to it by these and other names.

As a boy, Lincoln doubtless came under the influence of the predestinarian Baptist doctrines of his parents and neighbors. As a young man, perhaps in response to the rationalistic literature he read, he favored a rather abstract and mechanistic conception—the "Doctrine of Necessity"—which he argued with Herndon and which he mentioned in his campaign handbill of 1846. As he grew older, and especially after his elevation to the Presidency, Lincoln increasingly personified this moving force as God.

His changing attitude, as of 1842, is revealed in his correspondence with Speed. Lincoln had done the work of Cupid in helping to bring about the marriage of Speed and his beloved Fanny. Speed, finding wedded life blissful far beyond his expectations, wrote to thank Lincoln for the latter's help. "The truth is," Lincoln wrote back, "I am not sure there was any merit, with me, in the part I took in your difficulty; I was drawn to it as by fate; if I would, I could not have done less than I did. I always was superstitious; and as part of my superstition, I believe God made me one of the instruments of bringing your Fanny and you together, which union I have no doubt He had foreordained."

Eventually Lincoln came to feel that Fate had marked him for some much grander purpose. As President, he once told

Congressman Isaac N. Arnold how, years before, he had declined the governorship of Oregon Territory when it was offered him. Arnold observed: "If you had gone to Oregon, you might have come back as senator, but you would never have been President." Yes, said Lincoln, and with a pensive expression he added: "I have all my life been a fatalist. What is to be will be, or rather, I have found all my life as Hamlet says:

> *There is a divinity that shapes our ends,*
> *Rough-hew them how we will."*

President Lincoln considered himself "an instrument of Providence," as he reportedly said to a group of ministers who called on him at the end of 1862. Of course, he had his own opinions and purposes, he admitted. "But I am conscious every moment that all I am and all I have is subject to the control of a Higher Power."

Fatalistic though he was, Lincoln did not rule out all possibility of human will and human choice. "I believe in the supremacy of the human conscience," he was quoted as saying to the ministerial delegation of 1862. And in 1864 he wrote to a Quaker correspondent, Mrs. Eliza P. Gurney, that we must recognize God's wisdom and our own error. "Meanwhile we must work earnestly in the best light He gives us, trusting that so working still conduces to the great ends He ordains."

Thus Lincoln came to look upon himself, in all humility, as an agent of God upon earth. And he strove to make out the Almighty's purposes, so that he might best perform his own mission in giving effect to the supernal will. What was God's purpose in the Civil War?

"All will be well in the end, because our cause is just and God will be on our side." So (according to Dr. Gurley) Lincoln spoke to a delegation of clergymen who called at the White House during the darkest days of the war. At another time he wrote to an Illinois critic of his war methods: "Let us diligently apply the means, never doubting that a just God, in his own good time, will give us the rightful result." And yet Lincoln held to no simple and self-righteous belief that God was on his side, and the Devil on the other.

Not that he supposed the rebel cause was just or would win. To a Tennessee woman, who sought the release of her prisoner husband with the plea that he was a religious man, he said, "The religion that sets men to rebel and fight against their government, because, as they think, that government does not sufficiently help *some* men to eat their bread on the sweat of *other* men's faces, is not the sort of religion upon which people can get to heaven!" (He granted the pardon the woman wanted.)

But neither did Lincoln believe that wickedness was a monopoly of the South. In some of his proclamations he sounded like a latter-day Jeremiah calling his own people to account for their sins. Proclaiming a day of humiliation, fasting, and prayer in 1861, he reminded the nation that "fear of the Lord is the beginning of wisdom." In 1863 he said, "We have forgotten God."

As the war dragged on past the second summer, and Lincoln pondered the meaning of the bloodshed, he was more and more inclined to doubt that God was a fellow combatant. Once he jotted down his inmost thoughts on a piece of paper. He did not date this note, but it probably was written in September 1862. In it he wrote:

"The will of God prevails. In great contests each party claims to act in accordance with the will of God. Both *may* be, and one *must* be wrong. God can not be *for*, and *against* the same thing at the same time. In the present civil war it is quite possible that God's purpose is something different from the purpose of either party—and yet the human instrumentalities, working just as they do, are of the best adaptation to effect His purpose. I am almost ready to say this is probably true—that God wills this contest, and wills that it shall not end yet. By His mere quiet power, on the minds of the now contestants, He could have either *saved* or *destroyed* the Union without a human contest. Yet the contest began. And having begun He could give the final victory to either side any day. Yet the contest proceeds."

Often, as the slaughter increased and brought no end to war, Lincoln puzzled over the hidden aim of the Higher Power, but he did not doubt an aim was there. "The purposes of the Almighty are perfect, and must prevail, though we erring mortals may fail to accurately perceive them in advance," he wrote to his Quaker correspondent, Mrs. Gurney, in September, 1864—after Grant had fought his Wilderness campaign with staggering casualties and no decisive victory. "We hoped for a happy termination of this terrible war before this; but God knows best, and has ruled otherwise."

Finally Lincoln hit upon an explanation for the long continuance of the war. God must have been offended, and this must be His way of removing the offense. It must be, also, His way of punishing both Northerners and Southerners for a national sin—the sin of slavery. Lincoln expressed this opinion in his Second Inaugural. To the throng that stood before him on that sodden March day in 1865, he said:

"The Almighty has His own purposes. 'Woe unto the world because of offences! for it must needs be that offences come; but woe to that man by whom the offence cometh!' If we shall suppose that American slavery is one of those offences which, in the providence of God, must needs come, but which, having continued through His appointed time, He now wills to remove, and that He gives to both North and South, this terrible war, as the woe due to those by whom the offence came, shall we discern therein any departure from those divine attributes which the believers in a Living God always ascribe to Him?"

Congratulations upon this address came to Lincoln from the crafty, hard-bitten politician Thurlow Weed, of all people. Lincoln responded: "Men are not flattered by being shown that there has been a difference of purpose between the Almighty and them. To deny it, however, in this case, is to deny that there is a God governing the world. It is a truth which I thought needed to be told; and as whatever of humiliation there is in it, falls most directly on myself, I thought others might afford for me to tell it."

God moved in mysterious ways, but Lincoln the President did not question their wisdom, nor did he shrink from what he believed divine necessity required of him.

chapter 4

THE MAN WHO SAID NO

God willed the war. "Surely," Lincoln wrote in the midst of it, "He intends some great good to follow this mighty convulsion, which no mortal could make, and no mortal could stop." No man, then, was to blame for what had happened in 1860–1861. No one was responsible for the failure to effect a compromise that might have saved both the Union and the peace. So Lincoln afterward seemed to think.

Maybe he was mistaken. Maybe there *were* human beings who could have stopped the war—before it started. Maybe he was one of them. He, after all, had been President-elect during the winter of 1860–1861. To him and his party had belonged the responsibility of prospective power. His own election had set off the train of events which brought about the war crisis.

On election night, November 6, 1860, he stayed at the Springfield telegraph office to get the late returns, then went home and to bed with the knowledge that victory was his. True, he was not the choice of a majority of the American people. No one in the Deep South had voted for him, and fewer than forty out of a hundred in the country as a whole. The rest divided their votes among his three opponents: the Northern Democrat Stephen A. Douglas, the Southern Democrat John C. Breckinridge, and the Constitutional Unionist John Bell. Still, Lincoln won a clear and decisive majority in the electoral college. He was the duly elected President-to-be.

There had been the threat that he never would preside over all the United States. During the campaign some Southern politicians contended that, if such a "Black Republican" should win, the slave states ought to secede at once. This campaign oratory did not cause Lincoln much concern. He felt sure it did not represent the real opinion of most Southerners. One of them wrote to a friend in New York to say that he, a Virginian, would be happy enough to see Lincoln win, though he did not dare say so openly. The New Yorker sent this letter on to Springfield, and Lincoln returned his thanks for it. "It contains," he said, "one of the many assurances I receive from the South that in no probable event will there be any very formidable attempt to break up the Union." He thought the Southern people had "too much of good sense" for that.

Soon after election day he had cause for wonder. South Carolina seemed ready for disunion. Her legislature, on November 10, called a special convention to meet in December and declare the independence of the state. And men in other cotton states talked of following her example.

Even so, Lincoln persisted in doubting whether the seceders were in earnest. Several days after his victory, entertaining a supper guest at his house, he gave the impression that he considered the secession talk mostly bluff. A few Southerners were trying to scare the North, he said, and once they learned they could not do it, they would quiet down.

At first, he seemed to be in high good humor as he greeted the visitors who, day after day, flocked into Springfield. His law office could not accommodate the crowds, and neither could his house on Eighth Street. So he readily accepted when the Illinois governor offered the use of his rooms in the Statehouse. Up the dark steps to the second floor daily trooped the uninvited callers, a hundred and more at a time, inquiring newspapermen, job-seeking politicians, and the idly curious—farmers in muddy boots, ladies in their Sunday best. Their host shook the hands of one and all. He joked and told stories. If no women happened to be present, the stories were likely to be somewhat uncouth, though always to the point. At every opportunity he gave the occasion a light touch, as when he had a tall Missourian measured against the wall, to compare heights with him.

Some of his cronies suspected he was putting on airs, for he sported a new hat and suit, and was beginning to grow whiskers. But no one could have been more "common" and approachable than Old Abe, even though he soon was to be President of the United States. Or President of what might be left of them.

After several weeks a noticeable change came over him. Outwardly he remained as jocular as ever, but new lines of worry began to show on his face, and at times a deathly pallor. Inwardly he seemed to be growing more and more troubled. And finally he put an end to his daily receptions with their come-one-come-all hospitality. He had too many important visitors to see, too many important letters to write. He tried to confer by appointment only, at home or at the town's one decent hotel. Part of the time he hid out, alone, in a dingy back room above a store, across the street from the Capitol.

He had stacks of newspapers to check, bushels of mail to go through. From the South he received a number of letters reviling him and threatening his life, some of them hysterical, some of them obscene. From South Carolina came a package addressed not to him but to Mrs. Lincoln, and in it was a painting that crudely but unmistakably pictured the President-elect with tar and feathers all over him, chains on his feet, and a rope around his neck. Communications of this kind he could shrug off. Far more trying were the letters from politicians North and South, letters demanding decisions and answers.

Meanwhile, as closely and conscientiously as any man could do, Lincoln followed opinions and events, the nation over.

2

The nation spoke with many voices. Congressmen took up the debate after they had met in Washington, in the Capitol with its unfinished dome, the symbol, perhaps, of a Union in need of repair. In and out of Congress, Democrats and Republicans disagreed not only along party lines, but among themselves as well. Northerners did not all see eye to eye, and neither did Southerners.

Immediate secession was the cry of "fire-eaters" like Robert Barnwell Rhett of South Carolina, William L. Yancey of Alabama, and Howell Cobb of Georgia. They argued that, in the very act of electing Lincoln, the North had declared war against the South. The noble Declaration of Independence had been perverted as a thing of politics. "Mr. Lincoln and his party assert that this doctrine of equality applies to the Negro," said Cobb, "and necessarily there can exist no such thing as property in our equals." Rhett asserted: "The people of the North have not left us in doubt as to their designs and policy. United as a section in the late Presidential election, they have elected as the exponent of their policy one who has openly declared that all the States of the United States must be made Free States or Slave States." The latter, for their own safety, must quit the Union at once, the fire-eaters maintained.

Not all Southerners went so far or so fast. Many advocated delay, at least until Lincoln was in office and had committed some "overt act." If the South remained in the Union, the Republican party would not control Congress or the Supreme Court. Slavery was in no immediate danger, the moderates believed. So James H. Hammond of Virginia busied himself with writing letters to secessionists, urging them to do nothing until the North had had a chance to provide a remedy for the wrongs of which they complained. The Georgian Alexander H. Stephens delivered a powerful speech in behalf of the Union before the Legislature of his state. At a conference of Mississippians in Congress, Senator Jefferson Davis opposed secession so long as there was any hope for concessions from the North.

If men like Davis were Unionists for expediency and nothing more, there were others in the slave states, especially in those of the upper South, who really loved the Union and dreaded secession and war. If war should come, many a Tennesseean or Kentuckian would find himself in a most unhappy middle, with friends and economic connections on either side. In the presidential election, Southern Unionists had voted heartily for Douglas or for Bell, as the less extreme of the four candidates. Afterward these Bell and Douglas voters desperately looked for some kind of sectional truce.

So did the followers of Douglas and Bell in the North. And so did certain of the Lincoln men. "There were thousands and thousands of Conservative men in the North who voted for Lincoln, who would now yield much for the sake of peace and feel that they were not compromising principle thereby," one of these thousands wrote to Lincoln's friend, Senator Lyman Trumbull of Illinois. "Every year the North is gaining whilst the South loses political power." Time must be on the side of the North but, whether it was or not, "anything is better than Civil War."

Procompromise Republicans were most numerous in the cities of the Northeast, which faced a financial panic and the prospect of a business depression, brought on by the disunion threat. Banks closed, stocks fell, and factories stood idle while unsold goods piled up. Merchants and manufacturers dreaded the loss of their Southern markets. Creditors feared that debts owing from the South might never be paid. Apprehensive businessmen begged the politicians to appease the South and hold the Union together.

Some politicians responded. The leading Republicans of

New York began to plead for concession and compromise. The party boss of the state—the big, genial, shrewd Thurlow Weed—put all his influence into the cause of sectional harmony. His influence was great. He was the intimate friend and political partner of William H. Seward, the slight, hawk-nosed, cigar-chewing Senator from New York. Seward had been Lincoln's chief rival for the Republican nomination, and despite his loss to Lincoln he still thought of himself as the party leader, and thousands agreed with him. He, not Lincoln, appeared to be the Mr. Republican of the time. And Seward, taking his cue from Weed, was inclined toward compromise.

But most Republican politicians were not. They got their support from rural constituencies little concerned about the plight of business in Boston or New York, and much concerned about what they viewed as slave-power aggression. Generally, the Republican voters of the farms and small towns expected firmness from the men they had elected.

In the very suggestion of compromise, therefore, many an elected Republican could see only political death for himself and for his party. Among themselves, the politicians talked freely of their fears. "To yield one new guarantee to slavery will either destroy the Republican party or send to their political graves every Republican who lends his support or countenance to such a course." "It is the veriest suicide for the party leaders to yield to the demands of the fire-eaters, for it can only result in rending the party into a hundred wavering fragments." "I repeat, do not sacrifice the party. If we suffer the principles of the party to be compromised away, the party is dead. We won the victory—it is ours."

These fears, reiterated in countless letters and conversations, had a real, substantial basis. The Republican party was a heterogeneous grouping of men with divergent backgrounds: old Whigs and Know-Nothings, former Democrats, Liberty party members, thoroughgoing Free-Soilers, even abolitionists. The radicals were ready to abandon the party if it abandoned them and what they stood for.

"Sir, has it come to this?" Thaddeus Stevens of Pennsylvania demanded in the House of Representatives. "Cannot the people of the United States choose whom they please President, without stirring up rebellion, and requiring humiliation, concessions, and compromises to appease the insurgents?" The bewigged, clubfooted Stevens apologized for his poor health and his weak voice, but his sentiments were vigorous enough. "Sir," he went on, "I would take no steps to propitiate such a feeling. Rather than show repentance for the election of Mr. Lincoln, with all its consequences, I would see this Government crumble into a thousand atoms."

Stevens spoke the convictions of the great majority of Republicans. Probably as many as five in six of them agreed with him and not with Weed or Seward. Nevertheless, the comparatively few procompromise Republicans together with the numerous Douglas Democrats and the Bell adherents made up a Northern majority who desired some kind of adjustment with the South. This majority seemed to grow as the weeks went by. When the Democrats made gains in several local elections during the winter, the returns were interpreted as straws in the wind of conservative, conciliatory reaction.

The compromisers had behind them the weight of public opinion in the North, the border states, and much of the South itself. They also had the weight of tradition on their side. A policy of give-and-take between the sections had become hallowed as an essential element of the American way. Again and again the Union had been patched together by mutual concessions—in the Constitutional Convention of 1787, in the Missouri Compromise of 1820, in the Compromise Tariff after the nullification threat of 1832, and in the Compromise of 1850.

Now, in 1860, the President of the United States, James Buchanan, prayed that some kind of Union-saving, peace-keeping arrangement might be made once more. He saw no other hope. As he told Congress, it was unconstitutional for a state to secede, but it also was unconstitutional for the Federal government to use force against a seceding state. The future, though, was not Buchanan's to grasp, for he was a political has-been, on the way out. On behalf of the incoming Republicans, William H. Seward seemed eager to reenact the role of Henry Clay, to make himself the Great Pacificator, to go down in history as the sponsor of a Compromise of 1860. But the future was not necessarily Seward's, either. He was not the President-elect.

Lincoln was. Where did *he* stand? What would *he* do?

3

At the time Lincoln was elected, his position could not be inferred from his campaign speeches. He had taken no stand. His attitudes and purposes must be sought in speeches he had made earlier, particularly those he had delivered in his debates with Douglas in 1858. His purposes presumably could be discovered also in the platform his party had adopted at Chicago and he, as the party's presidential nominee, had run on.

On the troublesome questions of slavery and the territories, this Republican platform was not altogether clear. Like most documents of the kind, it included resolutions designed to appeal to a wide variety of voters. One plank, to please the radicals, quoted and endorsed the "all men are created equal" passage of the Declaration of Independence, though not mentioning the Negro. Another plank, to cater to conservatives, recognized the right of each state to order "its own domestic institutions" as it pleased (and "domestic institutions" was of course a euphemism for slavery). Still another plank, in somewhat equivocal wording, upheld the right and duty of Congress to legislate freedom in the territories—when necessary.

As for Lincoln's previous statements, they were not all of a piece. For example, in one speech (July 10, 1858) he said we should "discard all this quibbling" about men or races being inferior and should "stand up declaring that all men are created equal." In another speech (September 18, 1858) he averred that he was not and never had been "in favor of bringing about in any way the social and political equality of the white and black races." And in his often quoted "house divided" remark he was at least a little enigmatic in predicting that "this government cannot endure permanently half slave and half free."

After his election he knew full well that most of his fellow partisans expected him to stand his ground—or rather *their* ground—and make no retreat from even the most extreme implications of his own remarks and the party platform. He got too many letters from Republicans and talked with too many Republicans in person not to know what they were saying and thinking.

But he also heard from Southern Unionists and Northern friends of the South who urged him to make "a clear and definite exposition" of his views. These people thought of him as a conservative and expected his personal opinions, once he had clarified and broadcast them, to strengthen Unionism in the slave states. If he would only issue an authoritative statement, his correspondents advised, he might be able "to disarm mischief makers, to allay causeless anxiety, to compose the public mind." He might "assure all good citizens of the South" and "take away from the disunionists every excuse or pretext for treason." That is to say, he might leave the fire-eaters with little to rave about.

To all who thus appealed to him, Lincoln gave essentially the same reply. His views already were on record, in his party's platform and in his own published remarks. Repetition would do no good, he said. Upon this stock answer he sometimes elaborated.

To George D. Prentice, editor of the pro-Union *Louisville Journal,* he explained: "For the good men of the South—and I regard the majority of them as such—I have no objection to repeat seventy and seven times. But I have *bad* men also to deal with, both North and South, . . . men who would like to frighten me, or, at least, to fix upon me the character of timidity and cowardice. They would seize upon almost any letter I could write, as being an *'awful coming down.'* " By "bad men" in the North who would thus accuse him, he could have meant only abolitionists and radical Republicans.

In responding to John A. Gilmer, Unionist congressman from Greensboro, North Carolina, Lincoln seemed to bristle a bit. "Is it desired that I shall shift the ground upon which I have been elected? I can not do it. You need only to acquaint yourself with that ground, and press it on the attention of the South. It is all in print and easy of access." So Lincoln said, and he added that any "additional production" from him would be quite improper. "It would make me appear as if I repented the crime of having been elected, and was anxious to apologize and beg forgiveness." Yet Gilmer had not asked him to apologize or to shift his ground. He had asked him to clarify it.

In corresponding with Alexander H. Stephens, the man in Springfield was gentler but just as firm. The sad-eyed, wizened Stephens was an old and much-admired acquaintance of Lincoln's, a onetime fellow congressman and fellow Whig. Now, having seen reports of Stephens' Union speech in Georgia, Lincoln sent his congratulations and his thanks. Stephens wrote back with the invariable request of Southern Unionists, that the president-elect strike a blow for them by stating his real opinions. Lincoln countered: "Do the people of the South really entertain fears that a Republican administration would, *directly,* or *indirectly,* interfere with their slaves, or with them, about their slaves? If they do, I wish to assure you, as once a friend, and still, I hope, not an enemy, that there is no cause for such fears." Then Lincoln summed up the issue as he saw it. "You think slavery is *right* and ought to be extended; while we think it is *wrong* and ought to be restricted. That I suppose is the rub. It certainly is the only substantial difference between us." Having read this, Stephens hoped all the more that Lincoln would make a public statement. "A word fitly spoken by you now," Stephens wrote again, rather wistfully, "would be like 'apples of gold in pictures of silver.' "

To the editor of the *New York Times,* who had forwarded the report of a rabid anti-Lincoln harangue in the Mississippi

Legislature, Lincoln wrote to say that the Mississippi "madman" had quite misrepresented Lincoln's views. He was *not* "pledged to the ultimate extinction of slavery," and he did *not* "hold the black man to be the equal of the white man, unqualifiedly," as the fellow had asserted.

When a bold Mississippian came to Springfield and put in a startling appearance at one of Lincoln's receptions in the Statehouse, sullenly announcing that he was a secessionist, Lincoln frankly told him he was opposed to any interference with slavery where it already existed.

Lincoln gave the same sort of personal assurances to a number of his callers and correspondents—but always privately or even secretly. His letter to Stephens, for instance, was headed "For your eye only." Consistently he refused to make a public statement. Consistently he refused to let anyone else make one for him in his name.

He did write a few editorials, anonymously, for the *Illinois State Journal,* the Republican paper of Springfield. He also composed a few lines for the speech that Senator Trumbull delivered at the Republican victory celebration in Springfield on November 20. In these lines Lincoln pledged that "each and all" of the states would be "left in as complete control of their own affairs" as ever. But Trumbull was not free to say he was quoting Lincoln, and there was no way for the public to know whether the Senator spoke for anyone besides himself. On his own, he further stated that the Republicans were not at all the "advocates of Negro-equality or amalgamation" which "demagogues" had accused them of being. Yet he also said the Republicans would stick by their platform (and it contained a plank declaring that *all* men are created equal).

Lincoln's silences—and Trumbull's utterance—did nothing to help Unionism in the South, and the fire-eating secessionists made the most of them. "What are the facts to justify the hope that the Black Republicans will recede from their well-defined position of hostility to the South and her institutions?"

Thus demanded Howell Cobb (about to resign as Buchanan's Secretary of the Treasury) in an open letter to the people of Georgia. "Shall we look for this hope in the whispered intimation that, when secure of his office, Lincoln will prove faithless to the principles of his party? Or in the public announcement made by Senator Trumbull of Illinois, since the election, *in the presence* of Mr. Lincoln, that he, Lincoln, would *'maintain and carry forward the principles on which he was elected'?*"

The youthful *New York Herald* reporter Henry Villard, watching and listening in Springfield, gathered that Lincoln was convinced he could do absolutely nothing "to stem the tide of the times." Villard reported that the president-elect would have given in to what was asked of him "in the way of public definitions of his policy" if he could have believed it would alleviate the troubles of the nation. "But he considers all such demonstrations futile, as the South, to use his own language, 'has eyes but does not see, and ears but does not hear.' "

Lincoln came to this conclusion without having made a single try at public definition or redefinition of his policy.

4

In Congress, when it assembled about a month after the election, there were dozens of proposals for a sectional adjustment, and at the outset the spirit of compromise seemed to prevail. True, most of the Republicans refused to support a resolution—which passed—asking for the prompt approval of any constitutional amendments needed to soothe the injuries of the suffering South. And thereupon thirty of the Southerners issued a truculent manifesto, proclaiming that the time for secession already had come. "The argument is exhausted," the thirty said. "The Republicans are resolute in the purpose to grant nothing that will or ought to satisfy the South." Yet, in the House of Representatives, the majority of the Republicans and all the other members voted for the creation of a compromise committee of thirty-three, one from each state. In the Senate a committee of thirteen was set up to sift the numerous proposals that were in the air. And hopes for compromise continued.

The plan upon which attention centered was that of Senator John J. Crittenden of Kentucky. Tall but bowed with his seventy-three years, Crittenden had the same passionate concern for Union and peace as did most Kentuckians, who feared what for them would be literally a brothers' war. (Indeed, once the fighting had begun, one of Crittenden's sons was to be a Confederate general and another a general on the Union side.) Crittenden proposed a whole series of amendments to the Constitution. One of these guaranteed slavery against congressional action in the places where the institution already existed. The most important—and most controversial—divided the territories between freedom and slavery by reaffirming and extending the old Missouri Compromise line (36° 30′).

The Crittenden Compromise gained the instant and hearty support of many thousands throughout the country. They looked to it hopefully as the means of putting a final quietus on the sectional row. Prominent Republicans and Democrats, Northerners and Southerners, gave it their endorsement. The *New York Herald* and many other papers praised it in their editorials. Petitions favoring it swamped Congress. The numberless signers dreaded the horrible alternative, the looming consequences of the compromise's defeat. "War of a most bitter and sanguinary character will be sure to follow in a short time," Republican Senator James W. Grimes wrote to his wife in Iowa.

Nevertheless, Grimes and his fellow partisans were far from unanimous for the Crittenden plan. Some Republicans favored it, more of them opposed it, and others hesitated, unable to make up their minds. The two Illinois senators, Lyman Trumbull and Elihu B. Washburne, and the Illinois member of the House committee of thirty-three, William Kellogg, received instructions from an authoritative source. Each of them got a letter postmarked Springfield, Illinois, and signed by Abraham

Lincoln. Each letter was marked "private and confidential." And each contained the same message, with slight variations in wording. "Let there be no compromise on the question of *extending* slavery," the letter to Trumbull said. "Have none of it. Stand firm. The tug has to come, & better now, than any time hereafter."

Senator Seward of New York, thought to be a compromiser, also had mail from Springfield. It gave him no advice on policy but offered him the post of Secretary of State in Lincoln's cabinet. Seward left Washington for Albany, to confer with his partner in politics, Thurlow Weed. The two decided that Weed should go to Springfield and consult with Lincoln. While Seward waited at his home in Auburn, Weed took a train for Illinois, after writing an editorial for his *Albany Evening Journal,* in which he said the big question before the nation "must have a violent or peaceful solution" and urged his fellow Republicans to accept a division of the territories.

On Thursday, December 20, Weed and Lincoln talked for hours in Springfield. They were still talking when the telegraph brought news that the South Carolina convention, meeting in Charleston, had passed an ordinance of secession that same day. Neither this intelligence nor Weed's persuasive charm availed to budge Lincoln from the position he had taken. He was willing to approve Crittenden's constitutional amendment guaranteeing slavery within the states. He had no objection to the idea that Congress should recommend to the Northern states the repeal of their "personal liberty" laws, which hampered the return of fugitive slaves. But he would agree to no proposal that would "touch the territorial question." That night, Weed left Springfield with a written statement of Lincoln's views. These were not for publication. Lincoln wrote to Trumbull, reporting the conference with Weed, "Do not let my name be known in the matter."

On Saturday, December 22, traveling with Weed on a train between Syracuse and Albany, Seward learned of Lincoln's emphatic opposition to any territorial compromise. The same day in Washington the Senate committee of thirteen, of which Seward was a member, met without him. The four other Republican members of the committee voted against the territorial provision of the Crittenden plan. The two committeemen from the Deep South, Robert Toombs of Georgia and Jefferson Davis of Mississippi, also voted against it. The remaining six—three Northern Democrats, two Kentuckians and one Virginian—voted for it. Thus the vote was tied, and the proposal was defeated, for the committee had agreed that no action could be taken without the approval of a majority of the Republican members.

Despite this blow, moderates in Washington still counted upon the Crittenden plan. It *had* to go through, they thought. Otherwise, the states of Mississippi, Florida, Alabama, and Georgia certainly would join South Carolina in secession, and the states of Louisiana and Texas probably would follow. Now, the extreme secessionists of the lower South were not to be appeased by a partition of territory in the West. "The revolutionists in the Gulf States don't want to be satisfied with this," a *New York Tribune* man reported from the capital, "but the other slave States, or those in them who are opposed to dissolving the Union, consider that the concession would force the secessionists to desist."

The compromisers expected Seward to turn the trick. When he rejoined the Senate committee of thirteen, he could bring about a reconsideration. With his own vote and the votes of only two of his Republican colleagues—and surely he could prevail upon two of them—he could reverse the decision on the Crittenden plan. And if he did, the Georgia and Mississippi members of the committee would reconsider and approve also. At least, it was freely said that Toombs and Davis would vote yes if a majority of the Republicans did (though Davis already had signed the Southern manifesto which asserted that the time for compromise was past).

On Monday, December 24, Seward was back in Washington. Meeting with the committee, he did not suggest that his fellow

Republicans undo what they had done. He had his own vote recorded on the defeated motion of the previous Saturday. He voted no.

The compromisers, among them President Buchanan, were far from merry that Christmas Eve. They were becoming desperate, but they were not yet without hope. Despite Lincoln's secrecy, they gathered that the President-elect had had a part in stiffening the backs of Republicans. Indeed, they could read in the *New York Tribune* (December 22): "We are enabled to state, in the most positive terms, that Mr. Lincoln is utterly opposed to any concession or compromise that shall yield one iota of the position occupied by the Republican party on the subject of slavery in the territories." What was needed, then, was a direct appeal to Lincoln himself.

After Christmas, President Buchanan sent to Springfield a personal emissary, the Georgian Duff Green, who once had been in Andrew Jackson's "Kitchen Cabinet" and who longed to live out his few remaining years in a Union undivided. Green was careful to keep his mission absolutely secret, and somehow he succeeded in escaping the notice of newsmen. In Springfield, on December 28, he had a long conversation with Lincoln. He gave him a copy of Crittenden's resolutions, which Lincoln read and reread several times. Lincoln admitted that the territorial line might quiet agitation for the present. But he thought the trouble would be renewed in the future by demands for the annexation of Mexico, Cuba, and other new slave territories to the South. Green could not persuade him to endorse the Crittenden plan.

While Green was in Springfield, the senators on the committee of thirteen met for the last time and agreed that they could not agree. Throughout the South a message from Toombs to the people of Georgia was republished in the papers. "The test has been put fairly and frankly," Toombs said, "and it is decisive against the South." He was now an out-and-out secessionist. "The unconciliatory and defiant course of the Republican leaders has rendered the advocates of patience and steadiness in the South all but powerless," the Kentucky Unionist George D. Prentice wrote (December 31) in his *Louisville Journal.* On January 9, 1861, Mississippi seceded, and Jefferson Davis went with his state. By February 1 the five other wavering states had gone. Reviewing these events, an Ohio Democrat told the Senate: "At any time before January 1st, a two-thirds vote for the Crittenden resolutions in this chamber would have saved every state in the Union except South Carolina."

While the lower South was seceding, Republican friends of compromise made last-minute appeals to Lincoln. J. T. Hale, a Pennsylvania congressman on a border-state compromise committee, received this answer from him: "We have just carried an election on principles fairly stated to the people. Now we are told in advance, the government shall be broken up, unless we surrender to those we have beaten, before we take the offices. In this they are either attempting to play upon us, or they are in dead earnest. Either way, if we surrender, it is the end of us, and of the government. A year will not pass, till we shall have to take Cuba as a condition upon which they will stay in the Union." William Kellogg, the Illinois member of the committee of thirty-three, went to Springfield "in a good deal of anxiety" to see the President-elect. Lincoln made it clear: "I am inflexible." Any territorial division, he said, would "put us again on the highroad to a slave empire." Henry Villard, still covering events in Springfield, reported to the *New York Herald* that Lincoln looked "unfavorably" upon the Virginia scheme for holding a peace convention of the states, as a last resort. (This peace convention finally met in Washington but could accomplish nothing.)

After the secession of the lower South, this observation appeared in the *Lancaster Intelligencer,* the Democratic paper of Thaddeus Stevens' home town: "The plain question now presented to the North is, shall the Republican party or the Union break?" The party did not break, but the Union did, and the war came.

5

Suppose, after his election, Lincoln had given *in public* the same assurances he gave in private—that he had no intention of promoting, directly or indirectly, the abolition of slavery in the South or the establishment of complete racial equality anywhere. Suppose he openly and enthusiastically had championed a territorial compromise instead of secretly and resolutely opposing it. Would such a compromise have passed? Could secession have been headed off and war avoided?

To hypothetical questions of this kind, there can be no certain answers. There can be nothing more than guesses in terms of historical probability. In these terms the best answer to each of the questions seems to be—yes.

Not that Lincoln could have kept South Carolina from seceding. Once the Republicans had won the presidential election, Unionism, of whatever shade or degree, all but disappeared in that state. Almost nobody of prominence even held out for delay. Without company, however, South Carolina hardly could have defied the United States for very long.

Nor could Lincoln have appeased the most extreme and impatient secessionists in the other states of the Deep South. These men desired no reassuring words from the President-elect, no territorial concessions from Congress. These men already were hell-bent for secession, and the less that was done to conciliate, the better they liked it.

But in every state except South Carolina, the extremists had to contend with prominent men who advocated continuing the Union or, at least, delaying disunion. And in every state except South Carolina the people, or most of them, apparently were by no means ready for secession before the end of 1860—if, indeed, they were ready even after that.

Between the fire-eaters and their opponents the contest for a while was nip-and-tuck. In appealing to the undecided, the strongest argument the fire-eaters had was this: Lincoln and his party are Black Republicans, abolitionists, who will yield nothing to the honor and security of the South. If the Southern moderates could have pointed to unequivocal refutations in Lincoln's statements and his party's actions, the chances are that these moderates could have stemmed the secessionist tide.

Lincoln's party contained many men, besides himself, who were no more willing to offer territorial concessions than the Southern extremists were to receive them. But if *he* had taken a different stand, so would a number of his fellow partisans, including a few very influential ones. He probably could have carried enough of the Republicans with him to bring about the adoption of the Crittenden Compromise. Surely Seward would have favored this measure in the Senate committee of thirteen. Of the other four Republicans on that committee, at least two (Jacob Collamer and J. R. Doolittle) conceivably would have gone along with Seward and given in to Lincoln's wishes. Thus, in the committee, there would have been the requisite majority for compromise—even without the support of the Deep South members, Toombs and Davis, who may or may not have been sincere in giving the impression that they would approve if a majority of the Republicans did. Having passed the Senate committee, the Crittenden resolutions undoubtedly would have passed both houses of Congress with the two-thirds vote necessary for constitutional amendments.

All this is speculation. One can argue to the contrary, and some able historians have done so. Still, the evidence on the whole seems to point to the conclusion that, if Lincoln had granted the reassurance and concessions which he refused in 1860, there would have been no war in 1861.

6

Suppose there had been no hostilities, then or later. Suppose there had been no resistance to slavery extension on the part of Lincoln and the Republicans. Would slavery in time have overspread the territories? Or would slavery ultimately have disappeared, even in the Southern states? These questions can be answered with less confidence, even though some historians have given extremely confident answers, pro and con.

On the one hand, it has been argued that the South's "peculiar institution" already was on the way out before the war began. Not only was the institution outmoded by the progress of humanitarian, democratic principles throughout the civilized world. More important, it no longer paid as it formerly had done.

By 1860 slavery had reached its "natural frontiers" in the West. The Great Plains, the Rocky Mountains, and the desert basin beyond were unfit for the production of cotton, sugar, rice, tobacco—the staples adapted to the slave system of the South. In the 1850s no one, not even the most aggressive of the proslavery politicians, really expected the system to take root in either Kansas or Nebraska. The census of 1860 revealed the grand total of fifteen slaves in Nebraska and only *two* in Kansas. Surely the fears and hatreds and the fateful sectionalization of politics that led to secession and war make up one of the most tragic ironies of all history.

Westward, slavery had nowhere to go, and it could not expand to the southward, either. True, filibusterers looked from time to time to Cuba, Nicaragua, or Mexico, and a few planters had hopes of finding new lands for slave cultivation in those areas. But those lands, particularly in Mexico, were little if any more suitable for the cotton economy than those of the American West. The filibustering schemes were visionary, futile. Most planters were indifferent to them, seeing in them no real opportunity for benefit to slavery or the South.

Slavery had to expand if it was to prosper. It was an inefficient labor system which could thrive only with fresh and ever more fresh soil, only with an abundance of reasonably priced slaves, only with high prices for plantation products—cotton in particular. Costs in land and labor were rising, while the price of cotton, fixed by world-wide conditions of supply and demand, was entering upon an over-all downward trend. Suitable new lands were not to be had; neither were additional slaves in quantities sufficient to bring down the soaring price of prime field-hands. A few Southerners talked about reopening the African slave trade to replenish the labor market. They only talked. Most Southerners lacked interest in admitting slaves from Africa, and those Southerners who profited from selling slaves in interstate trade were opposed to any competition from abroad.

Slavery was not expanding—which meant it was declining. Around the edges, in the older states of the upper South and the border, slaves were being freed or sold away. Only on the rich, new lands of the Southwest (in Alabama, Mississippi, Louisiana, Arkansas, and eastern Texas) was the slave system still thriving. Only there could the planter invest in high-priced slaves and be assured of a handsome profit. The more the Southwest developed, the more the rest of the South was bound to decline. As cotton production rose in the newer, more bountiful states, the price would fall and further pinch the grower on the comparatively poor soil of the older areas. He would have to do what so many of his neighbors already were doing—free or sell his slaves and use Negroes (or whites) as hired laborers. The time was coming when the cycle of the older South would be repeated in the newer Southwest.

Slavery had reached its limits, and those limits would choke the institution. It had no economic future. Of its own accord, it would have died out in a little while, a single generation or even less. In the light of these "cold facts" there was simply no rational basis for the heated discussions of slavery in the territories, according to some historians, looking back from the perspective of a later day.

And certain statesmen of the time, without the benefit of hindsight, said essentially the same thing. In the debate on the Compromise of 1850 Daniel Webster, for one, contended that the whole question was a "mere abstraction." He said the excitement over it was compounded of "idle fears." Slavery already was prohibited in the West, outside of Texas, by a law more effective than any act of Congress could possibly be. This was a law of nature, of physical geography, which made the West unsuitable for the plantation system of the South. "I would not take pains," Webster declared, "uselessly to reaffirm an ordinance of nature, nor to re-enact the will of God." Stephen A. Douglas held the same belief when he proposed to stop the quarrel with his plan of "popular sovereignty," which would have allowed the actual settlers in the territories to decide whether or not slaves could be brought in. Lincoln steadfastly denounced the idea of "pop. sov." in his famous debates with Douglas and afterward.

If Webster, Douglas, and other men of like opinion were correct, then Lincoln and his fellow Republicans, in insisting that Congress must prohibit slavery in the West, were dealing with political phantoms. Douglas questioned the sincerity of the Republicans. In Congress, shortly before Lincoln's inauguration in 1861, they approved the organization of territorial governments for Colorado, Nevada, and Dakota *without a prohibition of slavery*. They seemed to think it needless. Now Douglas chided them, for he had been saying just that, all along. Reviewing the prewar controversy and the party's lapse from its own avowed principles, the Republican of Republicans James G. Blaine years afterward concluded that the worst of the sectional bitterness had "related to an imaginary Negro in an impossible place."

Meanwhile, in the 1860–1861 argument over compromise, Southerners in Congress charged the Republicans with endangering the Union over an empty and unreal issue about the territories. A Maine Republican replied with this *tu quoque:* "You say it is a mere abstraction for which we are contending, because slavery cannot possibly go there. And yet you regard this abstraction as of so much importance to you that you are willing to dissolve the Union . . . to secure it. If it is an abstraction with us, of course it must be an abstraction with you." In other words, we may be crazy, but you are just as crazy as we are. Perhaps, though, neither group had gone completely mad. Perhaps there *was* some kind of reality associated with the territorial issue. Perhaps the issue was at least a symbol of vital differences dividing Americans. Apparently large numbers of them, North and South, thought so at the time.

Certain recent historians have agreed with them. These historians concede that the question of the territories was a "peripheral" issue and in a sense an unreal one. Yes. But *why*, they ask, did such an issue so arouse the people? And they reply: not merely because agitators and fanatics played upon their feelings, but because the territorial question was related to a real issue, a matter of good and evil, of right and wrong. Slavery was wrong, and a society like the South, closed in defense of the institution, was evil. Between the North and the South there was a moral gulf, too broad to be bridged by compromise.

True, the continued existence of Southern society, unchanged, was not the question the politicians of 1860–1861 discussed. They could not easily have done so, since they were inhibited by the Constitution, with its implied sanction of slavery and its phrases about state rights. Nevertheless, the moral issue of slavery per se gave urgency and significance to the argument about slavery in the territories. In that argument, on the edges of the matter as it were, the ethical reality could be faced.

The abolitionists did not flay a dead or dying horse. Obsolete though it undoubtedly was, economically as well as morally, the "peculiar institution" of the South was not due for an early and natural death. The economic plight of many of the planters made them all the more desperate, all the more determined to keep slavery alive, to extend it, to make it pay. Many of them demanded access to the slave markets of Africa, complete elimination of the protective tariff, independence from Northern bankers and shippers, an end to measures that would build up the Northwest and unite it with the Northeast, and finally a program to check the rise of free states within the territories. If the discontented planters could not get all they wanted by remaining in the Union, they were bound to try the alternative of secession and a separate confederacy.

It is unthinkable that Southerners, even with economic prostration in the offing, ever would have undertaken to reform their own society. Throughout the South freedom of thought had disappeared long before the Civil War began. A native critic, the North Carolinian H. R. Helper, who wrote a book to show the economic wrongs of slavery, was hounded from his home and his writings were banned. Antislavery societies, numerous in the South in 1830, were nonexistent there by 1860. Proslavery propaganda closed the minds of Southerners, even those (the great majority) who never owned a slave. It taught them that the institution was not an evil at all but, in John C. Calhoun's words, "a good—a positive good." The more aggressive propagandists of the 1850s thought slavery was too good to be confined to the South or even to the Negroes. These writers, boldly pursuing the logic of their argument, recommended slavery as a sovereign cure for all the ills of competitive society, for labor troubles, strikes, and revolutionary isms in the North and throughout the world.

In the light of a century of world history, the assumption that slavery could not take root in the American West, that it could exist only under certain rare conditions of soil and enterprise, can no longer be confidently held. The argument that slavery, by 1860, was in an irreversible decline is based on the assumption that it was dependent upon the Southern plantation system. Slavery, we now know, is a highly adaptable institution which can take many forms. The labor camps of Germany and Russia provide a couple of reminders. It is possible that—with popular and governmental attitudes favoring it—slavery of a sort could be profitably adapted to the orchards, mines, and factories of the United States today.

If this was a possibility, Lincoln was not seeing a mere bogeyman in the possible territorial expansion of the "peculiar institution," but had the foresight of a prophet when he predicted that the nation could not forever remain half slave and half free. It became all free, but conceivably it might have become all slave. Who knows?

7

If we probe into Lincoln's motives, we may conclude that he made his great refusal in 1860–1861 partly because of a deep-seated and farsighted concern for the future of freedom in America. He was moved by a determination to keep slavery within bounds, so as to ensure its ultimate end, though for the time being he accepted slavery as an unpleasant fact and had no intention of encouraging abolition outright. "As to fugitive slaves, District of Columbia, slave trade among the slave states, and whatever springs of necessity from the fact that the institution is amongst us, I care but little, so that what is done be comely and not altogether outrageous," he wrote to Seward during the compromise debate. But this seems certain: he would consent to nothing which would extend slavery or prolong its life.

This principle, however, could not have been the only thing Lincoln had in mind. His motives appear to have been neither simple nor self-evident. In the case of any public man making a hard decision, the threads of thought and feeling are likely to be tangled and partly hidden, even from himself. So it probably was with Lincoln. In private conversations and correspondence during the secession crisis, he gave more than one reason for doing what he did. After the secession of seven states had become a *fait accompli,* he seemed to feel the need for explaining himself further to the people. On his way to Washington for the inauguration, he planned to cross into Kentucky, while stopping in Cincinnati, and speak briefly in his native state. So he wrote out a self-explanation for his fellow Kentuckians. As it happened, he did not appear in Covington and make the speech, but he incorporated the explanatory passage in the inaugural address which he delivered in Washington on March 4. These were his words:

"During the winter just closed, I have been greatly urged, by many patriotic men, to lend the influence of my position to some compromise, by which I was, to some extent, to shift the ground upon which I had been elected. This I steadily refused. I so refused, not from any party wantonness, nor from any indifference to the troubles of the country. I thought such a refusal was demanded by the view that if, when a Chief Magistrate is constitutionally elected, he cannot be inaugurated till he betrays those who elected him, by breaking his pledges, and surrendering, to those who tried and failed to defeat him at the polls, this government and all popular government is already at an end. Demands for such surrender, once recognized, are without limit, as to nature, extent and repetition. They break the only bond of faith between public and public servant; and they distinctly set the minority over the majority."

This matter of majority rule seemed to bother him. After all, he had *not* been elected by a majority of the voters, and everybody knew it. Nor had a majority of the people taken the same view of compromise that he, privately, had taken. In an early draft of the inaugural he wrote: "A constitutional majority is the only true sovereign of a free people." Before delivering the address he changed the opening words of that sentence to read: "A constitutionally expressed majority." Which, of course, he could rightfully claim—in the electoral college. Under the circumstances, the point was a rather delicate one. Nevertheless, Lincoln seemed to feel that he had been compelled to take an uncompromising stand in order to vindicate the principle of government by the people.

Apparently he also had convinced himself that he was bound by his "pledges," which must have meant the planks in the Republican platform, since he had not committed himself by any statement of his own during the campaign. His devotion to the platform was unusual, for it had not been customary for an election winner to take his party's campaign resolutions more seriously than was expedient, nor has it become customary since. At any rate, the 1860 plank on slavery in the territories was by no means so clear-cut as the 1856 plank had been.

The 1856 resolution called upon Congress to "prohibit" slavery in the territories. The 1860 wording was rather involved; it said that freedom was the "normal condition" of the territories and that Congress had a duty to maintain this freedom by legislation, "whenever such legislation is necessary." The change in wording is significant. Here was a loophole for any Republican who thought it wise to make a territorial deal. Such a Republican did not have to abandon the platform but only to reinterpret it. He could argue, to himself and his fellow partisans, that a law prohibiting slavery in all the lands of the West was *unnecessary* at the moment.

Lincoln, in the inaugural, disclaimed "party wantonness" as a reason for his stand. Yet he certainly had been aware of what so many Republicans were saying to one another—that any yielding on the territories would mean the death of the Republican party. He himself had used much the same language, as when he wrote to a fellow Republican that "surrender" would mean "the end of us."

Finally, as we may see by reading between some of Lincoln's lines, he was motivated by personal pride. Humble though he was in his way, he had no stomach for the self-abasement that would have been involved in the appeasement of his political foes. He had worked hard for the Presidency. He had won it fairly. It was *his*. And he could see no good reason for wheedling his way into the unimpaired rights and honors of the office.

Lincoln, it seems, was quite conscious of the dangers that lurked on the one side of his dilemma. If he yielded to pressure, he might sacrifice his own self-respect, the future of his party, the integrity of popular government, and the long-run freedom of the nation. On the other side, if he *refused* to yield, he ran the risk of war. But, apparently, he did not allow himself to dwell upon this danger, to realize how imminent hostilities might be, or how long they might last, or how costly of human life they might become.

Afterward, as the war dragged on from year to year, his fatalistic philosophy must have been a partial comfort to him.

If what was to be *would* be, then nothing he could have done would have made any difference. If God planned the war, mere mortals were powerless to have made it, or to have stopped it. But sometimes Lincoln seemed to protest too much. Sometimes, perhaps, he wondered. If he had tried to do otherwise during those critical months when he was President-elect. . . . Or, for that matter, if he had tried to do something else than what he did during his first weeks as President, when Americans North and South focused their attention on Fort Sumter, and watched, and waited. . . .

chapter 5

THE BRINGER OF WAR

Watching events from Springfield during the winter of 1860–1861, Lincoln had reason to expect that, if war should come once he had been inaugurated, he might be blamed for starting it. Not that he could see eighty and more years ahead, when a future President would be charged with maneuvering the nation into war, at Pearl Harbor. But he could look back only twelve or fifteen years to the time when a previous President had been accused of contriving hostilities, along the Rio Grande.

Indeed, Lincoln himself had been one of the most persistent accusers of President James K. Polk. In 1846, having ordered an army into disputed territory, Polk asked Congress for a declaration of war after the Mexicans fired upon the troops. War exists, he said, and by the act of Mexico herself, "American blood has been shed upon American soil." Throughout the Mexican War the Whig opposition kept denouncing Polk as both provocator and prevaricator. Lincoln, as a Whig congressman, got national publicity with his "spot resolutions" which called upon the President to point out the exact spot where blood had been shed. Lincoln aimed thus to show that the shooting had not begun on "American" soil at all. It had not begun with Mexican aggression. It had begun in consequence of Polk's trickery.

Afterward, Lincoln did not forget this war-maneuver thesis. As late as June of 1860, when writing his autobiographical sketch for a campaign biography, he took pains to justify his earlier stand against the Polk administration. He now said of Polk that "the President had sent Genl. Taylor into an uninhabited part of the country belonging to Mexico, and not to the U. S. and thereby had provoked the first act of hostility—in fact the commencement of the war." All this had been "*unnecessary,* inasmuch as Mexico was in no way molesting, or menacing the U. S. or the people thereof," and it had been "*unconstitutional,* because the power of levying war is vested in Congress, and not in the President." And Lincoln asserted that Polk had been impelled by an ulterior motive, a political one. Polk had intended "to divert public attention" from his failure to secure the whole of the Oregon country from Great Britain.

Less than half a year after writing this, Lincoln himself faced the question of sending armed forces into disputed territory. When South Carolina seceded she claimed all the Federal forts, arsenals, and other property within her borders as rightfully hers. She was willing to pay the Federal government for the improvements it had made, or at least for a share of the cost. But she insisted that the sites now belonged to the state, which could no longer tolerate the presence of a "foreign" power upon her soil. The rest of the seceding states took the same position.

Thus a hard choice loomed for Lincoln, months before he

was due to occupy the White House. If, as President, he used force to hold or take the properties the Federal government claimed, and if the South resisted, he might be accused of bringing on a war. But if he let those properties go, he would risk the charge of cowardice and a whole train of possible disasters.

He did not hesitate in making his first and fundamental decision. At about the time he received the news of the South Carolina secession ordinance (December 20, 1860) he also learned the opinions of Winfield Scott, the seventy-four-year-old veteran of the War of 1812 and the war with Mexico, now general in chief of the United States Army. General Scott had given President Buchanan advice about the forts in Charleston harbor. Fort Moultrie, the General believed, was open to attack from the land side and was almost impossible to defend, yet Major Robert Anderson and his small garrison were stationed there. Fort Sumter, on a tiny island in the harbor, was far more defensible even though still under construction. The garrison should be reinforced, and moved to Fort Sumter. So Scott told Buchanan. He reminded him that, at the time of South Carolina's nullification threat in 1832–1833, President Jackson had sent reinforcements. Jackson had remarked that he was not making war on South Carolina, but that if South Carolina attacked she would be making war on the United States. Scott was afraid Buchanan might give up the Charleston forts. Scott's views were relayed to Lincoln both by mail and by special messenger. "Please present my respects to the General," Lincoln replied to one of his informants, "and tell him, confidentially, I shall be obliged to him to be as well prepared as he can to either *hold,* or *retake,* the forts, as the case may require, at, and after the inaugeration [*sic*]."

It soon appeared that Buchanan was not going to abandon the forts without at least a gesture toward making them secure. On December 26 Major Anderson, finding authority for the move in his vague orders from the War Department, transferred his men from Moultrie to Sumter. As the old year ended and the new one began, the Southern, prosecession members of Buchanan's cabinet were replaced by Northern Unionists. On January 8, 1861, the merchant steamer *Star of the West,* chartered by the government to carry provisions and (below deck) troops for Fort Sumter, attempted to enter Charleston harbor. Hostile batteries guarding the ship channel fired upon the vessel, and she turned and steamed away, while soldiers on the Sumter parapets impatiently looked on. Had Anderson ordered them to use their own guns, he might have had at once the war which, as a Kentuckian and a peace-loving soldier, he wished desperately to avoid.

Many Americans North and South were ready for a fight; many others shared the feelings of Major Anderson. Most Republicans insisted that the Federal government must maintain its rights and enforce its laws. Most people in the upper South and the border area agreed with those of the lower South that "coercion" of a state was unconstitutional and unthinkable. North Carolina, Virginia, Tennessee, Arkansas, Kentucky, and three other slave states remained for the time being in the Union. Some or all of them might be lost if an attempt were made to "coerce" a sister state. They might join the Confederacy which had its beginnings in Montgomery, Alabama, on February 4—exactly a month before the day set for Lincoln's inauguration.

So Lincoln would need to be careful of what he said when the time came for him to speak out—on March 4. Before he left Springfield he completed a draft of his inaugural address, in the dusty back room where he hid from time-wasting visitors. He did not want to dribble his message out beforehand, but on his slow, zigzag journey by special train to Washington (February 11–23) he found a crowd of eager listeners at every stop. Usually he managed to hold himself to a few joking and rather pointless remarks. At certain of his appearances, though, he let out strong hints of what he intended to do and how he intended it to be viewed.

In Indianapolis, speaking from the balcony of the leading

hotel, the Bates House, he referred to the arguments against coercing a state. "But," he asked, "if the Government, for instance, but simply insists upon holding its own forts, or retaking those forts which belong to it"—here he was interrupted by cheers from his audience—"or the enforcement of the laws of the United States in the collection of duties upon foreign importations"—he had to pause again while the cheering was renewed—"would any or all of these things be coercion?"

In Trenton, addressing the General Assembly of New Jersey, he said: "The man does not live who is more devoted to peace than I am. None who would do more to preserve it. But it may be necessary to put the foot down firmly." At this, the legislators broke into a bedlam of applause.

In Philadelphia, at a Washington's Birthday flag-raising in Independence Hall, he declared there was "no need of bloodshed and war." And there would be no bloodshed, he promised, unless it should be forced upon the government. "The Government will not use force unless force is used against it." Again, prolonged applause.

In Harrisburg he was impressed by the fine marching of the State militiamen on the streets. He told the Pennsylvania General Assembly that he was gratified to see such a display of "military force" and such willingness to use it in case of emergency. But he said he hoped to have no need for the troops. After waiting for the applause to stop, he continued: "I promise that (in so far as I may have wisdom to direct) if so painful a result shall in any wise be brought about, it shall be through no fault of mine."

While in Harrisburg, he was warned that it would not be safe for him to stop, as planned, in Baltimore. There was talk of an assassination plot. So he went through Baltimore at night, to arrive in Washington a day ahead of schedule. There were rumors of impending violence in Washington also.

During the ten days before the inauguration, Lincoln was besieged by clamorous callers at Willard's Hotel, and he had last-minute problems of patronage to worry about, in addition to the big problem that no one could forget for a moment, particularly in the capital. He showed the draft of his inaugural to his Illinois friend O. H. Browning, and to the man he had named as his Secretary of State, William H. Seward. They suggested that he soften the phrasing of certain passages, and he made a number of changes, striking out the words "All the power at my disposal will be used to reclaim the public property and places which have fallen. . . ."

Day broke on March 4 with a balmy promise of spring, and then the morning turned cloudy and raw. Punctually President Buchanan called at Willard's and escorted Lincoln to a waiting carriage, while policemen opened a path through the throng about the doorway. The carriage was open, so all could observe as the rugged, black-haired Lincoln rode through the chill air down packed Pennsylvania Avenue beside the stately, white-haired Buchanan, whose wry neck gave a dignified tilt to his head. Along the way, hidden on rooftops, were soldiers with rifles ready, and at strategic points artillery and cavalry were stationed. General Scott took no chances.

When, on the platform rigged up for the occasion at the east entrance of the Capitol, Lincoln stood to begin the reading of his address, he faced an audience variously estimated at ten to thirty thousand. Throughout the country people waited to read reports of what he had to say. He was prepared to discuss the secession crisis in its manifold aspects, but what his hearers and readers wanted particularly to know was his policy regarding Fort Sumter. They wanted to know if he brought tidings of disunion or reunion, of continued peace or threatened war.

Regarding the forts, he said: "The power confided in me, will be used to hold, occupy, and possess the property, and places belonging to the government, and to collect the duties and imposts; but beyond what may be necessary for these objects, there will be no invasion—no using of force against, or among the people anywhere."

Then, near the end, addressing the absent Southerners: "In

your hands, my dissatisfied fellow countrymen, and not in *mine*, is the momentous issue of civil war. The government will not assail *you*. You can have no conflict, without being yourselves the aggressors."

2

By the time Lincoln had taken the oath as President, the United States still held actual possession of only four forts inside the Confederate States. In Florida there were Forts Taylor, Jefferson, and Pickens, of which the first two, at least, seemed safe enough. In South Carolina there was Fort Sumter, almost encircled by hostile guns on Morris Island and elsewhere around the harbor. The Confederate government, relieving the individual states of jurisdiction, demanded the surrender of *all* the Union-held forts. A Confederate commissioner already had arrived in Washington for diplomatic negotiations with the United States, and two other commissioners were on the way. Poised between the Union and the Confederacy stood the states of the upper South and the border. As Virginia went, so would at least three others. In Virginia, a secession convention had met and had neither voted for disunion nor adjourned. Its members waited to see what the new President would do. Privately and publicly he had expressed his determination to hold the forts.

His Secretary of State, the cheerful and ingratiating Seward, had other ideas. More than ever, Seward was ambitious now to be the savior of both the Union and the peace. He thought the Federal government needed to do nothing except wait. Give the Southerners time, and they would come to their senses. Let the forts go. If the people of the Confederacy were left to themselves, their old love for the Union eventually would prevail, and they would rebel against the rebellion. Hence Seward opposed any kind of provocative action. He confidently expected his do-nothing policy to be carried out. Though during the winter he had yielded to Lincoln on the question of compromise,

Seward now looked upon himself as the administration's prime minister and guiding spirit.

On the first day that Lincoln woke in the White House, March 5, Seward had news for him. He brought a big handful of documents, including several letters from Major Anderson to the War Department and a note from General Scott to the new President. According to Anderson, the time had passed to do much, if anything, to help Fort Sumter. Only a very "large and well appointed" force could hope to relieve the garrison now. And supplies were running out, with enough left for only six weeks, if that long. On the basis of this information, Scott advised: "I now see no alternative but a surrender, in some weeks."

Seward saw no alternative, either. The next day he told the Confederate commissioners so. He dared not communicate with them directly for that would imply official recognition of the Confederacy, but through a go-between he informed them that the forts would be abandoned.

He did not speak for Lincoln. During his first week in office, the President gave orders for Scott to "exercise all possible vigilance for the maintenance of all the places within the military department of the United States." He declined to approve Scott's draft of a message directing that Anderson "peacefully evacuate Fort Sumter." And he ordered the strengthening of Fort Pickens. Having learned that reinforcements were aboard a ship in Pensacola harbor, but had not been landed because of a truce arranged under Buchanan's administration, he sent instructions for their immediate transferral to the fort.

That, presumably, would take care of Pickens, but as yet Lincoln did nothing about Sumter. A second and a third week passed after his inauguration, and still he gave no sign that he had made up his mind. He did not lack advice. From military and naval men, from members of the Cabinet, from newspapers and private citizens, he got a wide selection.

Seward and Scott forwarded to the President letters they received from Southerners and Northerners pleading that the Sumter garrison be withdrawn. "A collision between the Federal Government and any of the seceded States would leave us powerless," wrote a Virginian on behalf of the Unionists of his state. "South Carolina is kept apprised of our position and will seize the slightest pretext for a collision." From Boston a conservative Republican warned: "The object of the Secessionists is to make the United States Government the aggressor, so that if Civil War ensue, it may not be charged on them. They have already been disappointed that they have no act of the Government of which they can really complain, or upon which they can rouse the people of the border States to join them. They are looking to Fort Sumpter [*sic*] for such an act. They do not wish to attack it first—but if they could, by their batteries, intercept a reinforcement or supplies, and thereby call out a response from the guns of Major Anderson, they would have what *they* would call an affirmative act of aggression on the part of the United States, and would so make their people believe."

Writing directly to the President, many Republicans volunteered the opinion that most members of the party would accept the evacuation of Sumter as a military necessity, so long as Pickens continued to be held. But other Republicans said just the opposite. "Give up Sumpter, Sir, & you are as dead politically as John Brown is physically," one of the more warlike assured Lincoln. "You have got to fight." Another wrote: "Thirty days more of '*Peace Policy*' at Washington—and not only the Republican party but the Government itself will be gone to destruction or placed beyond remedy." And the German-born Carl Schurz, who had Lincoln's permission to sample popular feeling, reported: "As soon as one vigorous blow is struck, as soon as, for instance, Fort Sumter is reinforced, public opinion in the free States will at once rally to your support."

Thus opinions differed about the advisability of strengthening and holding Fort Sumter; they also differed about the feasibility of it. In his daily mail Lincoln received a number of suggestions, some the fantastic imaginings of crackpots, one of whom offered to outfit his own expedition and guaranteed to hold the fort for a year—for five million dollars! Not all the suggestions were crazy. J. Watson Webb, the publisher of the *New York Courier and Enquirer,* proposed this thought-provoking plan:

"Charter three steamers. Freight two of them with the necessary provisions and stores for Fort Sumpter for the next six months or a year. Divide the troops to be sent equally among the *three;* and let the expedition sail under sealed orders. *Do this publicly and let the destination and purpose of the expedition be proclaimed.* [Italics added.] When within thirty miles of Charleston, let the *orders* be opened, and the Officer in Command (I wish I were he) remove every soldier from the steamer not freighted with stores—leaving on board only the necessary persons to navigate her. Let the *three* then sail for Sumpter, *every man below*—the empty or decoy steamer leading at least one mile. All the steamers presenting the same aspect, the battery from Morris Island will of course open upon the leading steamer, and possibly destroy her. The fire having been thus opened by the Rebels upon Government vessels, nobody will censure Major Anderson or the Government if he promptly, as he can, destroys *Moultrie* and the battery on Morris Island."

Of all the volunteer planners, the most thoughtful and thorough was a retired naval officer serving as a textile-mill agent in Massachusetts. This man, Gustavus Vasa Fox, had urged his ideas upon President Buchanan, in vain. Fox happened to be a son-in-law of old Francis P. Blair, once a member of Andrew Jackson's "Kitchen Cabinet," now living in the Washington suburb Silver Spring and acting as a self-appointed adviser of Presidents. Blair's son Montgomery was Lincoln's Postmaster General and, on the Sumter issue, was Seward's strongest and most persistent adversary in the cabinet. Suspecting Seward and Scott of weakness that bordered on treason, the Postmaster General was determined to offset their influence. He and his father worked together. Old man Blair called on Lincoln to argue against Scott's evacuation proposal, saying that withdrawal would be an ignominious "surrender of the Union" unless it were done in the face of "irresistible force." He counseled Lincoln to be like Jackson, to put forth a Union proclamation as Jackson had done at the time of South Carolina's nullification threat. Montgomery Blair wired his brother-in-law Fox to hurry to Washington.

Arriving promptly in the capital, the enterprising Fox explained his plan to Lincoln. He proposed an expedition consisting of a troop transport, warships, and fast steam tugs. Off Charleston harbor the reinforcements were to shift from the transport to the tugs and speed past the Confederate shore batteries at night. Fox thought the risks slight, the prospects good. The Navy officers agreed with him. The Army officers did not.

Lincoln considered the possibility of sending only supplies, without the troops that Fox was thinking of. He put the question to his cabinet (March 15): "Assuming it is possible to now provision Fort Sumter, under the circumstances is it wise to attempt it?" Blair answered yes. All the others, no. The Secretary of the Navy, Gideon Welles, whose copious beard made him look the part of Neptune, explained that the fort or the warships or both might have to fire upon enemy gunboats in order to protect the provisioning tugs. And Welles had a question of his own: "If this is done, will it not be claimed that aggressive war has been commenced by us upon the State and its citizens in their own harbor?" Seward took the cabinet vote as a vindication for himself, a defeat for Blair.

But Lincoln had not given up. He found himself in the midst of a welter of conflicting views. On the one hand, there were several "considerations in favor of withdrawing the Troops." On the other hand, there were at least two strong objections: first, "The danger of demoralizing the Republican party by a measure which might seem to many to indicate timidity;" second, "The danger of the movement being construed by the Secessionists as a yielding from necessity, and in so far a victory on their part." Lincoln needed information. He sent several men to Charleston to look things over on the spot. One was Fox, who visited Fort Sumter. Another was Stephen A. Hurlbut, an Illinois friend of Lincoln's who had been born in Charleston and who now revisited his home town on the pretext of seeing relatives. Hurlbut reported back:

"The power in that State and in the Southern Confederacy is now in the hands of the Conservatives—of men who desire no war." But "there exists a large minority indefatigably active and reckless who desire to precipitate collision, inaugurate war & unite the Southern Confederacy by that means." The question for the President is "one involving Peace or War, with this unfortunate contingency that it is by no means certain that any thing less than unqualified recognition of absolute Independence and of course unqualified surrender of Jurisdiction will satisfy. . . . I have no doubt that a ship known to contain *only provisions* for Sumpter would be stopped & refused admittance. Even the moderate men who desire not to open fire, [who] believe in the safer policy of time and starvation"—even these men would approve of firing if a ship were sent, though the ship were known to contain provisions only.

On March 28, the day after Hurlbut made this report, Lincoln reached the verge of a decision. That day General Scott advised him to give up *both* Pickens and Sumter, on the grounds that "the evacuation of both the forts would instantly soothe and give confidence to the eight remaining slave-holding states, and render their cordial adherence to the Union perpetual." This was Seward's argument. This was political and not military reasoning. No one before had intimated that Pickens, as distinct from Sumter, was militarily untenable, nor was Scott suggesting it now. That evening Lincoln held his first state dinner in the White House, and he seemed his usual joking, storytelling self, as if he had not a care in the world. After dinner he called his Cabinet members aside and informed them of Scott's latest proposal. All except Seward were aghast.

The next day Lincoln polled the Secretaries a second time for their written advice. They now reversed their earlier vote.

All except Seward agreed that both Sumter and Pickens should be held. "The dispatch of an expedition to supply or reinforce Sumter would provoke an attack and so involve a *war at that point,*" Seward objected. "The fact of preparation for such an expedition would inevitably transpire, and would therefore precipitate the war, and probably defeat the object." The others were equally convinced that the effort could not be made without provoking resistance. "But," as Welles said, "armed resistance to a peaceable attempt to send provisions to one of our own forts will justify the government in using all the powers at its command. . . ." That same March 29 Lincoln sent notes to the War and Navy Secretaries instructing them to get an expedition ready. Later he decided on two expeditions, one for Sumter and the other for Pickens.

Seward now found himself in a most embarrassing predicament. He had committed himself to the optimistic assumption that *his* policy would prevail, that Fort Sumter would certainly be evacuated. He had given repeated promises to the Confederacy through its commissioners, waiting in Washington.

On April 1 he made a desperate attempt to get his way. He handed Lincoln a long memorandum saying the administration had no policy, offering to take charge, suggesting foreign war, and proposing that the issue at home be changed from "Slavery" to "Union" by yielding Sumter and holding Pickens.

That same day Lincoln wrote out a reply, rejecting all Seward's propositions. The administration *had* a policy, he said, the policy laid down in the inaugural and in the early order to Scott to look vigilantly to the maintenance of all Federal places. This "comprises the exact domestic policy you now urge, with the single exception, that it does not propose to abandon Fort Sumpter." Furthermore, "I do not perceive how the re-inforcement of Fort Sumpter would be done on a slavery, or party issue, while that of Fort Pickens would be on a more national, and patriotic one."

Three days later, on April 4, Lincoln talked with John B. Baldwin, a Unionist member of the Virginia convention, but made no record of the conversation. He also gave orders to Gustavus Fox to proceed with the Sumter expedition. This was to include three warships (one, through error, was diverted to the Pickens force), a gunboat, three tugs, and a chartered steamer with two hundred soldiers and provisions to supply the fort for a year. On April 4 the President drafted a message for Major Anderson, to inform him of Fox's coming.

On April 6 Lincoln learned that, because of an error, his earlier order for the reinforcement of Fort Pickens had not been carried out. This day, he also wrote out a notice to be delivered to Governor Francis W. Pickens of South Carolina. The President's messenger was to say: "I am directed by the President of the United States to notify you to expect an attempt will be made to supply Fort-Sumpter with provisions only; and that, if such attempt be not resisted, no effort to throw in men, arms, or ammunition, will be made, without further notice, or in case of an attack upon the Fort."

The messenger read this notice to Governor Pickens on April 8. That evening, on a ship anchored near New York and ready to sail at daylight, Fox dashed off a note for his brother-in-law Blair: "We ought to be off Charleston the night of the 11th and make the attempt the night of the 12th."

Early on the morning of April 12, without waiting for Fox's expedition, the Confederates began to shell Fort Sumter.

On the next day, while the bombardment was still going on, Lincoln received a delegation of Virginia Unionists at the White House. He reminded them of his inaugural pledge that there would be "no invasion—no using of force" beyond what was necessary to hold government places and collect the customs. "But if, as now appears to be true, an unprovoked assault has been made upon Fort-Sumpter, I shall hold myself at liberty to repossess, if I can, like places which had been seized before the Government was devolved upon me."

Thereafter Lincoln called upon the states for soldiers. Refusing, Virginia joined the Confederacy, and so did Tennessee, Arkansas, and North Carolina, while the border slave states continued to waver. Throughout the North, in a frenzy of patriotism, men volunteered to defend the flag. The war was on.

3

Such are the bare facts of the Sumter incident—facts known or knowable from the records of the time itself. The rest is afterthought and controversy.

For all the endless argument, nobody really knows what Lincoln intended or expected when he made up his mind to let that fateful expedition go. There are those who say he intended and expected war. They have been saying it ever since Fort Sumter fell. There are others who say he intended and expected a peaceful provisioning of the fort, that he based his whole policy on an earnest wish to restore the Union without a bloody conflict, and failed.

In looking back upon events, Lincoln himself did not seem to think of the Sumter expedition as an utter failure. A few weeks after the firing on the fort he wrote a letter to cheer up Captain Fox, the commander of the expedition, who had not managed to enter the harbor and relieve the garrison. Lincoln said: "You and I both anticipated that the cause of the country would be advanced by making the attempt to provision Fort Sumter, even if it should fail; and it is no small consolation now to feel that our anticipation is justified by the result."

Lincoln explained and defended his Sumter policy in the message he prepared for the special session of Congress which he called for July 4, 1861. "Starvation was not yet upon the [Sumter] garrison; and ere it would be reached, *Fort Pickens* might be reinforced," he wrote. "This last [the reinforcement of Pickens] would be a clear indication of policy, and would enable the country to accept the evacuation of Fort Sumter, as a military *necessity*." Just one week before the fall of Sumter, he said, he received the news that the troops previously sent to Pickens had not been landed there. "To now re-inforce Fort Pickens, before a crisis was reached at Fort Sumter, was impossible." Against such a contingency the government had readied the Sumter expedition, "which expedition was intended to be ultimately used, or not, according to the circumstances." Once the notice had been given to the South Carolina Governor, Fort Sumter was attacked even before the ships arrived. Thus, clearly, the assailants did not act in self-defense. "They knew—they were expressly notified—that the giving of bread to the few brave and hungry men of the garrison was all which would on that occasion be attempted, unless themselves, by resisting so much, should provoke more."

Referring to himself in the third person, as "the Executive," Lincoln added: ". . . having said to them in the inaugural address, 'You can have no conflict without being yourselves the aggressors,' he took pains, not only to keep this declaration good, but also to keep the case so free from the power of ingenious sophistry, as that the world should not be able to misunderstand it. By the affair at Fort Sumter, with its surrounding circumstances, that point was reached. Then, and thereby, the assailants of the Government began the conflict of arms. . . ."

The message concluded: "And having thus chosen our course, without guile, and with pure purpose, let us renew our trust in God, and go forward without fear, and with manly hearts." Obviously Lincoln expected to be accused, with "ingenious sophistry," of bringing on hostilities and making the other side appear to be the aggressor.

On July 3, the eve of the assembling of Congress, Lincoln chatted in the White House with his friend O. H. Browning, the new Senator from Illinois. Lincoln read the forthcoming message to him, then told him, as Browning recorded in his diary: "He himself conceived the idea, and proposed sending supplies, without an attempt to reinforce giving notice of the fact to Gov Pickens of S. C. The plan succeeded. They attacked Sumter—it fell, and thus, did more service than it otherwise could."

As the Presidential message put it, Lincoln had taken pains to keep his inaugural declaration good, and ultimately a point had been reached where it *was* made good. In this respect he did not fail, by his own official account. Having listened to it, that evening of July 3, Browning would have had little cause for wonderment when he heard Lincoln go on to remark that his plan had succeeded when Sumter was attacked and fell. Browning might have had cause to wonder about the words "without guile" in the closing sentence of the message, if he had noticed them.

But Lincoln, in justifying his policy afterward, did not describe it as an unqualified success. In the message to Congress he indicated that he would have been willing to withdraw from Sumter if he could have been sure of holding Pickens. At other times he gave the impression that he would have been willing to withdraw from Sumter if he could have been sure of keeping Virginia in the Union. Three days after his White House interview with the Virginia Unionist John B. Baldwin he told another Virginia Unionist, John Minor Botts (April 7, 1861), that he had offered Baldwin to swap the fort for the state, to give up Sumter if the state's secession convention would adjourn without taking action. At least, that was the story Botts told years afterward. A Philadelphian by the name of George Plumer Smith heard Lincoln say the same thing to him, soon after Virginia had seceded, or so Smith remembered. In 1863 he asked John Hay to find out if Lincoln could verify the recollection. Lincoln could and did, according to Hay's reply to Smith, but asked that the information be kept confidential. Thus Lincoln himself was given as authority for the story that he had failed in his hopes for avoiding conflict by finding an equivalent which would have made it possible for him to abandon Sumter without appearing to abandon the Union cause completely.

In after years most Lincoln biographers and most Northern historians accepted and elaborated upon his own retrospective version of his policy. They differ in their emphasis upon his success or failure. J. G. Nicolay and John Hay contend that it is "reasonably certain" he "expected resistance and hostilities" when he sent the Sumter expedition, and they praise him for his statesmanship in managing affairs so that "the rebellion should be put in the wrong." They feel, however, that he would have yielded Sumter if he could have been guaranteed a substitute for it: "Pickens once triumphantly secured, the loss of Sumter could be borne." Other authorities—such as David M. Potter, James G. Randall, and Benjamin P. Thomas—agree with Nicolay and Hay about the Pickens-for-Sumter proposition but disagree about Lincoln's bold acceptance of war once he was satisfied the rebels would be put clearly in the wrong. These more recent writers maintain that Lincoln, to the last, counted upon peace (and hence, essentially, failed). They say his notice to the South Carolina Governor was designed to make clear his nonaggressive intent and to remove the possibility of provocative surprise. Thomas points to Lincoln's 1863 confirmation of the Botts story as positive proof that Lincoln would have been content with a Sumter-for-Virginia deal if it could have been arranged.

On reexamination, however, Lincoln's version of the Virginia matter appears to be questionable, as does his account of his Pickens plans, to say nothing of the interpretations which Lincoln-defending historians have put upon his own defense.

The Virginian Baldwin, to whom the offer of a fort for a state supposedly was made, reported no such proposal to the Virginia convention at the time, and afterward he always denied that Lincoln had given him any sort of pledge. According to Baldwin's testimony, Lincoln merely had asked that the Unionists adjourn the convention and go home, and Baldwin had replied that adjournment would do no good, that another and more radical convention then would meet. Baldwin apparently was a sincere Unionist, who voted against secession to the last. It is difficult to see why he would have kept the President's proposal secret, if indeed such a proposal ever was made.

In considering the Pickens-for-Sumter question, there is a tricky problem of timing. In his July 4 message to Congress, Lincoln said he had decided to let the Sumter expedition go only after learning of the disobedience of his order to land troops at Fort Pickens. In the same message he said he learned of this a week before Sumter's surrender. The surrender occurred on April 14; one week before that would have been April 7. Certainly Lincoln did not hear about the matter before April 6. But, according to Fox's testimony, he had given Fox his final instructions two days earlier—on April 4! And Lincoln's note to Major Anderson, telling him relief was coming, was dated April 4!

Lincoln's defenders explain away this time discrepancy with the following argument: The key date is not April 4 but April 6. Until April 6 Lincoln could have recalled the Sumter expedition, which did not actually depart for two more days (it left early on the morning of April 9). As for Fox's statement about having received his final orders on the fourth, he may well have been mistaken, at least about their finality. As for the note to Anderson, it was written and dated on the fourth but was not dispatched until the sixth. As proof for this, there still exists a copy of the letter with the following endorsement on the envelope in Lincoln's own hand: "This was sent by Capt Talbot, on April 6, 1861, to be delivered to Maj. Anderson if permitted. On reaching Charleston, he was refused permission to deliver it to Major Anderson."

But the fact is that other copies of the letter had been made and one of these, sent by regular mail instead of special messenger, reached Anderson on April 7. This copy must have been mailed before the previous day. And it *was,* according to Nicolay and Hay, who were the President's private secretaries at the time. They say that a copy was put in the mail for Anderson immediately after the letter had been written and copied in quadruplicate, on April 4.

This question of timing is more than a mere technicality. Upon it depends the thesis that Lincoln was willing to give up Sumter for Pickens and decided on the Sumter expedition only *after* he had received information causing him to doubt whether Pickens could be held. (Incidentally, Pickens *was* held. It did not fall, as Sumter did.) The conflicting evidence casts doubt on the Lincoln version.

And there is still stronger evidence against Lincoln's explanation, if not actual disproof. On April 1—three days before he composed the note for Anderson and at least *five* days before he heard about the miscarriage of his previous Pickens order—Lincoln wrote the reply to Seward in which he said his own domestic policy was the same as Seward's "with the single exception, that it does not propose to abandon Fort Sumter." Yet afterward, on July 4, Lincoln gave Congress to understand that he *had* proposed to abandon Fort Sumter if Fort Pickens could be made secure!

Now, if Lincoln told the truth in April, he was not telling the truth in July. And if he was not telling the truth in July, only two inferences are left to be drawn. Either he had a poor memory and had forgotten a great deal in three months, or he was rationalizing for Congress and the country.

In reporting to Congress he may have been sensitive to the differences of opinion which his incoming correspondence during March and early April had revealed. On the one hand, Republicans from Maine to Illinois then assured him that they and their fellows were quite willing to accept the evacuation of Sumter as a military necessity but were chagrined at rumors of the possible evacuation of Pickens also. On the other hand, Republicans in larger numbers warned him that he must not flinch from making a stand at Sumter, if he valued the party and the government itself. After he finally had made the Sumter effort he no longer needed to justify himself to the advocates of boldness and vigor. But he may have felt it advisable to assure the more timid and hesitant that he had exhausted the possibilities of peace and, in particular, had considered carefully the Pickens-for-Sumter alternative.

Be that as it may, the evidence on the whole makes it hard to believe that Lincoln could have counted on a peaceful provisioning of Fort Sumter. He knew well what had happened to Buchanan's attempt to send supplies in a lone, unarmed merchant steamer, the *Star of the West*. He had little reason to expect a more friendly welcome for his own much larger expedition, which included warships. He was acquainted with the opinion of Hurlbut who, after his flying visit to Charleston, reported that "a ship known to contain *only provisions* for Sumter" would be fired upon. In the light of this information Lincoln would have had cause to wonder whether his advance notice to the South Carolina Governor would mollify the Confederates even if he had confined it to a simple announcement that he would attempt to supply "provisions only" and had said nothing about throwing in arms, ammunition, and men. Lincoln must have thought armed resistance a probability, as his Cabinet advisers did.

From all this, however, it does not necessarily follow that he preferred war to peace, that he willfully contrived to bring about hostilities, or that he was the real "aggressor."

4

"He chose to draw the sword," the *Daily Express* of Petersburg, Virginia, said during the war, "but by a dirty trick succeeded in throwing upon the South the *seeming* blame of firing the first gun."

This was hardly news to that paper's readers. It passed for common knowledge, at least in the Confederacy.

When Alexander H. Stephens afterward wrote his book about "the late war," he had no doubt as to who the real aggressor had been in 1861. In the book the former Confederate Vice President conducted an imaginary colloquium:

"Do you mean to say, Mr. Stephens, that the war was inaugurated by Mr. Lincoln?"

"Most assuredly I do."

"Why, how in the world . . . ?"

"It is a fact that the *first gun* was fired by the Confederates," Stephens conceded to his incredulous questioner. Then he patiently explained: "The *aggressor* in a war is not the *first* who *uses force* but the first who renders force *necessary*."

On this point Jefferson Davis agreed with his former Vice President, though the two men agreed about little else. Since the time of Davis and Stephens, Southern historians have elaborated the Confederate view. The most thorough of them, Charles W. Ramsdell, sums up the charge thus:

"Lincoln, having decided that there was no other way than war for the salvation of his administration, his party, and the Union, maneuvered the Confederates into firing the first shot in order that they, rather than he, should take the blame of beginning bloodshed."

According to the Ramsdell argument, Davis and the rest of the Confederate leaders desired peace. They were ready to negotiate a settlement. But Lincoln, not so peaceably inclined, refused to deal with them.

During the weeks that followed his inauguration he was beset on two sides. Coercionists demanded that he act to save Fort Sumter. Others counseled him to yield. If he acted, he stood to lose the upper South, if not the border also. If he yielded, he would lose his own party. While he hesitated, his fellow Republicans bickered among themselves, his administration threatened to fall apart, and the country drifted toward ruin. He had to make up his mind soon, before the Sumter garrison was starved out.

At last he hit upon a way out of his dilemma. The thought occurred to him—*must have* occurred to him—that he could induce the Confederates to attack the fort. Then, the flag having been fired upon, he would gain all the benefits of an aroused patriotism. Republicans and Democrats would forget their quarrels of party and faction, the border states would respond with an upsurge of loyalty, and wavering millions throughout the North would rally to the Union cause. The party, the administration, and the Union would be saved.

The stratagem was a shrewd one, worthy of the shrewd man that Lincoln was. He decided to send the expedition and—most cleverly—to give advance notice. A genius with words, he could make them mean different things to different people. This is what he did with the words he addressed to the Governor of South Carolina. To Northerners these words would seem quite innocent. The government was taking groceries to hungry men and would not use force unless it had to. That was all. To Southerners the same words carried a threat, indeed a double threat. First, Sumter was going to be provisioned so it could hold out. Second, if resistance was attempted, arms and men as well as food were going to be supplied!

The notice was timed as carefully as it was phrased. It was delivered on the day that the first ships of the expedition left New York. These could not reach their destination for three days at least, so the Confederates would have plenty of time to take counteraction before the ships arrived. Already the Confederates had news that a sizable expedition was being prepared, and they were left to suppose that the entire force (including the part of it actually being dispatched to Fort Pickens in Florida) was heading for Charleston. With such a large force presumed to be on the way, they had all the more reason for a quick move.

The ruse worked perfectly. True, the expedition neither provisioned nor reinforced Sumter; it gave the garrison no support at all. But that was not the object. The object was to provoke a shot that would rouse the North to fight.

In this Ramsdell thesis there undoubtedly is a certain element of truth, but there is even more that is fallacious. Ramsdell—like Davis, Stephens, and others before him—makes Lincoln appear too much the warmonger, the Confederates too much the unoffending devotees of peace. Ramsdell also pictures Lincoln as too much the controlling force, the Confederates as too much the helpless, passive agents.

After all, the Confederates themselves had something to do with the firing on Fort Sumter.

Even assuming that Lincoln had some kind of "maneuver" in mind, he could not have made it work without the cooperation of the Confederates. And it is fair enough to suppose that the maneuver idea in some form did occur to him, since he received so much advice about decoying the enemy into shooting first, and since he was familiar with the idea as applied to President Polk. But the point is that Lincoln could have had no sure foreknowledge that an expedition, no matter how planned and carried out, would have the desired effect. It might have exactly the opposite effect, and indeed he received counter advice telling him so. There was, for instance, that letter from the cautious Bostonian who warned that if the secessionists could "intercept a reinforcement or supplies, and thereby call out a response from the guns of Major Anderson, they would have what *they* would call an affirmative act of aggression on the part of the United States," and this would become *their* "rallying cry."

So far as Lincoln could know ahead of time, the result of the Sumter expedition might have been just what this correspondent predicted. If the Confederates had withheld their fire upon the fort, if they had waited for the arrival of the ships and had merely tried to head them off, and if the fort then had opened fire on the installations in the harbor, the Confederates might have had a rallying cry indeed, a cry that would have won them many friends in the North as well as the border states. Lincoln could not depend upon the Confederates' convicting themselves of aggression (or seeming in the eyes of the North to do so) by firing the first shot and firing it not at the approaching fleet but at Anderson's men in the unoffending fort (as Northerners would see it).

There were still other dangers—for Lincoln. If for any reason his expedition was bungled, and the Confederates waited and withheld their fire, then Lincoln and the Union would suffer a psychological blow. And the expedition was in fact bungled, but of course the Confederates did not withhold their fire.

When they did fire, they did not necessarily become the aggressors because of that. To this extent Stephens was correct. By the same token, however, Lincoln did not necessarily become the aggressor when he sent the expedition.

From the Confederate point of view the United States had made itself the aggressor long before Lincoln acted to reinforce any fort. It was aggression when, on December 26, 1860, Major

Anderson moved his troops from Moultrie to the more defensible Sumter. Indeed, it was a continuing act of aggression every day that Union forces remained in Sumter or any other place within the bounds of the Confederacy. And from the Union point of view the Confederacy had committed and was committing aggression by its very claim to existence, to say nothing of its seizures of Federal property, its occupation of Fort Moultrie, and its construction of a semicircle of harbor batteries with Sumter as their target.

There is little reason to suppose, and there was little reason for Lincoln to suppose, that he could escape either war or the charge of warmonger by giving up Sumter and holding Pickens as a substitute symbol of the national authority. The Confederate commissioners in Washington had instructions to obtain the cession of Pickens and other places as well as Sumter. Lincoln's fact-finding emissary to Charleston, Hurlbut, reported back that conflict could not be averted by Sumter's abandonment. "Undoubtedly this will be followed by a demand for Pickens and the Keys of the Gulf," Hurlbut opined. Indeed, Seward himself at the last did not really believe that Pickens, in contrast to Sumter, could be held and reinforced without war. He merely thought a better case for war could be made in consequence of an incident at Pickens. "I do not think it wise to provoke a Civil War beginning at Charleston and in rescue of an untenable position," he said in his Cabinet opinion of March 29. "I would . . . at once and at any cost prepare for war at Pensacola and Texas, to be [under]taken however only as a consequence of maintaining the possession and authority of the United States."

No matter which way he turned, Lincoln could find no clear and unobstructed path away from the danger of war. As Hurlbut told him, and as various signs indicated, the sacrifice of Sumter would mean no guarantee of continued peace. "Nor do I believe," Hurlbut added, "that any policy which may be adopted by the Government will prevent the possibility of armed collision."

Of course, a surrender to the Confederate demands might have prevented, or at least postponed, the shooting. When the Confederates talked of peace, that is what they meant—a surrender on Lincoln's part. They wanted peace with the recognition of the Confederacy and the transfer to it of all the property the United States claimed within Confederate boundaries. No doubt Lincoln longed for peace. But peace to him was meaningless without the preservation of the Union.

And even if he had been willing to yield all that the seceders for the moment demanded, he had no assurance that the result would be anything more than a postponement of war, a prolongation of the truce. One possibility is this: the rest of the slave states might have remained in the Union, and the seven states of the stunted Confederacy might have had eventually no good choice but to abandon their experiment in rebellion. But there is another possibility: the Union and the Confederacy might have come into conflict over any one of several points, and an incident arising therefrom might have precipitated the secession of the upper South. As a matter of fact, not all the secessionist leaders were satisfied with the extent of the Confederacy as it was at the start. Hotheads in South Carolina—and in Virginia too—hoped for a clash that would bring new members to the Confederacy. A couple of the rabid Virginians, Roger A. Pryor and Edmund Ruffin, went to Charleston before the Sumter attack and did all they could to stir up trouble, with the idea that Virginia would go to South Carolina's aid once trouble came. Lincoln, if he had let the Confederacy have its way in April, 1861, would doubtless have had to contend thereafter with a continuation of this deliberate troublemaking.

Thus Lincoln was far less a plotter of war-bringing maneuvers than some of the Confederates themselves. And he was no more the aggressor in the conflict than any of the Confederates were.

5

If Lincoln neither sought war nor counted upon peace, what did he have in mind when he made his Sumter decision? The answer can be no more than a guess based on extensive but conflicting information.

Lincoln was devoted to the Union and determined to preserve it. He also was devoted to his party and unwilling to stand by and see it go to smash. In the circumstances it seemed that the party and the Union must stand or fall together, for without the party behind him he would have been powerless to save the Union, or to do anything else of much consequence. He felt it his duty to hold, occupy, and possess the Federal property in the South, and he never seriously considered relinquishing any of it, except in the face of superior force. At the same time he was conscious of the need to avoid all appearance of aggression on the part of the government.

To do his duty as President, he was convinced he had to make a stand sooner or later, and he concluded he might as well make it at Sumter. In doing so, his primary aim was neither to provoke war nor to maintain peace. He thought that hostilities might follow, but if they did, it would be a short war, quickly won. He did not foresee the long years of bloody conflict. And he thought there was at least a bare chance of provisioning and holding Sumter without general hostilities.

He was pursuing what Kenneth M. Stampp has described as a policy of "calculated risk." In preserving the Union, Lincoln would have been glad to preserve the peace also, but he was ready to risk a war.

chapter 6

THE MILITARY GENIUS

o far as appearances went, it was a most unmilitary man who, y virtue of his office as President of the United States, was ommander in Chief of the Army and the Navy during the ur years of the Civil War. Abraham Lincoln had neither e bearing of a soldier nor the background of one.

Once, as a young man of twenty-three, he had been briefly a ldier of sorts. When Chief Black Hawk, with his hungry Sac nd Fox tribesmen, recrossed the Mississippi River to "plant rn" on old tribal lands, Lincoln answered the Illinois Govrnor's call for militiamen to repel the invaders from the state. incoln was elected captain by his comrades in a Sangamon ounty company. He always prized this honor, yet he hardly took his military life seriously, if he is to be judged by th stories he afterward told about it.

The first time that Captain Lincoln gave an order, the r sponse he got was, "Go to the devil, sir." He seems to have ha considerable trouble with his orders. At the head of his com pany he came one day to a narrow gate and could not think o the right command for telling his men to form a column so the could get through. "Halt!" he finally shouted. "This compan will break ranks for two minutes and form again on the oth side of the gate."

"By the way, Mr. Speaker," he joked in Congress sixteen yea later, "did you know I am a military hero? Yes sir; in the da of the Black Hawk War, I fought, bled, and came away." Tru he saw no "live, fighting Indians," but he had "a good man bloody struggles with the mosquitoes."

In that same campaign against the Indians there served, i the Regular Army, a young West Point graduate by the name o Jefferson Davis. So far as is known, Lieutenant Davis and Ca tain Lincoln did not meet. There is a story that Davis admi istered to Lincoln the oath of allegiance to the United Stat when Lincoln brought his Illinois volunteers into the Feder service. Too bad the story is not true, since it has a certai ironical fitness.

Afterward Davis went on to military glory. Commanding th Mississippi Rifles in the Mexican War, he distinguished him self by his heroism and resourcefulness in the battle of Buen Vista. The Mexicans attacked with far superior numbers, an Davis threw them into retreat with a V-shaped formation h improvised for the occasion.

He won fame not only as a battlefield tactician but also as a army administrator. When Franklin Pierce was President, Dav was Secretary of War, and he made a record for efficiency an good sense which gave him a reputation as one of the greate of all heads of the War Department.

Such was the man who, in the Confederate States of Americ held the office which, in the United States, was occupied by veteran of many a skirmish with mosquitoes in the Black Hawk War.

Besides having a military professional as president, the Confederacy had as generals far more than its fair share of the men who had been schooled at West Point and battle-tested on the fields of Mexico. Above all, the Confederacy had Thomas J. Jackson and Robert E. Lee.

On the Union side, Lincoln could call on men whose experience was great, but whose talents have been more open to question.

Winfield Scott, the man who had led the Army to victory in Mexico, boasted more years in service than any Confederate. Scott was a real soldier, of proved ability. But by the time of the Civil War he was weighted down with years and excess flesh.

George B. McClellan, who took Scott's place for a while, possessed the vigor of youth. He was not yet thirty-five when he took command in 1861. For one so young, he was well versed at least in some phases of war. After his service in the Mexican War he returned to West Point to teach the cadets military engineering. Then he made surveys and directed construction projects for the Army in various parts of the United States and in Santo Domingo. Later he toured Europe with a board of officers to study military organizations abroad. During the Crimean War he watched the siege of Sevastapol and afterward wrote an excellent report. He recommended, and the cavalry adopted, what became known as the McClellan saddle.

Henry W. Halleck, who followed McClellan as Lincoln's top general, was the author of a textbook on the art of warfare. Though little more than a translation, the book indicated Halleck's familiarity with what was considered the best of military science in Europe. Halleck was known by the nickname "Old Brains," and even if some people thought it should be Old Woodenhead, he was a knowledgeable soldier.

Ulysses S. Grant, the General in Chief for the last year of the war, proved his military abilities only after forty years of failure in the Army and in civilian life. He was careless of dress in a way that Scott—"Old Fuss and Feathers"—never would have been. He slouched about as no one ever saw the erect and self-conscious McClellan do. Yet Grant possessed the instincts as well as the training of a great commander.

After getting rid of Simon Cameron, Lincoln had in Edwin M. Stanton a Secretary of War who, though not a military man, at least exhibited the brusque manner of an army martinet. But Lincoln himself seemed oddly out of place in soldier gatherings. Reviewing McClellan's troops near Washington early in the war, he rode with his long legs braced in low-slung stirrups, his coattails flapping, his stovepipe hat perched precariously atop his head, while the immaculately uniformed McClellan sat his horse like a centaur. Visiting Grant's army near Richmond late in the war, the President still had his quaint, civilian air as he stalked along beside the grizzled general who looked every inch the hard campaigner he had become.

An amateur among professionals, a novice among the initiated, Lincoln again and again confessed his ignorance and showed his willingness to learn. He talked with officers to draw out their views. He studied tactics and strategy, gathering a small library of books and poring and puzzling over them night after night. Through the four years of the war he followed events with an absorption no mere spectator could approach.

Lincoln learned. How much he learned—and how much he contributed to the success of the Union war effort—are questions which have divided military experts ever since they began to refight the Civil War.

Says Lord Wolseley, the outstanding soldier of Great Britain in the Victorian era: "Mr. Lincoln, though doubtless one of the greatest men who has ruled the United States, was entirely ignorant of war. Able and wise as he was in all matters of civil government, he failed here most disastrously."

A leader among nineteenth-century American military historians, John Codman Ropes, agrees with Wolseley. "Few men at the head of affairs during a great war," Ropes maintains, "have ever given such evidence of an entire unfitness to have any general direction over military men as Mr. Lincoln and Mr. Stanton. And this inaptitude for war the former retained to the end of his life."

But Francis V. Greene, a Major General of United States Volunteers, contends: "Lincoln had that faculty of intense application and clear insight, so rare that we call it genius; and he applied it as successfully to military affairs as to politics."

And Brigadier General Colin R. Ballard of the British Army writes in *The Military Genius of Abraham Lincoln:* "My belief is that Lincoln was solely responsible for the strategy of the North and proved himself a very capable strategist."

The experts disagree and the debate goes on and on. Since the points at issue are matters of *judgment* rather than of *fact,* it will probably go on forever. Meanwhile a brief review of certain controversial points in Lincoln's conduct of the war will at least give some idea of what the argument is all about.

2

Military authorities, whether or not they approve Lincoln's strategy as a whole, find no fault with the first big decision he had to make as Commander in Chief. This was, of course, his decision in regard to Fort Sumter, and in making it he rejected the advice of his general in chief, Scott. Even G. F. R. Henderson, Stonewall Jackson's admiring biographer and Lincoln's severe critic, concedes that, in "forcing the Confederates to become the aggressors, and to fire on the national ensign," Lincoln "created a united North" and thus scored an important point.

Authorities also agree in endorsing Lincoln's next big decision after his call for three-months volunteers to put down the rebellion. This was his decision to impose a blockade, which he announced just one week after the first shell exploded over Sumter. The blockade was his own idea (and Seward's); it was not the suggestion of any of his generals. "Judicious indeed," says Henderson, "was the policy which, at the very outset of the war, brought the tremendous pressure of the sea-power to bear against the South; and, had her statesmen possessed the knowledge of what that pressure meant, they must have realized that Abraham Lincoln was no ordinary foe."

But authorities differ about the wisdom of his early strategic thinking in general, and his Bull Run decision in particular. Some hold that he was too much the politician and too little the strategist, that too often political rather than military considerations determined his battle plans.

For more than three months after the war began, no large-scale fighting took place. A few optimists in the North expected to win with no shooting, or practically none.

Lincoln's patriarchal attorney general, Edward Bates, had a scheme which he said "would not necessarily lead to the shedding of a drop of blood" and yet would be "very promising of success." His proposal was simply to discontinue the Southern mails, guard the Mississippi River, make the blockade effective —and sit tight.

General Scott conceived a strategy almost as passive as that of Bates. According to Scott's "Anaconda" plan, Union forces should move down the Mississippi River so as to split the Confederacy. Then, with the coast blockaded and the Mississippi closed, the Southeast would be caught in a gigantic squeeze. No further large-scale offensive would be necessary—only a holding action. Eventually the rebels would come to their senses and lose their will to fight.

Most Northerners, however, grew increasingly impatient with the sitting war as spring turned to summer in 1861. They wanted and expected a quick campaign which would smash the rebellion with a single blow. It was time to act. By the end of July many of the three-months enlistments would terminate and the army of Union volunteers would melt away. On July 20 the Confederate Congress was scheduled to meet in Richmond; it must not be allowed to do so. "Forward to Richmond! On to Richmond!" was the daily slogan of Horace Greeley's *New York Tribune*. Radical Republicans in the United States Congress took up the cry. Some of them insinuated that Scott, a

Virginian, held back the Union offensive because he did not wish to see his fellow Southerners killed.

General Irvin McDowell, drilling raw troops near Washington, considered them unready for offensive action. Agreeing with McDowell, the general in chief advised Lincoln that no forward movement should be made until the fall, and that the advance then should be projected down the Mississippi, not toward Richmond. Once more Lincoln rejected Scott's advice. So Scott submitted a plan that McDowell had prepared for a Virginia operation aimed at Manassas Junction, an important railroad point some thirty miles from Washington. Lincoln ordered that McDowell's plan be promptly carried out.

The first news from Bull Run, where the Confederates were engaged on July 21, was heartening to Lincoln as he waited anxiously at the War Department telegraph. Sure of victory, he went out for a Sunday drive. By the time he returned, tidings of disaster had come in. Soon the fleetest soldiers of McDowell's fleeing army neared the comparative safety of the capital. For a time, Washingtonians wondered whether the city itself was safe.

Days of crimination and recrimination followed. Scott confessed himself "the greatest coward in America" for yielding to the clamor of the politicians and the press. "I deserve removal," he said, "because I did not stand up, when my army was not in condition for fighting, and resist . . . to the last."

Had Lincoln succumbed to political pressure? Some historians say so, but others deny it. According to Ballard, the President in his Manassas decision was guided by strictly military considerations, though at this and other times he allowed the politicians to believe they exerted influence upon him. The North at the moment had a chance to bring superior numbers to bear upon a strategic point, and Lincoln realized it. His planning, Greene adds, was not proved wrong by the fact that the Federals were routed at Bull Run. From the Union view "it was one of the best planned battles of the war, but one of the worst fought," as William Tecumseh Sherman once said.

The plan had depended upon keeping two Confederate

armies apart. The Union general, Robert Patterson, was supposed to engage Joseph E. Johnston at Winchester, and prevent his going to the aid of P. G. T. Beauregard at Manassas. But Johnston, with the Jackson who was to gain the sobriquet of "Stonewall" on the Manassas field, managed to slip away.

The night of the Bull Run defeat, Lincoln did not go to bed. He began to jot down with a pencil the lessons to be learned. His ideas were his own. Unlike his general in chief, he started with the assumption that the war would have to be *fought* if it ever was to be won. After a succession of more or less sleepless nights he produced two memoranda on military policy. Then he demoted McDowell and called McClellan from a victorious though rather minor campaign in western Virginia to take command of the forces in the vicinity of Washington.

Lincoln's memoranda of July 23 and 27, 1861, have been hailed as conclusive evidence of his brilliance as a strategist. According to Greene, they provided "the first definite and coherent plan for the prosecution of the war." Throughout the conflict the President "never swerved" from these principles. Eventually all of them were put into effect, and the war was won.

It is a little disappointing to turn from such high praise to the actual words that Lincoln jotted down. He recommended these steps: tighten the blockade, drill the volunteers at Fort Monroe, hold Baltimore, strengthen the forces in the Virginia mountains and in Missouri, reorganize the Manassas remnants, discharge the unwilling three-months men, and bring up new volunteers as fast as possible, training them in two camps, one on each side of the Potomac.

"When the foregoing have been substantially attended to—

"1. Let Manassas Junction (or some point on one or other of the railroads near it) and Strasburg, be seized, and permanently held, with an open line from Washington to Manassas; and an open line from Harper's Ferry to Strasburg—the military men to find the way of doing these.

"2. This done, a joint movement from Cairo on Memphis; and from Cincinnati on East Tennessee."

These were merely Lincoln's thoughts: he hesitated to issue them as outright orders. In November he accepted the resignation of Scott and elevated McClellan to the position of general in chief. Through the winter Lincoln continued to think of the Bull Run lessons as they applied to his big political-military problem—how to advance against the Confederate armies and at the same time hold and use the support of Unionists in Missouri, Kentucky, western Virginia, and eastern Tennessee. He refrained, at first, from telling McClellan or the generals in the field what they had to do. But he did suggest to them what he believed they ought to do. And he was especially eager that Halleck in Missouri and Don Carlos Buell in Kentucky should act together on a sensible plan.

"In the midst of my many cares, I have not seen, or asked to see, Gen. McClellan's letters to you," he wrote Buell, January 13, 1862. "For my own views, I have not offered, and do not now offer them as orders. . . . With this preliminary, I state my general idea of this war to be that we have the *greater* numbers, and the enemy has the *greater* facility of concentrating forces upon points of collision; that we must fail, unless we can find some way of making *our* advantage an overmatch for *his;* and that this can only be done by menacing him with superior forces at *different* points, at the *same* time; so that we can safely attack, one, or both, if he makes no change; and if he *weakens* one to *strengthen* the other, forbear to attack the strengthened one, but seize, and hold the weakened one, gaining so much. To illustrate, suppose last summer, when Winchester ran away to reinforce Manassas, we had forborne to attack Manassas, but had seized and held Winchester."

So, now, Buell should threaten eastern Tennessee while Halleck threatened western Kentucky and "down river." No matter where the enemy chose to concentrate, the Union would gain a point. Thus Lincoln argued, and he seemed especially eager that something be done to open communications with the loyal element of the Tennessee mountains.

In appraising these strategic views of Lincoln's, the latter-day authorities have seen either a wise or an unwise devotion to nonmilitary ends. And they have seen either a sound or an unsound preference for a rather wide deployment of the Union armies. But the experts have wrangled loudest and longest about the differences which in 1862 developed between Lincoln and McClellan in regard to the management of the fighting on the Virginia front. To make the issues clear, it may help to tell the story twice—first from the pro-McClellan, anti-Lincoln view; then from the pro-Lincoln, anti-McClellan side.

3

Afterward, McClellan wrote in an official report: "In the arrangement and conduct of campaigns the direction should be left to professional soldiers. A statesman may, perhaps, be more competent than a soldier to determine the political objects and direction of a campaign; but those once decided upon, everything should be left to the responsible military head, without interference from civilians."

What had happened to McClellan illustrates the evils of civilian interference at their worst, according to those who dispute Lincoln's greatness as a commander in chief.

Now, McClellan had his faults. Though fond of Napoleonic poses, he lacked the fighting blood of Bonaparte. He was slow, overcautious, duped by his spies' fantastic exaggerations of enemy strength. Yet he had real abilities, particularly in drilling troops and inspiring them with loyalty and trust. To some extent his faults were merely defects of his virtues. He sought to make the most of the Union preponderance in men and resources—to win the war by strategy, not butchery. Gather an army of tremendous numbers, train it to perfection, and equip it with the best. Then, when all is ready, but not a day before, overwhelm the enemy in a single campaign. That was McClellan's idea, and that was the reason for his long delay in taking the field.

His greatest weakness, the one that led to his ultimate undoing, was political, not military. He was a Democrat, a conservative who wished no damage to slave or other property of the civilian South. The Radical Republicans, however, demanded what they called a "vigorous prosecution" of the war, with abolition as a leading aim. They did not want hostilities to end too soon for emancipation, nor did they welcome victory at the hands of a general whose glory would redound to the advantage of the Democratic party. Better years of defeat than a quick success for McClellan, these Radicals believed. So they schemed to frustrate him, working in the Congress through their Committee on the Conduct of the War and in the Cabinet through their two-faced ally Stanton, who pretended all along to be McClellan's friend.

Having put McClellan in supreme command, Lincoln might well have given him a fair, unfettered chance, but the President could not close his ears to the harping of the Radicals. For months he wavered between the self-interested badgering of the politicians and the professional advice of his general in chief. No wonder that, meanwhile, disasters came.

His patience frayed, Lincoln with his General Order Number One commanded McClellan to advance from Washington, setting a day for the movement to begin—and thus, incidentally, betraying his naïveté in military affairs. As if the start of a campaign could be timed by nothing more than a glance at the calendar! McClellan knew, if Lincoln did not, that there were preparations still be made and that Virginia roads still lay deep in mud.

Lincoln preferred an overland march by way of Manassas (as before, when an ill-trained army went forth to Bull Run and hastily returned) but McClellan proposed to go as far as possible by water, transporting his army down the Potomac River and Chesapeake Bay, landing it on the Peninsula between the York and the James, then moving it against Richmond from the east. His plan had its advantages. It would free him from the dangers of a long communications line through hostile territory. It would enable him, with the cooperation of the Navy, to bring up heavy guns for the bombardment of Richmond. But the plan appeared to have a serious flaw. To nervous civilians, including the President, the plan seemed to uncover Washington, exposing it to capture by the Confederates. McClellan knew better. He knew that the Confederates dared not risk a major blow at the Union capital while their own capital was under siege. And he was going to leave sufficient forces in and around Washington to make it safe against diversionary raids.

Once McClellan had got his Peninsula campaign under way, both the Radical politicians and the Confederate strategists began to play upon Lincoln's fears in the hope of causing the campaign to fail.

The Radicals complained that McClellan had left too few troops behind to garrison the capital. They insinuated that he had done so deliberately and treacherously—to let the rebels take Washington at will. Yielding to the Radical pressure, Lincoln demoted McClellan from general in chief of all the armies to commander of the Army of the Potomac alone. And he cut McClellan's army, holding back a division and then a whole corps, for the defense of Washington. He simply did not understand McClellan's arrangements for the capital's protection; he counted only the soldiers manning the works in the immediate vicinity, ignoring the force already stationed in the Shenandoah Valley, the one feasible route for a Confederate thrust to the north. The corps he had detached—McDowell's—he placed between Washington and Richmond with the thought that McDowell might cooperate with McClellan by moving toward Richmond while screening Washington. The President appeared to be reverting to his own strategy of an overland approach and doing his best to combine it with McClellan's plan, which he reluctantly had approved.

Then, while McClellan with his weakened army was struggling on the Peninsula, Stonewall Jackson struck with a series of lightning maneuvers at the Union forces in the Valley. Suddenly Lincoln ordered McDowell to turn away from Richmond and go off in pursuit of Stonewall Jackson. McDowell, though himself a Radical in politics, knew the foolishness and futility of such a chase. He protested the order but obeyed it.

As the Washington panic grew, Lincoln wired McClellan about the objective of Jackson: "I think the movement is a general and concerted one, such as would not be if he was acting upon the purpose of a very desperate defense of Richmond. I think the time is near when you must either attack Richmond or give up the job and come to the defense of Washington." Calmly McClellan replied: "The object of the movement is probably to prevent reinforcements being sent me." In a letter to his wife, noting that the President was "terribly scared about Washington," he exclaimed: "Heaven save a country governed by such counsels!"

Lincoln was wrong and McClellan right. Jackson's movement in the Valley was *not* "a general and concerted one" aiming at the capture of Washington. It *was* a diversion intended to keep aid from going to McClellan. Lincoln had fallen—or rather the Radicals had pushed him—into a Confederate trap.

From start to finish he botched the Peninsula campaign for McClellan. The latter had counted on McDowell's corps for the specific task of turning the enemy fortifications at Yorktown and opening the way for the rest of the army to advance up the Peninsula before the Confederates could mass their forces for the defense of Richmond. Without McDowell's corps (and without the naval aid he had desired) McClellan felt it necessary to invest the Yorktown works. Thus he lost a precious month. By the time he reached the outskirts of Richmond, he had an army only two-thirds as large as he originally had planned for, an army scarcely larger than the Confederates now assembled. Yet he needed at least a three-to-two edge to launch a successful offensive under the circumstances. And he was compelled to deploy his forces awkwardly on both sides of the Chickahominy River, since he had to extend his right far to the north so as to make contact with McDowell, who was supposed to be moving toward him overland. Even so, McClellan took the worst that Lee could throw against him. He frustrated Lee's scheme to cut his communications and destroy him in detail. In the course of the hard-fought Seven Days he saved the bulk of his army and its supplies and, staging successfully one of the most difficult maneuvers known to warfare, shifted his base in mid-campaign from the York across the Peninsula to the James.

As the Seven Days battle was drawing to a close, Lincoln seemed to appreciate some of the difficulties under which McClellan was laboring. "We protected Washington and the enemy concentrated on you," he said in a consoling message to McClellan. "Had we stripped Washington he would have been upon us before the troops sent could have got to you." And yet, as these words showed, Lincoln still had failed to grasp the essentials of the situation. In fact, Washington had not been threatened, and McClellan never had proposed that it be "stripped" of defending troops. That was not the issue.

After the Seven Days McClellan begged for reinforcements with which to begin an assault upon Richmond from his new base on the James. But Lincoln could not comprehend the need for additional troops. Even after visiting McClellan at Harrison's Landing, he told Stanton that the Army of the Potomac was "still a large one, and in good condition, although much diminished, consisting when it was sent there of 160,000 men." Later he made the famous remark that sending men to McClellan's army was "like shoveling fleas across a barnyard—not half of them get there." The truth is that Lincoln had not been sending men to McClellan's army; he had been taking them away. That army, after its arrival on the Peninsula, never numbered 160,000 or anywhere near so many, though McClellan had planned on a force of approximately that size, before the President began to interfere. Lincoln was compounding error with error.

Again the Radical politicians and the Confederate authorities combined to work on the anxieties of the President. The Radicals' favorite, General John Pope, having been given an independent command in northern Virginia, added his voice to the cry that McClellan's army be withdrawn from the Peninsula. And Stonewall Jackson, after having joined in the defense of Richmond, was sent back to the Valley to renew his threats from there. Again Lincoln gave in to his fears, recalling McClellan, calling off his campaign.

Afterward McClellan said that the President, if not satisfied with him, should have left the army where it was, given it adequate reinforcements, and put at its head either Pope or some other general who had the confidence of the administration. For the Federals, as Confederate General Richard Taylor observed in retrospect, "the true line of attack was on the south of the James, where Grant was subsequently forced by the ability of Lee." McClellan was there already, in the summer of 1862. Not for two long and bitter years was a Union army again to be so close to Richmond.

On his return to the Washington area, McClellan became a general without an army, his forces being transferred piecemeal to the command of General Pope. At the second battle of Manassas the boastful Pope was deflated by the foxy generalship of Jackson and Lee. Pope and his Radical friends tried to shift the blame somehow to McClellan, though the latter was without responsibility, and was miles away. In the emergency Lincoln had no choice but to appeal to McClellan and, though receiving no clear-cut authority from the President, McClellan forgot his grievances and heeded only the call of patriotism. He rallied and reorganized Pope's shattered army, pushed energetically through the passes of South Mountain, and met the invading enemy at Antietam. Only the hesitancy of one of his corps commanders, Ambrose E. Burnside, prevented McClellan from coordinating his attack so as to smash beyond repair the smaller army of the bold if not foolhardy Lee. As it was, McClellan in the war's bloodiest day won a strategic success which forced Lee to retreat and headed off a threatened move of European powers to recognize and aid the Confederacy. Not Gettysburg nor Vicksburg but Antietam was the turning point of the Civil War.

"General," said Lincoln to McClellan on a visit to the army camp soon afterward, "you have saved the country. You must remain in command and carry us through to the end."

"That will be impossible," the General replied. "We need time. The influences at Washington will be too strong for you, Mr. President. I will not be allowed the required time for preparation."

That was how McClellan remembered the talk, and that was how the future was to be. Egged on by the Radicals, Lincoln began to complain of McClellan's requests for additional supplies, of his slowness in moving out and making contact with Lee. Lincoln was generous only with advice. Head for Richmond, he suggested. Cut in between Lee and his capital, thus threatening his communication line. The well-meaning President failed to see that if McClellan could threaten Lee's communications, Lee could endanger McClellan's even more. Failed to realize that Lee had an alternative base and was not dependent on Richmond. Failed to understand that marching and countermarching McClellan's cumbrous host was no simple task. Lincoln, it would appear, was an armchair strategist. But Lee, whom McClellan had to face, was not.

Finally, when McClellan was starting out in the direction that Lincoln had indicated, he suddenly was handed a message removing him from all command. Why, nobody really knows, though the Radical clamor had risen to its highest pitch. From a military point of view, the moment was most inopportune. And bad as McClellan's dismissal was, the choice of his successor was even worse. Burnside, the man who had delayed so disastrously at Antietam! In the course of time, by his insane assaults at Fredericksburg (December, 1862), Burnside proved to others what in his heart he had known all along, that he was utterly unfit to lead the Army of the Potomac. After Burnside—Joseph Hooker. And "Fighting Joe" fought little better when his turn came, at Chancellorsville in May of 1863.

If McClellan was a comparatively good general, Lincoln in his dealings with him must have been a correspondingly poor Commander in Chief. And McClellan *was* a good general, according to many a well-informed military man. "The best general the Army of the Potomac ever had," opined General

Francis W. Palfrey, a hardheaded authority on the battle of Antietam. While the Confederacy was young and yet unwearied, McClellan "fought a good, wary, damaging, respectable fight" against it. He learned as he fought. "With longer possession of command, greater things might fairly have been expected of him." Thus Palfrey, and another and far more imposing authority may be quoted in McClellan's favor. The man who should have known best, the man who had opposed Grant as well as McClellan, is reported as declaring his opinion in no uncertain terms. When, after Appomattox, he was asked to name the ablest general he had faced in the war, Robert E. Lee did not hesitate. Lee pounded his fist on the desk and exclaimed: "McClellan by all odds!"

4

And now the other side.

During the Civil War and after, the partisans of Little Mac, including himself, overdid their efforts to make him appear the innocent victim of political discrimination. Lincoln, in his dealings with the general, was guided by considerations of military policy, not by those of party politics.

In his argument with McClellan over the prospective route of the latter's first offensive—directly overland or roundabout by water—Lincoln took the more sensible view. The practical thing to do was to attack and defeat the Confederate army at Manassas, and this was what Lincoln favored. He was not convinced by the case for the Peninsula approach, but he had no general of proved capacity to put in McClellan's place, and he hesitated to impose upon McClellan a plan the latter so obstinately opposed. McClellan's main reason for favoring the Peninsula was this, in his own words: "The roads in that region are passable at all seasons." Supposedly he knew what he was talking about, for was he not an engineering expert? Yet, once he had landed on the Peninsula, he floundered for weeks in mud and bog. Then his tedious cry, his excuse for going so slowly, became the wetness of the accursed terrain.

As for Lincoln's withholding part of the army, this may or may not have been a mistake. Certainly he was right in insisting upon the safety of the capital, for its loss would have been a very serious psychological, political, and diplomatic setback. Perhaps he was wrong in his calculation of the troops available for protecting Washington. If so, McClellan was to blame. He should have taken the President into his confidence, explaining fully and frankly his defensive arrangements. This he did not do. "He seems to have considered," says Sir Frederick Maurice, 1915–1918 director of British military operations, "that his ipse dixit should have been sufficient for Lincoln, whose sole function, as far as military affairs were concerned, was to comply with his demands without asking stupid questions." After all, an army head has some responsibilities in his treatment of the head of government, as well as the other way around.

With respect to McDowell's corps, after keeping it back from the departing Peninsula force Lincoln did not blunder in deciding on the Valley venture to deal with Stonewall Jackson instead of the Richmond movement to aid McClellan. The President was by no means so panicky as he has been portrayed. At the moment he was thinking more of attack than of defense. His order to McDowell read: "Your object will be to capture the forces of Jackson and Ewell. . . ." To *capture* the forces of Stonewall Jackson! This does not sound like timidity. Nor was it a harebrained enterprise, despite McDowell's and McClellan's protests. If luck had been a little better, if McDowell had moved a little faster, if Generals Fremont and Banks had cooperated a little more effectively, the Confederates might well have been surrounded and the elusive Stonewall brought to bay.

Even though it failed, the effort in the Valley was a better gamble than a reinforcement of McClellan would have been. McDowell's 35,000 men, if sent on to McClellan, might have put him in a position to gain a decisive victory, but the question remains whether he actually would have gone ahead to gain it.

Lincoln had cause to doubt whether McClellan had in him the aggressiveness to make a determined assault. "Starting from the premise that McClellan would not attack, it is only a short step to the next argument," Kenneth P. Williams points out. *"Lincoln knew that McClellan would not attack."* Why, then, should Lincoln have wasted additional troops on him?

After the Seven Days the President had all the more reason for doubting whether McClellan ever would fight a hard-hitting aggressive battle, no matter what reinforcements he might get. The general insisted that, if given 20,000 fresh troops, he could take Richmond. He already had about 90,000. By his estimates, however, the enemy before him had 200,000! Even with the reinforcements he demanded, McClellan still, in his own mind, would be hopelessly outnumbered. Lincoln suspected that, if the Peninsula army were increased to more than 200,000, McClellan even then would not move. He would double his estimate of enemy strength, beg for further reinforcements, and wait. No wonder the President resolved to call off the whole campaign.

If there is any fault to find in Lincoln's handling of military matters, between McClellan's withdrawal from the Peninsula and his final dismissal, it is only that Lincoln was too patient in putting up with McClellan so long and allowing him to act on plans that Lincoln did not approve. This patience may be interpreted as weakness. Or it may be explained by the fact that there were no clear alternatives, or that there were political exigencies to be taken into account. The fall elections were coming up, and many voters might be offended by the removal of McClellan who, be it remembered, was a Democrat.

Whatever the reasons for his long forebearance (and he forbore till after the elections) Lincoln did not dismiss McClellan because of politics. True, the Radicals were pressuring the President more strongly than ever, but he would have stood unmoved behind his general if he had thought him the fighting, winning kind. He did not consider him as capable of treason, despite the politicians' charges of pro-Southern plotting. No, he got rid of McClellan for the best of all possible reasons, the one that by itself was all-sufficient. At last he simply could not escape the conclusion that McClellan was unfit to command an army in an offensive undertaking.

The failure of the next two commanders of the Army of the Potomac, Burnside and Hooker, does nothing to prove that Lincoln should have hung on to McClellan. They are wrong who say: "McClellan ought not to have been removed unless the Government were prepared to put in his place some other officer whom they knew to be at least his equal in capacity." In choosing his successive commanders Lincoln did the only thing he could. He chose each one on the basis of previous success in some independent command, and that was all he had to go on. McClellan, Pope, Burnside, Hooker—each had distinguished himself on some field. And the assumption that McClellan was any better than the rest of the lot is at least arguable.

The subsequent appraisals of McClellan as a great or even a good general are worth no more than the judgment of the presumed experts uttering them. In any case, the name of Robert E. Lee should be stricken from the roster of the eulogists. Though Lee has been quoted as saying McClellan was the best of the generals he opposed, the quotation comes not from a contemporary and authentic document but from a second-hand recollection written down after Lee was dead. There is a good probability Lee never said it. He did show his opinion of McClellan, however, by his actions in the field against him. It was not a high opinion. Only against a most unenterprising opponent would Lee, with his smaller army, have dared to take the risks he did in front of Richmond and along Antietam Creek.

"Surely the verdict must be: McClellan was not a real general," Kenneth P. Williams concludes. "McClellan was merely an attractive but vain and unstable man, with considerable military knowledge, who sat a horse well and wanted to be President."

This Lincoln-or-McClellan question is not to be answered by facts alone, though controversialists on each side can prove their opponents wrong, or at least weak, on certain factual points. The answer depends upon inferences as well as facts. It depends upon guesses. We have to guess what McClellan *might have done if* he had been given a full chance, or what Lincoln *must have known* McClellan would do or leave undone.

The Philadelphia newspaperman Alexander K. McClure, once an acquaintance of both Lincoln and McClellan, wrote a generation after Appomatox: "Not until all the lingering personal, political, and military passions of the war shall have perished can the impartial historian tell the true story of Abraham Lincoln's relations to George B. McClellan, nor will the just estimate of McClellan as a military chieftain be recorded until the future historian comes to his task entirely free from the prejudices of the present."

Two more generations now have passed since McClure wrote. He is long dead, as are his contemporaries who took part in the controversies of the Civil War. Those men are dead, but the passions and prejudices of their time are not. McClellan still possesses a rare power to inspire either admiration or contempt, and nowhere in sight as yet is that impartial historian whom McClure looked for.

5

After demoting McClellan at the start of the Peninsula campaign, Lincoln got along for a few months without a general in chief. In July, 1862 he returned from his conference with McClellan near Richmond and then went hastily north to West Point to consult with the retired General Scott. Back in Washington again, Lincoln gave the supreme command to Henry W. Halleck. Though accepting, Halleck shrank from responsibility and never served as more than a nominal general in chief. For nearly two years—until the elevation of U. S. Grant in March, 1864—the Union armies had no real unity of command. President Lincoln, General Halleck, and Secretary Stanton acted as an informal council of war. For the period that they did so, it is not always possible to find out where actual responsibility lay.

The President transmitted official orders to his generals through Halleck. Sometimes he also communicated directly with the generals, sending personal "suggestions" in his own name.

In the spring of 1863, when Lee was beginning the campaign that was to culminate at Gettysburg, Lincoln telegraphed to Hooker: "I have but one idea which I think worth suggesting to you, and that is in case you find Lee coming to the north of the Rappahannock, I would by no means cross to the south of it. If he should leave a rear force at Fredericksburg, tempting you to fall upon it, it would fight in intrenchments, and have you at disadvantage, and so, man for man, worst you at that point, while his main force would in some way be getting an advantage of you northward. In one word, I would not take any risk of being entangled upon the river, like an ox jumped half over a fence, and liable to be torn by dogs, front and rear, without a fair chance to gore one way or kick the other."

Several days later the President wired again: "I think *Lee's* army, and not *Richmond,* is your true objective point. If he comes towards the Upper Potomac, follow on his flank, and on the inside track, shortening your lines, whilst he lengthens his. Fight him when opportunity offers. If he stays where he is, fret him, and fret him."

In the midst of Hooker's pursuit of the Confederate invaders, Lincoln switched generals, replacing Hooker with George Gordon Meade. Lincoln was elated by the news that later came from Gettysburg—and at the same time from Vicksburg. "We have certain information that Vicksburg surrendered to General Grant on the 4th of July," he wrote to Halleck (not to Meade) on July 7. "Now, if General Meade can complete his work, so gloriously prosecuted thus far, by the literal or subtantial destruction of Lee's army, the rebellion will be over."

But Lee got away. Afterward, in anger born of frustration and disappointment, Lincoln penned a letter for Meade, then put it away, unsent. "Again, my dear general," the President wrote, "I do not believe you appreciate the magnitude of the misfortune involved in Lee's escape. He was within your easy grasp, and to have closed upon him would, in connection with our other late successes, have ended the war."

Even some of Lincoln's severest critics find good sense in his advice to his generals. He showed he had "military insight of a kind" when he cautioned Hooker not to get entangled on the river like an ox jumped half over the fence. He was wiser than his generals in seeing that the object was to destroy Lee's army, not to capture Richmond or to drive the invader from Northern soil.

Even some of Lincoln's warmest defenders concede, however, that he was at fault in failing to centralize responsibility and provide a clear and unconfused chain of command. If, for example, he had sent positive orders to Meade in his own vigorous style, instead of communicating his hopes through Halleck, quite possibly he could have "spurred Meade to such exertions as would," in Greene's words, "have caused the desired result." Certainly it was poor policy to issue official orders through Halleck and at the same time to send the generals personal suggestions and advice. "This," as Greene mildly puts it, "is not the way in which military operations are successfully conducted."

Many pro-Lincoln and anti-Lincoln writers also agree that, with the appointment of Grant to supreme command, Lincoln wisely stepped aside and let Grant run the war thereafter. During the final year Lincoln "looked on quietly" while Grant went to work, Ballard says. "This closes the chapter of Lincoln's active part as Strategist of the North." Lord Wolseley writes that "the Northern prospects did not begin to brighten until Mr. Lincoln, in March, 1864, with the unselfish intelligence which distinguished him, abdicated his military functions in favour of General Grant." Lincoln, it would seem, commanded best when he commanded least.

But did he?

6

According to the prevailing view, Grant had shown his understanding of grand strategy by his campaigns in the West, before taking over as general in chief. Certainly he handled his Vicksburg campaign with a brilliance that most military experts have admired.

Lincoln himself admired it. Nine days after the Vicksburg surrender he sent Grant a "grateful acknowledgment for the almost inestimable service" he had done the country. He sent also an admission of his own error. He said he had expected Grant to by-pass Vicksburg and go on down the Mississippi, instead of crossing the river and turning back to approach Vicksburg from the rear. "I feared it was a mistake," Lincoln wrote in his letter of congratulation. "I now wish to make the personal acknowledgment that you were right, and I was wrong."

According to Grant's later reputation, however, he had done more than merely look to his immediate command. All along, he had seen beyond his theater of operations to comprehend the war as a whole. He had kept in mind, as no one else had done, the true object of all the fighting—to destroy the military power of the foe.

And, once in charge of all the armies, he continued to apply his unique knowledge of warfare, without even explaining the mysteries of his art to the President, who continued to acknowledge his own incompetence in military affairs.

Grant himself made this quite plain in his memoirs, as he told of his relationship with the Commander in Chief, from the time he went east for his promotion.

"In my first interview with Mr. Lincoln alone," Grant recalled, "he stated to me that he had never professed to be a military man or to know how campaigns should be conducted, and never wanted to interfere in them; but that procrastination on the part of commanders, and the pressure from the people at the North and Congress, *which was always with him,* forced him into issuing his series of 'Military Orders'—one, two, three, etc." He never had wanted to interfere. All he had wanted was for someone to take the responsibility and act, calling on him for government aid and support.

Grant assured him he would do the best he could, without "annoying" him any more than necessary.

Lincoln said he did not care to know what Grant proposed to do, and when Grant saw Secretary Stanton and General Halleck, both of them warned him not to tell the President his plans. They explained that Lincoln was "so kind-hearted, so averse to refusing anything asked of him," that he could not be trusted with confidential information. A word to the wise was enough. Never (till the war was practically over) did Grant communicate his plans to the President—nor for that matter to the Secretary of War or the Chief of Staff.

Though, at that first private interview, Lincoln confessed his shortcomings as a strategist, he made bold to suggest to Grant his own plan of operations, with the understanding that the general of course could do as he pleased about it. According to Grant, "He brought out a map of Virginia on which he had evidently marked every position occupied by the Federal and Confederate armies up to that time. He pointed out on the map two streams which empty into the Potomac, and suggested that the army might be moved on boats and landed between the mouths of these streams. We would then have the Potomac to bring our supplies, and the tributaries would protect our flanks while we moved out." Respectfully Grant listened, and tactfully he refrained from indicating to Lincoln the obvious defect in the plan. Those same streams, which supposedly would "protect our flanks while we moved out," also would "protect Lee's flanks while he was shutting us up."

While Grant, with his headquarters at Culpeper, was preparing for his great offensive, he visited the President in Washington every week. At the last meetings, as the Wilderness campaign was about to begin, Grant revealed just a little of the strategy he was going to follow. Naturally, Lincoln had at least a vague idea of what was in the wind. "He had of course become acquainted with the fact that a general movement had been ordered all along the line, and seemed to think it a new feature in war." A general movement a new feature in war! The President's amazement was a measure of his limited progress in military science. It would take a patient and rather elementary explanation to make him understand. Grant obliged. "I explained to him that it was necessary to have a great number of troops to guard and hold the territory we had captured, and to prevent incursions into the Northern States. These troops could perform this service just as well by advancing as by remaining still; and by advancing they would compel the enemy to keep detachments to hold them back, or else lay his own territory open to invasion." Once it had been so carefully explained to him, Lincoln quickly grasped the meaning of a cooperative advance on several fronts. "His answer was: 'Oh, yes! I see that. As we say out West, if a man can't skin he must hold a leg while somebody else does.' "

After Grant, months later, had forced Lee into Richmond and begun to press a siege, he acted decisively to frustrate Lee's efforts to distract him. Lee sent Jubal A. Early up the Valley to worry Washington (much as Stonewall Jackson had done when McClellan was outside Richmond) and after raiding around the capital Early got away because of confusion in the Lincoln government. The Shenandoah invasion route long had been a problem, "chiefly because of interference from Washington." Stanton and Halleck had been so concerned about keeping a defensive army between the enemy and the capital that again and again they had lost track of the worrisome Confederates. "I determined to put a stop to this," Grant recollected. He assigned Philip Sheridan to the task of driving the foe clear out of the Valley. The President, who apparently saw few of Grant's orders, "in some way or other got to see this dispatch" directing that Sheridan take the field against Early. Lincoln in a message to Grant said the move never would be carried out unless Grant himself saw to it every day and every hour. The President, a bystander though an interested one, seemed to be depending on his general in chief for everything.

Still as nervous and fearful as ever, Lincoln (to quote Grant again) "became very much frightened" lest Sheridan get too far away and be cut off by Early. Grant sent Lincoln the calming news that he would keep reinforcements away from Early by attacking on the Richmond front. Lincoln lost his nerve again when Sherman proposed his daring march to the sea. "Even when it came to the time of starting, the greatest apprehension, as to the propriety of the campaign he was about to commence, filled the mind of the President, induced no doubt by his advisers." They had been informed by a member of Grant's staff who opposed the march. Grant, favoring Sherman's plan from the outset, finally managed to see it carried through.

Almost to the end, Grant continued to keep secrets from the President. The latter was nearby, at City Point, when Grant launched the final push that drove the defenders out of Richmond and Petersburg. "I would have let him know what I contemplated doing," Grant wrote afterward, "only while I felt a strong conviction that the move was going to be successful, yet it might not prove so; and then I would have only added another to the many disappointments he had been suffering for the past three years." On the morning after Petersburg fell, Grant telegraphed Lincoln to meet him there. On arrival Lincoln said: "Do you know, general, that I have had a sort of a sneaking idea for some days that you intended to do something like this." And now, at long last, Grant confided his hopes and plans, which already were hastening the enemy to surrender at Appomattox.

But there is another side to the story of Grant and Lincoln. The version in the *Personal Memoirs* of U. S. Grant should not go unchallenged. In the decades between Appomattox and the writing of those volumes, Grant forgot much that had happened during the war, and he remembered some things that probably never happened. He wrote under the influence of a postwar myth which depicted him as the Great Strategist and Lincoln as the Great Statesman in the preservation of the Union. This is the argument of, among others, T. Harry Williams.

According to Williams, Grant actually was Lincoln's inferior in overall strategic planning. Before his rise to the top command the general seldom looked beyond the Western theater or calculated in terms of the entire war. In January 1864, wishing to know what Grant would do if and when he was appointed general in chief, Lincoln through Halleck asked for his opinions about the East. Grant replied that he had not been disposed to give advice on strategy outside his own area "or even to think much about the matter." And when he got around to presenting his plans, he demonstrated convincingly enough that he had given them little thought. One of his proposals called for landing 60,000 men on the North Carolina coast and using them to cut the railroad connections between Richmond and the lower South. What Lincoln thought, when he saw this, is not recorded, but he must have been disappointed. For the plan had many faults, in principle and in detail. The detachment of the 60,000 men would weaken the Army of the Potomac, and their invasion of North Carolina would expose them to the mercy of rebels converging from Georgia and Virginia. Still worse, the mere suggestion of such a scheme showed that Grant, like McClellan and McClellan's successors, was thinking of Richmond and not Lee's army as the main objective. After his promotion and his conversations with Lincoln, Grant changed both his aims and his methods. The plain inference is that, instead of Lincoln's taking a few trivial lessons in warfare from his general, Grant learned some fundamental points from his Commander in Chief.

In that first interview with Grant, Lincoln could not have said he cared nothing about knowing the general's plans. In a letter to Grant several weeks afterward (April 30, 1864) the President did say: "The particulars of your plans I neither know nor seek to know." The *particulars.* Lincoln doubtless meant that he did not want Grant to throw upon him the responsibility for decisions on tactical and other details—as Hooker, for one, had tried to do. Lincoln's disinterest in particulars shows he already was familiar with the broad plans. He must have been. They were essentially his. How much he contributed to the specific form they took—to the plan for coordinated movements by Grant, Butler, and Sherman—it is hard to say.

Certainly the idea of a general advance on several fronts at a time was nothing new to Lincoln. Often in the past he had urged his various commanders, East and West, to engage the foe concurrently so as to take advantage of numerical superiority and prevent the Confederates from shifting troops from place to place. The Presidential secretary John Hay noted in his diary that Lincoln, commenting on Grant's strategy, said it reminded him of the suggestions he previously had made. In the light of Hay's diary and other contemporary records, Grant's long-delayed recollections are nonsense when they tell of Lincoln's wonderment at hearing of such a thing as a general movement of several armies at once. Lincoln no doubt used the analogy of skinning and holding a leg, but not in the circumstances related by Grant.

If as a rule the President let Grant have his own way, that was due to the fact that, as a rule, Grant's way was also the President's. But Grant was not always left to do as he pleased. At the time of Early's Washington raid, Grant blundered in failing to make proper provisions for the defense of the capital. When the capital was threatened, Lincoln intervened by prodding Grant to take effective steps (not by issuing orders on his own, as he had done with McClellan in 1862). Lincoln was aware, as Grant at first was not, that the general at his headquarters near Richmond was too far away to assume direct charge of the Washington defenses. Lincoln took the initiative in bringing about a reorganization of the command system so as to locate responsibility for the direction of troops around the capital. He also gave the necessary stimulus to Sheridan's campaign for clearing the Shenandoah Valley. He had to tell Grant, bluntly, to see to it that Sheridan got his orders and carried them out. It was no mere accident that Lincoln saw Grant's dispatch regarding Sheridan's orders. Lincoln watched Grant closely all the time.

He disagreed with Grant about the fitness of George H. Thomas, in command of the Union army at Nashville, Tennessee. In December, 1864 Thomas seemed too slow in attacking the Confederates in front of him. Grant determined to remove Thomas, and Lincoln, after trying to dissuade Grant, reluctantly gave in. Lincoln thought that Thomas, on the ground, was better able to decide when to move than Grant, hundreds of miles away, was able to decide for him. Before Grant could effect the removal, Thomas suddenly launched an offensive which routed and almost annihilated the enemy. This battle of Nashville gained the most decisive Union victory thus far in the entire war. Thomas was vindicated, and so was Lincoln. "Again," as Williams says, "the President had been more right than Grant."

Lincoln overruled Grant less often than McClellan, but that was only because Grant was more willing to fight the war along Lincolnian lines than McClellan had been.

7

The greatest—or one of the most inept. A military genius—or a meddler with generals who knew much better than he how to fight the war. The main issues are sharply drawn indeed.

In this debate the weight of authority seems at present to be on the side of Lincoln's military greatness. Still, it would be rash to award the decision outright to either side. Most likely, the truth lies somewhere between the two extremes.

A great deal can safely be conceded to those who praise Lincoln as a war leader. Certainly he was much more effective as Commander in Chief the last year than the first. He grew.

His very lack of military background may well have been an advantage to him. By the same token, knowledge of the accepted rules of warfare may well have been a disadvantage to Jefferson Davis and to many of the generals, both North and South. Times change, and so does strategy. Wars may be lost by blind adherence to the rules of previous wars. At the time of the Civil War the generals with formal military training knew best the principles that Jomini, the great French authority, had derived from Napoleon's campaigns. These principles had served Napoleon well, but on occasion they could handicap a man who half a century later insisted upon following them too closely. Lincoln, though he read the textbooks, never mastered them. And they never mastered him.

In the widespread deployment of his armies, Lincoln violated the old and orthodox rule of concentration of force. But he had justification, both political and military. He could not and did not ignore politics in the broad (as distinct from the narrow, partisan) sense. He had to protect the Northern people against invasion, prevent the defection of wavering border states, and hold on to that priceless symbol, the capital of the Union. Only by spreading out his forces could he achieve these "political" objectives.

And only by doing so could he make the best use of his soldiers from a strictly military point of view. Napoleon's theory of the "offensive mass," and McClellan's notion of an army of 300,000 for campaigning in Virginia, might have been good enough as abstract propositions. But these ideas did not fit the facts. The facts were that the Union had to start out with raw troops and a poorly trained staff, and that Virginia offered difficult terrain for the maneuverings of a massive army, and provided inadequate subsistence for its living off the country. Such an army would have been unwieldy, tied too closely to its base of supplies.

Nearly three years passed before Lincoln's plan for a coordinated offensive on many fronts began fully to materialize. The long delay was due not so much to defects in the plan as to the lack of means for carrying it out. Lincoln had to build an army, find a general to direct it, and develop a unified and workable system of command. While doing these things he never lost sight of his basic strategy, though from necessity he yielded at times to the judgment of his professional soldiers. At last he found Grant, and with him such qualified subordinates as Sherman, Sheridan, and Thomas. Then Grant put into effect those parts of Lincoln's plan that remained to be carried out.

Grant was only a member, though an important one, of a top-command arrangement that Lincoln finally had devised. Overseeing everything was Lincoln himself, the Commander in Chief. Taking the responsibility for men and supplies was Stanton, the Secretary of War. Serving as a Presidential adviser and as a liaison with military men was Halleck, the Chief of Staff. And directing all the armies, while accompanying the Army of the Potomac, was Grant, the general in chief.

Lincoln pioneered in the creation of a high command, an organization for amassing all the energies and resources of a people in the grand strategy of total war. He combined statecraft with military art, and (on the whole) most effectively. In the light of this, it seems rather absurd to cavil at civilian interference in military concerns. Someone, somehow, has to guide the effort as a whole and coordinate the parts. There *must* be "political" interference with strategy. Democracy demands it.

In the Civil War Lincoln was doing what American politicians have done in wartime before and since. Congress "interfered" in the conduct of the Revolutionary War. Presidents Madison and Polk, with their Cabinets, ran respectively the

War of 1812 and the war with Mexico. And Franklin D. Roosevelt, in cooperation with Winston Churchill, seldom hesitating to overrule the highest brass, shaped and directed strategy in World War II. These civilian leaders acted essentially as Lincoln did, but, considering the peculiar difficulty of his task, he stands out above them all.

chapter 7

THE TENDER-HEARTED

One winter night an Indiana congressman, Schuyler Colfax, left his business at the Capitol and went to the White House to plead for the son of one of his constituents. The boy, convicted of desertion, had been sentenced to die before a firing squad at Davenport Barracks, Iowa. Colfax told the story to President Lincoln, who listened patiently, then replied:

"Some of my generals complain that I impair discipline by my frequent pardons and reprieves; but it rests me, after a day's hard work, that I can find some excuse for saving some poor fellow's life, and I shall go to bed happy tonight as I think how joyous the signing of this name will make himself, his family and friends."

With a smile enlivening his care-furrowed face, the President signed his name and saved a life.

A Pennsylvania congressman, the dour, clubfooted, bewigged Thaddeus Stevens, once visited the White House with an old woman from his Lancaster district. She wished a pardon for her son, condemned to die for sleeping at his post. For Stevens, the mission was somewhat embarrassing, since he often had denounced the President for being too free with pardons. But Stevens knew that hundreds of his constituents were waiting to see how the old woman's Washington pilgrimage turned out. He also knew that any congressman, to stay in office, had to please the folks back home. And so he supported the mother's appeal. "Now, Thad, what would you do in this case if you happened to be President?" Lincoln asked him. Stevens answered that, knowing the extenuating circumstances as he did, he would certainly grant the request. "Well, then," Lincoln said, after a pause while he penned a few lines, "here, madam, is your son's pardon."

Judge Advocate General Joseph Holt brought to Lincoln the case of a soldier who in the midst of battle had demoralized his regiment by throwing down his gun and hiding behind a friendly stump. When court-martialed, the soldier offered no defense. He was found to be a habitual thief as well as a coward. And he had no living father or mother, no wife, no child, no known relative.

"Here," said Judge Holt in presenting the sentence to Lincoln for review, "is a case which comes exactly within your requirements. He does not deny his guilt; he will better serve the country dead than living, as he has no relations to mourn for him, and he is not fit to be in the ranks of patriots, at any rate."

Holt expected the President to approve the execution without further ado, but Lincoln sat a while in thought, running his hand through his hair. Finally he said:

"Well, after all, Judge, I think I must put this with my leg cases."

"Leg cases," Holt repeated. "What do you mean?"

"Why," Lincoln explained, "do you see those papers crowded into those pigeon-holes? They are the cases that you call by that long title, 'cowardice in the face of the enemy,' but I call them, for short, my 'leg cases.' But I put it to you, and I leave it for you to decide for yourself: if Almighty God gives a man a cowardly pair of legs how can he help their running away with him?"

One day a congressman, going to the White House for some business with the President, passed through an anteroom crowded with supplicants. An old man, crouching in a corner by himself, wept as if his heart would break. The congressman stopped to ask the trouble. The old man explained that his son, a private in the army of General Benjamin F. Butler, had been convicted of some crime and had been sentenced to be shot. The congressman, his sympathy enlisted, took the sobbing father into the President's office.

"I am sorry to say I can do nothing for you," Lincoln said, his face clouding with sorrow. "Listen to this telegram received from General Butler yesterday: 'President Lincoln, I pray you not to interfere with the courts-martial of the army. You will destroy all discipline among our soldiers.' "

The old man, his hopes aroused and then suddenly dashed, wailed and writhed in grief. Lincoln watched a while, then exclaimed: "By jingo, Butler or no Butler, here goes!" He wrote a few words and handed them to the man, who was cheered—and then again saddened when he read the note: "Job Smith is not to be shot until further orders from me.—Abraham Lincoln."

"Why," protested the old man, "I thought it was to be a pardon; but you say, 'not to be shot till further orders,' and you may order him to be shot next week."

Lincoln smiled and said: "Well, my old friend, I see you are not very well acquainted with me. If your son never looks on death till further orders come from me to shoot him, he will live to be a great deal older than Methuselah."

On a gloomy, rainy day in the winter of 1863–1864 Representative Daniel W. Voorhees of Indiana visited the White House with two Indiana senators, a fellow congressman, and a Mr. and Mrs. Bullitt. The latter's father, a Southern-born preacher in his seventies, had been convicted of conspiring in Tennessee to procure ammunition and quinine for the enemy. He was to be shot within forty-eight hours. The evidence indicated that the preacher, having lost a fortune on account of the war, was not in his right mind. Besides, he had been enticed by overeager detectives into the trading plot. Lincoln, as one of the senators presented the case, had a sad, preoccupied, faraway look. Then Mrs. Bullitt, sitting near him, spoke. He looked at the pale little woman, his face lighting up with a kindly expression, and he paid close attention to her every word. Suddenly he asked her father's name, and she told him.

"Why, he preached in Springfield years ago, didn't he?" Yes, he had. "Well, this is wonderful!" Lincoln said. "I knew this man well; I have heard him preach; he was a tall, angular man like I am, and I have been mistaken for him on the streets. Did you say he was to be shot day after tomorrow? No, no! There will be no shooting nor hanging in this case."

Stories of this kind—with an erring son or father or husband, a tearful appeal, and a last-minute reprieve or pardon—have been told and retold in almost countless numbers. Some of the stories have gained drama in the retelling.

One of the most dramatic is that of Private William Scott of the Vermont Volunteers. According to legend, Lincoln suddenly remembered the plea of a delegation of Vermonters who had called upon him earlier during a busy day. Time was running out; the soldier was scheduled soon to face the firing squad. Taking a carriage, the President hurried to the army camp outside Washington, found the tent where Scott was being held, and managed to rescue him after getting a promise of soldierly behavior in the future. Private Scott kept his promise. The next spring he was fatally wounded while leading a charge with rare valor, and as he died he said to tell the President he had not forgotten.

Myth aside, the well-attested accounts of Lincoln's clemency would fill a thick book. A lovesick Ohioan, having been refused a furlough to go home and see his fiancée, went home anyhow and married her, then was convicted as a deserter. He was pardoned. Another soldier fled to Canada, then got religion and repentance and went back to his regiment. He received no penalty except a prison term of the same number of days as his absence, the term to be served after his enlistment had expired. A New Yorker, besides deserting twice, had poisoned his prison guard and was sentenced to death for murder. He was granted a reprieve for a medical examination when one of the New York senators gave evidence to show that he was insane.

Not only did Lincoln deal leniently with Union soldiers—sleeping sentinels, homesick runaways, cowards, and criminals. He also exhibited mercy toward many Confederates. He freed on parole a number of war prisoners, including at least one of John Morgan's raiders, who had terrorized the people of southern Indiana and Ohio in the summer of 1863. He pardoned some spies and saboteurs, among them Lieutenant (C.S.A.) Samuel B. Davis of Delaware, a distant relative of Jefferson Davis, and Captain (C.S.A.) John B. Castleman of Kentucky. Both Davis and Castleman had been engaged in plots to foment uprisings, liberate prisoners, destroy railroads, and burn cities in the North. Davis won an eleventh-hour reprieve. At Johnson's Island in Lake Erie the scaffold and the rope were ready for an early morning execution when, in the middle of the night, a messenger arived with Lincoln's order.

Lincoln was indeed a pardoning President. "No man clothed with such vast power ever wielded it more tenderly and forbearingly," Schuyler Colfax declared. "No man holding in his hands the key of life and death ever pardoned so many offenders, and so easily."

"No man on earth hated blood as Lincoln did, and he seized eagerly upon any excuse to pardon a man when the charge could possibly justifiy it." So wrote David R. Locke, a friend of Lincoln's and (under the pen name Petroleum V. Nasby) one of his favorite humorists. Locke added: "The generals always wanted an execution carried out before it could possibly be brought before the President. He was as tenderhearted as a girl."

Attorney General Edward Bates said that Lincoln once referred to himself as "pigeon-hearted." Bates told F. B. Carpenter, the artist in residence at the White House, that Lincoln was nearly perfect as a wartime President—except for one thing. "His deficiency is in the element of *will.* I have sometimes told him, for instance, that he was unfit to be trusted with the pardoning power. Why, if a man comes to him with a touching story, his judgment is almost certain to be affected by it. Should the applicant be a *woman*—a wife, or mother, or a sister—in nine cases out of ten, her tears, if nothing else, are sure to prevail."

Some of Lincoln's generals thought the final victory was delayed because of the President's leniency. General Butler blamed his own losses on the President and, when asked why victory was so long postponed, gave the terse reply: "Pusillanimity and want of executive force of the government." General Daniel Tyler reportedly complained to Lincoln that Union reverses were due to his generosity. The Confederate commander Braxton Bragg shot his deserters, Tyler said. But "if we attempt to shoot a deserter, you pardon him and our army is without discipline." Supposedly the victorious Northern generals won their victories only by forestalling the pardon-prone Lincoln. "How did you carry out the sentences of your courts-martial and escape Lincoln's pardons?" Sherman was asked. He answered: "I shot them first."

The Radical Republicans in and out of Congress argued continually that Lincoln was too soft and weak for the exigencies of the time. After his death a number of citizens wrote to his successor, Andrew Johnson, to say the country needed a stronger President and sterner measures than it had had during the war. "We believe that Abraham Lincoln's work was done," an

Ohioan declared; "he was not the man to administer justice, he was always too merciful and kind."

Afterward instances from his early life were recalled to show that Lincoln, boy and man, was quite remarkable for his sensitivity and humaneness. He suffered at the thought of any creature in pain. As a youth he could not pass by the six lost little pigs he once saw along the path; he picked them up and restored them to their mother sow. He grieved when his own pet hog was slaughtered. On the trek to Illinois he waded back through an icy stream to rescue a dog that had been left behind. Indignantly he stopped the sport of boys who got fun from prodding turtles with firebrands. Such were the stories told about the young Lincoln, and whether or not they all are literally true, they illustrate a truth about him. He *was* humane.

Yet, as President, he led the nation to victory in war, and wars are not won by sheer kindliness and humanity. There must have been something besides tenderness in his heart.

2

Of course, large numbers of court-martialed soldiers actually were executed during the Civil War. At times the sound of the firing squad in a nearby camp could be heard in the White House, and Lincoln heard it, with much troubling of his spirit, but the work went on. Never did he go out of his way to look for men to pardon; the cases had to be brought to him. And, despite the humble tears and high-placed influences, he did not always intervene.

There were several bounty-jumpers whose claim to mercy he apparently could not justify, even to himself. There was the Missouri bushwhacker who was said to pour gunpowder into the ears of his Unionist captives and then light it and explode their heads. There was the Virginia physician and gentleman who provoked an altercation with a Negro officer of United States Cavalry on parade in Norfolk, then shot him dead.

In this case Lincoln postponed the execution until alienists could examine the doctor, and meanwhile he kept the doctor's wife away from the White House. "It would be useless for Mrs. Dr. Wright to come here," he explained. "The subject is a very painful one, but the case is settled." To the end the doctor's friends hoped for a last-minute telegram from the President. None arrived. None was sent.

There was also the case of John Y. Beall, a youthful Confederate captain who seized a boat on Lake Erie and tried to free the rebel prisoners on Johnson's Island, then turned to railroad sabotage in New York. Beall was captured and, since he was not in uniform, was sentenced to be hanged, even though Jefferson Davis took responsibility and avowed that Beall had acted under a Confederate military commission. The case of Beall, the son of a rich and prominent Virginia family, aroused tremendous sympathy in the North as well as the South. Among others, six senators and ninety-one congressmen including Thaddeus Stevens petitioned Lincoln for clemency. On the day before the execution Orville H. Browning made a last personal appeal to his friend the President and found him looking and feeling bad—"apparently more distressed" than Browning ever had seen him in the White House. Still, Lincoln did not give in, and Beall was hanged.

In the numerous other instances in which the President did issue a pardon or reprieve, he was not necessarily indulging a merciful whim or yielding to entreaties he did not have the heart to resist. As often as not, he probably was guided by *policy* considerations. Mercy in some ways was a very useful policy.

In dealing with Confederates, Lincoln used forgiveness as a means of weakening their desire to fight. From the start he released numbers of them on parole, in the prisons of the North and in the conquered areas of the South, once they had sworn an oath of renewed loyalty to the United States. Facing the prospect of parole rather than a fear of punishment, rebels of wavering faith were encouraged to desert. Lincoln made it a policy to deplete the enemy ranks by thus stimulating desertion. He acted upon military calculations more than sentimental impulse.

To some extent, his military calculations may have been wrong. General Grant thought they were. He believed that Lincoln should not free so many prisoners who were willing to take the loyalty oath. These men, the ones with loyal inclinations, should not be released but should be returned to the Confederacy to be exchanged for captured Union soldiers. The converted rebels thus sent South would represent little gain to the Confederacy and little loss to the United States. "They can afterward come into our lines," Grant explained, "if they do not wish to fight."

On certain occasions Lincoln gave in to the arguments of the military regarding prisoner exchanges. In the fall of 1863, when the demand was especially great for the return of captured Federals, the practice of paroling imprisoned Confederates was, for the time being, nearly stopped. Yet, in the course of the first three years of the war, many a gray-clad soldier took advantage of Lincoln's clemency to abandon a cause he never had quite believed in.

While releasing individual Confederates, Lincoln was hesitant to offer amnesty to all soldiers and civilians who would take the required oath. Again and again he was urged to do so. General Benjamin F. Butler, in command of occupied New Orleans, reported that thousands of Louisianans were "tired and sick of the war" and "would gladly return to their allegiance if, by some authoritative act, they could be assured that the past would be forgiven." Fernando Wood, the New York Peace Democrat, contended that the Southern people as a whole soon would give up if a full amnesty were proclaimed. Lincoln delayed because he doubted whether, in 1862, the time had come for an amnesty proclamation to have its greatest effect. Better to wait until the fortunes of battle unequivocally favored the Union. Then, in the minds of Southerners, the prospect of ultimate defeat might give real charm to Lincoln's promises.

By the end of 1863, after Gettysburg and Vicksburg and Chattanooga, the moment seemed to have arrived. In December of that year Lincoln put forth his proclamation of amnesty along with his "ten per cent" reconstruction plan. To all rebels —with certain exceptions—he offered to remit most of the penalties of rebellion in return for the oath of future loyalty. Persons of the excepted classes (mainly the Confederate leaders) could apply to him for individual pardons. His generosity was well known.

Yet, in one sense, he himself saw the proclamation as having a comparatively limited scope. Immediately the case arose of a man under sentence to be hanged as a spy. Lincoln maintained that his offer of amnesty did not include this man or any other already convicted of a crime, nor did it apply to prisoners of war. In the words of a government spokesman, the President had not intended a "general jail-clearing." But the Federal circuit court for northern California disagreed. The judges held that the proclamation, like any law, was to be interpreted in the light of its own words, "irrespective of any opinion" or "unexpressed intention" of its author. They ruled that the spy in question was entitled to a pardon. So Lincoln issued an explanatory proclamation in which he said the amnesty extended only to those "being yet at large and free from arrest, confinement, or duress."

What Lincoln had intended, instead of a general jail-clearing in the North, was a general stimulus to disaffection and desertion in the South. So Southerners understood, and Jefferson Davis and others denounced both the President and his proclamation. "Is even Lincoln base enough," the Richmond *Sentinel* demanded, "to imagine that people such as the Confederates have proven themselves, would . . . prove traitors to the men whom they have called to lead them?" More soberly, a Savannah newspaper with the somewhat ironic name *Republican* pointed out that Lincoln was trying to hasten the end of the war and that his proclamation revealed the rising confidence of the North. This confidence was of course a "delusion." And yet, the *Republican* warned, "It shows that we are a doomed people unless we . . . summon all our patriotism and energies. . . ." Thus Confederates committed to their cause saw Machiavellianism rather than mercy in what Lincoln had proclaimed. And they were not entirely mistaken.

How effective Lincoln's offer of pardon and amnesty was in weakening the enemy, it is hard to say. "During the year," he announced in his annual message of December, 1864, "many have availed themselves of the general provision, and many more would, only that the signs of bad faith in some have led to such precautionary measures as rendered the practical process less easy and certain." He also said he had granted special pardons to "individuals of the excepted classes" and had denied no "voluntary application"—no application coming from a person who was at large. He did not say what he thought the effect on Confederate morale had been. Probably the effect was less than he had hoped.

As if to hurry the laggards into taking the oath, Lincoln in the message of 1864 warned that his amnesty offer might not continue to stand indefinitely. The door had been practically wide open for a full year, he reminded all who might choose to listen. "It is still so open to all," he added. "But the time may come—probably will come—when public duty shall demand that it be closed; and that, in lieu, more rigorous measures than heretofore shall be adopted."

In dealing with Union soldiers, as in dealing with Confederates, Lincoln may well have believed that there were real military gains to be had from a liberal pardon policy.

Of course, he himself realized, at least in the abstract, the need for stern discipline. "Long experience has shown that armies cannot be maintained unless desertion shall be punished by the severe penalty of death," he once said. "The case requires and the law and the Constitution sanction this punishment."

Yet, in raising and maintaining armies, there was another consideration to be taken into account, as Lincoln seems to have been aware. He had to deal with an army consisting mainly of citizen soldiers, who were slow to drop the prepossessions of civilian life. With such men as these, frequent pardons may have been bad for discipline, but the regimen of the regular army, if unrelieved, might have been even worse for morale. The service needed to be made as popular and attractive as it could be, and Lincoln's clemency made it less unattractive than it otherwise would have been. Thus, within limits, the pardon policy made sense even from a realistic military point of view.

It made sense also from the point of view of politics. With pardons as with patronage, there were political foes to be appeased, political friends to be rewarded. Time and again, in sparing a youthful constituent, Lincoln was doing a favor for some congressman or senator. Almost all the stories of his life-saving mercy tell of politicians who intervened with him before he intervened with the army. Often, to record the identity of the supplicating politician, he required him to endorse the pardon request. Donn Piatt, the soldier-son of a wealthy Cincinnati family, a man who was acquainted personally with Lincoln, believed he always acted from ulterior motives in his deeds of clemency.

Some of the shrewdness and calculation in his pardon policy seems to be reflected in the remarkable relationship between him and his Secretary of War, Edwin M. Stanton. The two were opposites.

As Grant contrasted them, Lincoln "gained influence over men by making them feel that it was a pleasure to serve him," and he "preferred yielding his own wish to gratify others," but Stanton "cared nothing for the feelings of others. In fact it seemed to be pleasanter to him to disappoint than to gratify." Grant noted further: "It was generally supposed that these two officials formed the complement of each other. The Secretary was required to prevent the President's being imposed upon. The President was required in the more responsible place of seeing that injustice was not done to others."

Though Grant questioned this supposition, Lincoln himself has been quoted in its support. "I want to oblige everybody when I can," John P. Usher, Attorney General from 1863 to 1865, reported Lincoln as saying, "and Stanton and I have an understanding that if I send an order to him which cannot consistently be granted, he is to refuse it."

Such apparently was the division of labor between Lincoln and Stanton, between lenity and the law. If a life was spared, Lincoln could get the credit. If not, Stanton with grim satisfaction might take the blame.

3

Thus, in the matter of pardons, Lincoln does not appear to have been hopelessly sentimental and soft, as many of his acquaintances pictured him for posterity. He appears to have been still less so when his absorbing interest in weapons is taken into account.

Like the typical American of his time, Lincoln had a fondness for mechanical inventions. Once, before the war, he had gone around delivering a lecture on the subject. He was something of an inventor, himself. From his experience with navigation problems on the uncertain Sangamon River, he got an idea for a device to lift river boats over shoals. He patented the thing, but it was unworkable and was never used.

After the war had begun, thousands of ingenious Yankees came forward with new or improved weapons with which presumably to win it. Many of these inventions were as useless as Lincoln's had been. Some were downright crazy. Others had real promise. But War Department bureaucrats and army officers in the field were inclined to look upon all technological innovations with distrust. These people preferred the old and familiar and, with good reason, wished as far as possible to keep arms and ammunition standardized. There was no agency created for the purpose of sorting out and developing the better inventions—no agency comparable to the Office of cientific Research and Development which did this work during World War II.

During the Civil War, Lincoln himself acted as a kind of one-man OSRD. Inventors and promoters, eager for the prize of a government contract, brought their drawings and models o him. Time and again he arranged for the demonstration of some new weapon, and often he fired an experimental gun, himself. To the Army and Navy ordnance officials he recommended the adoption of weapons he approved. He was receptive o new ideas—too receptive, some of his critics thought, too frequently imposed upon by schemers and cranks. Yet he contributed much to wartime progress in military technology.

As compared with the single-shot muzzle-loader, which most Union soldiers used throughout the war, he readily saw the advantages of the breech-loading, repeating rifle, which in one form or another was available before the war began. Offered one of the improved Marsh breechloaders, he tried it out in a weedy lot between the White House and the Washington Monument, a place that often served as his personal rifle range and proving ground. He was so pleased with the weapon that he recommended another trial for it at West Point. Finally, overruling the Army Chief of Ordnance, he directed him to buy 25,000 of the Marsh rifles.

Again, he attended a testing of the even better Sharps repeater at McClellan's camp near Washington. He laughed with delight when the marksman, at 600 yards, hit the right eye of a target, the figure of a man labeled "Jeff Davis." Then and thereafter he pressed the adoption and the increased use of the Sharps rifle.

For another repeating breechloader, the Spencer carbine, he whittled out an improved sight from a stick of pine and, using this sight, scored a dozen hits in fourteen shots at a letter he had taken from his pocket for a target. He saw to the adoption of the carbine with an order for 10,000.

Guns like the Marsh, the Sharps, and the Spencer, though

they saw only limited use, added greatly to the deadliness of the firing on the Union side. They would have been much more widely used if Lincoln had had his way.

In the loft of a carriage shop across the street from Willard's Hotel he was shown a queer field gun with a hopper and a crank. He turned the crank and, in the words of Robert V. Bruce, the authority on Lincoln and the tools of war, "delightedly watched the cartridge cases drop one by one into the grooves of a revolving cylinder, while the mechanism automatically tripped the firing pin." He named this the "Coffee Mill Gun" and gave McClellan a most enthusiastic account of it as a "wonderful new repeating battery of rifled guns, shooting fifty balls a minute." He thought it would enable McClellan at last to advance, and he even suggested going out, himself, and standing or falling with the army. Actually the Coffee Mill Gun was to have little use in the Civil War. Yet it was the ancestor of the machine gun of later wars, and Lincoln's order for its purchase gave rise to what has been called the first known sale of machine guns in all history. "And like the breech-loading rifle," says Bruce, "the machine gun owed its first chance to a man who would 'take the responsibility' when others flinched."

Grimly, during the winter of 1861–62, Lincoln pushed the development of mortars for Halleck's and Foote's Mississippi River campaign. "Now," he said, "I am going to devote a part of every day to these mortars and I won't leave off until it fairly rains bombs." Foote was told that the President wished him to be sure, when he opened fire, to "rain the rebels out," to "treat them to a refreshing shower of sulphur and brimstone." Foote was told also that the President "is evidently a practical man, understands precisely what he wants, and is not turned aside by anyone when he has his work before him."

Not only in the opening of the Mississippi but throughout the war the mortars, which owed so much to Lincoln's determination, served with telling effect. In the trenches around

Petersburg, at the beginning of the long siege in July, 1864, a North Carolina trooper in a letter to his wife noted the death-dealing efficiency of the mortar-equipped Yankees. "They kill and wound more men with Morter Shell than any other way for the last few weeks," this Tarheel wrote. "They throw them up and Drop them Right into the trenches when they Explode and tare to pieces all around them."

Lincoln played a part in the decision to use another kind of ammunition that would tear to pieces—an explosive bullet, or rifle shell. A New Yorker by the name of Samuel Gardiner, Jr., had invented what he considered an improved bullet of that kind, one that was exploded by a time fuse rather than the usual percussion fuse. Some bullets of the percussion type already were being employed here and there. Supposedly they were well adapted to penetrating and blowing up ammunition boxes, but they also had the effect of penetrating and bursting within human flesh. The Confederates occasionally used them. "To my dying day," a *New York Tribune* correspondent reported, "I shall have in my ears the wailing shrieks of a private of the 1st Long Island, shot dead beside my horse with a percussion musket-ball, whose explosion within its wound I distinctly heard."

Just three days after that explosion the inventor Gardiner called at the White House with samples of his supposedly more effective musket shell. Carefully looking over the bullets, Lincoln seemed to think they constituted an improvement on solid shot. He penned a note for James W. Ripley, the Army Chief of Ordnance: "Will Gen. Ripley please consider whether this musket-shell, would be a valuable missile in battle?" Ripley felt that the bullet had impracticable features and that, in any case, an ordinary Minié ball would put a man out of action just as effectively and far less brutally. Nevertheless, Gardiner secured from the War Department an order for more than 100,000 of his bullets.

Ten thousand of these fell into rebel hands. At Gettysburg

some Confederates as well as Federals fired them. And the Federals occasionally employed them on Sherman's march and in Grant's Richmond campaign.

Apparently unaware of the whole story, Grant accused the rebels of using explosive bullets at Vicksburg; he protested that such bullets were "barbarous" because they produced "increased suffering without any corresponding advantage to those using them." After the war a new chief of ordnance condemned them as "inexcusable among any people above the grade of ignorant savages." European nations outlawed them as inhumane. But Lincoln did not forbid their use.

Nor did he have any scruples against making war with fire and flame, though General McClellan believed that "such means of destruction" were "hardly within the category of those recognized in civilized warfare." Recommending the inventor of an incendiary shell, Lincoln wrote a note for army ordnance: "He thinks he can make a very destructive missile, and, if not too much trouble to you, I shall be obliged, if you can accommodate him." Lincoln arranged for several demonstrations of Greek fire, one of them (which turned out to be a fizzle) on the snow-covered lawn of the White House. In April 1862 he telegraphed to McClellan on the peninsula and offered to send him a batch of "fire shells." These were sent but failed to reach McClellan, and ten barrels of incendiary fluid arrived too late for him to try out. In the spring of 1863 Lincoln personally took charge of plans for General Hooker to experiment with 100-pounder shells of liquid fire in battle use. He started for Hooker's camp to see for himself, then changed his mind when Lee undertook to invade the North. Still, though the Army's Chief of Ordnance was reluctant, Lincoln insisted upon an order for 1,000 incendiary shells.

Such shells, he thought, would be especially valuable in siege operations, as at Vicksburg and Charleston. Accordingly, from gunboats on the Mississippi, Admiral Porter threw a few shells filled with one brand of Greek fire into the sky above

Vicksburg and started fires that burned a number of houses and quantities of military stores.

Vicksburg surrendered before a thorough test could be made, but behind Fort Sumter the city of Charleston remained exasperatingly out of reach. After a long-range, 200-pounder Parrott gun (the "Swamp Angel") had been set up on Morris Island, Lincoln himself gave the order to shoot into the city with incendiary shells. Charlestonians awoke to a rain of fire in the middle of the night. Promptly General Beauregard, in command of the local defenses, denounced the Federals for throwing "a number of the most destructive missiles ever used in war into the midst of a city, taken unawares and filled with sleeping women and children."

Only after these missiles had proved ineffective in reducing Charleston—and extremely dangerous to the Union soldiers manning the guns—did Lincoln lose interest in the tactics of conflagration.

4

"Mr. Lincoln was tender-hearted *when in the presence* of suffering or when it was enthusiastically or poetically described to him; he had great charity for the weaknesses of his fellow-man; his nature was merciful and it sprang into manifestations quickly on *the presentation* of a proper subject under proper conditions; he had no imagination to invoke, through the distances, suffering, nor fancy to paint it. The subject of mercy must be presented to him."

Such was the retrospective judgment of William H. Herndon, that long-time law partner and subsequent interpreter of Lincoln. Some of Herndon's analyses of Lincoln's personality no doubt are wide of the mark. But this one appears to be remarkably shrewd, in light of Lincoln's pardon policy on the one hand and his creative interest in new weapons on the other. Herndon's conclusion makes more sense than do the opinions of those who thought Lincoln entirely too kind and merciful for his job. So does Herndon's prospective judgment, written in 1860 after his partner's election to the Presidency: "Lincoln is a man of heart—aye, as gentle as a woman's and as tender—but he has a will strong as iron."

Some years after the war Donn Piatt tried to debunk the "popular belief that Abraham Lincoln was of so kind and forgiving a nature that his gentler impulses interfered with his duty." Piatt contended that people were misled by the man's good-natured way. "It covered as firm a character as nature ever clad with human flesh, and I doubt whether Mr. Lincoln had at all a kind, forgiving nature. Such traits are not common to successful leaders."

Piatt, who admired "this strange, quaint, great man," undoubtedly overstated the case. But there can be no doubt of Lincoln's essential firmness and strong will. Though he did not always agree with the methods of the radical Republicans, who kept demanding from him a "vigorous prosecution" of the war, he was as determined as anyone to win that war. Indeed, he was perhaps the most determined of all. He never wavered from his firm resolve. More than anything else—far more than his melancholy or his mercy—his determination accounts for what he did or left undone during the four long years from Sumter to Appomattox.

"I expect to maintain this contest until successful, or till I die, or am conquered, or my term expires, or Congress or the country forsakes me . . . ," he confided to Seward at the moment of one of his greatest disappointments, in the summer of 1862, when he had lost all hope that McClellan ever would take Richmond.

To a Louisiana Unionist, who asked that the occupying army be removed from Louisiana, he expostulated in the fall of 1862:

"What would you do in my position? Would you drop the war where it is? Or, would you prosecute it in future with elder-stalk squirts, charged with rose water? Would you deal lighter blows rather than heavier ones? Would you give up the contest, leaving any available means unapplied?

"I am in no boastful mood. I shall not do *more* than I can, and I shall do *all* I can to save the government, which is my sworn duty as well as my personal inclination. I shall do nothing in malice. What I deal with is too vast for malicious dealing."

At the very outset of the war, Lincoln had felt it necessary to act quickly and decisively to save the capital and hold Maryland as well as the other border states. On the way to the rescue of Washington, the boys of the Sixth Massachusetts were mobbed in Baltimore, and promptly a delegation from the Baltimore YMCA called upon Lincoln with a request that he provoke no more riots. "You express great horror of bloodshed," he replied, "and yet you would not lay a straw in the way of those who are organizing in Virginia and elsewhere to capture this city." He reminded his petitioners of his oath of office. "You would have me break my oath and surrender the government without a blow. There is no Washington in that—no Jackson in that—no manhood nor honor in that." A Maryland Unionist warned him that he would "crush all Union feeling" in the state if he tried to bring additional troops over her soil. He brought more troops, and he suspended the writ of habeas corpus, so that obstreperous Marylanders could be arrested and held without trial. He lost neither Washington nor Maryland.

On other occasions and in other places he authorized his generals to make arbitrary arrests. Before the war was over, tens of thousands of citizens had been thrown in jail, to stay for weeks and months without written charges or a chance to be heard. Many of these inmates of the "American Bastille" were quite guiltless; comparatively few ever were proved guilty of crime or criminal intent. They and their families suffered heavily at the hands of the Lincoln administration, and Democratic politicians made a partisan issue of their plight. The politicans clamored that the government was a tyranny, Lincoln a tyrant.

Admitting that he was "ultimately responsible," Lincoln defended the program of military arrests as justified by the Constitution and by the circumstances of the time. He explained that the would-be destroyers of the Union had planned to take advantage of the Constitution in order to achieve their aim "Under cover of 'Liberty of speech' 'Liberty of the press' and 'Habeas Corpus' they hoped to keep on foot amongst us a most efficient corps of spies, informers, suppliers, and aiders and abettors of their cause in a thousand ways." The Constitution provided that the writ of habeas corpus should not be suspended except when, in case of rebellion or invasion, the public safety might require it. The present case was one of rebellion. The aim in arresting persons and holding them without trial was prevention, not punishment. So Lincoln argued, and he named Robert E. Lee and other prominent Confederates as examples of "traitors" who should have been seized *before* they had an opportunity to commit their crime.

"I further say," he concluded, "that as the war progresses, it appears to me, opinion and action, which were in great confusion at first, take shape and fall into more regular channels; so that the necessity for arbitrary dealing with them gradually decreases. I have every reason to desire that it would cease altogether. . . . Still, I must continue to do as much as may seem to be required by the public safety."

Sorely tried though he was by what seemed the necessities of war, Lincoln did not allow himself the comfort of delusions about an early and easy peace. From 1863 on, the Peace Democrats continually cried for some kind of conference or negotiation with the enemy to stop the fighting—on the unexamined assumption that somehow the Union automatically would be restored. "There are those who are dissatisfied with me," Lincoln said in a communication to a rally of Peace Democrats at home in Springfield, Illinois. "To such I would say; You desire peace; and you blame me that we do not have it. But how can we attain it?" And he gave his own answer, that to have peace and Union there was only one way, and that way was "to suppress the rebellion by force of arms." Again, in his annual message of December, 1864, he said of the enemy: "He cannot voluntarily re-accept the Union; we cannot voluntarily yield it. Between him and us the issue is distinct, simple, and inflexible. It is an issue which can only be tried by war, and decided by victory."

Victory meant continued war. It meant continued killing. "The North responds to the proclamation sufficiently in breath," Lincoln remarked after his preliminary emancipation decree; "but breath kills no rebels." Only the relentless advance of the Union armies could kill enough rebels to bring final victory.

From first to last, Lincoln urged his generals on—to fight, to win. "And, once more let me tell you, it is indispensable to *you* that you strike a blow," he told the procrastinating McClellan after a winter of delay. "And now, beware of rashness," he admonished Hooker when appointing him to take McClellan's place at the head of the Army of the Potomac. "Beware of rashness, but with energy, and sleepless vigilance, go forward, and give us victories." Meanwhile, to gossipy critics of Grant, he gave the silencing retort: "He fights." When Grant had fought his way futilely through the Wilderness and had laid siege to Richmond and Petersburg, Lincoln counseled him: "Hold on with a bull-dog grip, and chew & choke, as much as possible." Finally, when Lee had fled Richmond with the Federals in close pursuit, Lincoln from nearby City Point sent the laconic dispatch to Grant: "Gen. Sheridan says 'If the thing is pressed I think that Lee will surrender.' Let the *thing* be pressed."

Mere breath, mere talk, killed no rebels, as Lincoln said. Squirts of rose water would not do the job. What would kill rebels was the muzzle-loader and Minié ball or, better yet, the repeating rifle, the mortar, or the machine gun. What would kill them was the exploding bullet or the incendiary shell. Hence Lincoln's personal interest in all this gadgetry of death.

He was humane, but he was also human. Whatever would

win the war most quickly, he seemed to think, would win it most humanely.

If, in the 1860s, Yankee ingenuity had been equal to producing such a weapon, would he have withheld the atom bomb? Or if, in the 1940s, he had been in Harry Truman's place, would he have spared Hiroshima?

chapter 8

THE MASTER POLITICIAN

Among Americans the words *politics* and *politician* long have been terms of reproach. Politics generally means "dirty" politics, whether the adjective is used or not. Politicians, then, are dirty politicians unless they happen to be statesmen, and in that case they are not politicians at all.

A well-known American once defined politicians as "a set of men who have interests aside from the interests of the people, and who, to say the most of them, are, taken as a class, at least one long step removed from honest men." The author of this definition was Abraham Lincoln, and at the time he made it he was a twenty-eight-year-old member of the Illinois Legislature. He added: "I say this with the greater freedom because, being a politician myself, none can regard it as personal."

After his death Lincoln was hailed almost universally as a statesman, one of the greatest—if not the greatest—the countr or the world had ever seen. To many of his admirers it seeme unthinkable that he had been at any time a practitioner o politics. He, after all, was "Honest Abe." He must have bee above that sort of thing.

But some of his acquaintances and friends had thought o him as a master of the politician's art. In time historians looke carefully into his political interests and techniques, noting fo example the day-to-day attention that, as President, he gave to dividing the spoils of government jobs and patronage. The defenders of Lincoln do not infer, however, that he was a mere grubby spoilsman. "In being a competent politician," the conclude, "he became a statesman."

No longer are many people likely to be shocked by the picture of Lincoln busy at a politician's chores. It is taken fo granted that politics for him was a consuming interest. But hi expertness remains a subject of some dispute.

What were his strengths—and weaknesses? How successfu was he, really, as a politician?

2

If Lincoln as President proved himself a political wizard, thi could not have been due to native shrewdness or sagacity alone As a genius, if indeed he was one, he must have been made, no born. This is borne out by the record of his apprentice year in national politics.

"His ambition," Herndon thought, "was a little engine tha knew no rest." Besides his ambition he had experience in the State Legislature but almost nothing else to justify him when as a young man in his thirties, he looked longingly toward a seat in the House of Representatives. He had no platform, no program. "You know that my only argument is that 'turn abou is fair play,' " he stated frankly to a follower. He and two othe hopefuls, adopting in this case the opposition party's principle of rotation in office, had agreed to take turns as the Whig candidate in their district. His turn had come, and he was determined to have it.

During his single term in Congress (1847–1849) the lone Whig from Illinois left no monument of constructive legislation, large or small. He put together, but did not press, a plan for the gradual, compensated emancipation of slaves in the District of Columbia, the plan to take effect only with the approval of the voters in the District. On the whole he gave little attention to legislative matters as such. His big concern was Presidential politics, and his congressional speechmaking was mostly campaign oratory. He devoted a great deal of time to unmaking one President, a Democrat, and making another, a Whig.

He found an issue and a candidate in the Mexican War. The war, just getting under way when he ran for Congress, appeared to be extremely popular in Illinois. Whigs and Democrats alike waved the flag and volunteered for service at the front. What Candidate Lincoln said on the subject is not recorded, but the *Sangamo Journal* of Springfield, a newspaper that was thought to express his views, took a consistently patriotic, pro-war stand. More than a year later, when the congressman-elect arrived in Washington, he saw that the Whig leaders of the nation were bent on condemning the war and denouncing the President, James K. Polk, as the author of it. If Lincoln ever had approved the war, he no longer did so. Soon he was out-Whigging most of his fellow Whigs.

Within a few weeks after he had taken his seat, he introduced his "spot" resolutions, in which he challenged Polk's statement that Mexico had started the war by invading the United States and shedding American blood upon American soil. The point of these resolutions the new congressman drove home when he got to the floor for his maiden speech. If the President could not or would not answer the inquiries satisfactorily, his silence would prove that he was deeply conscious of being in the wrong. It would prove that "he feels the blood of this war, like the blood of Abel, is crying to Heaven against him." It would prove that for some ulterior motive he had plunged the nation into a war, into a needless, hopeless conflict, the end of which was nowhere in sight.

The war President, busy with strategy and with plans for peace, did not bother to reply. He did not rise to Lincoln's baiting, nor, apparently, did he even notice it. Indeed, in all the pages of his voluminous diary, Polk never so much as mentioned Lincoln's name. And less than two weeks after the latter's speech on the endless war, a treaty of peace with Mexico was signed.

Lincoln was but following the party line—voting to condemn Polk and the war while voting supplies for it—yet his course in Congress made him unpopular with his constituents in Illinois. Whigs as well as Democrats muttered about him. They or their friends or relatives had fought in the war and had come home as heroes, dead or alive. They did not relish being told that they or their fallen comrades had made all the effort and the sacrifice in an unworthy cause, a war unnecessarily and unconstitutionally begun.

Herndon wrote to warn his friend and partner that his principles were wrong and his politics unwise. Lincoln insisted that his principles, at least, were right. "I will stake my life, that if you had been in my place, you would have voted just as I did," he assured Herndon. "You are compelled to speak; and your only alternative is to tell the *truth* or tell a lie." Politics, Lincoln was saying, must take second place to honor, truth, and right.

And yet, in other letters he wrote, Lincoln made it plain that the Whig attitude toward Polk and the war had a very direct bearing on the Whig prospects in the Presidential election of 1848. The Whigs were ready to use the war both ways—to their own advantage and to the disadvantage of the Democrats—by condemning the war President while running a war hero as the Whig candidate. Lincoln was an early and eager worker for the nomination of the victorious general, Zachary Taylor. The thing to do, as Lincoln saw it, was to approve Taylor and his part in the war without approving Polk and *his* part in it. "You should simply go for Genl. Taylor," Lincoln advised a fellow Whig; "because by this, you can take some Democrats, and lose no Whigs; but if you go also for Mr. Polk on the origin and mode of prosecuting the war, you will still take some Democrats, but you will lose more Whigs, so that in the sum of the operation you will be loser." These look like the words of a calculating politician, not those of an inflexible supporter of right principle.

At the nominating convention in 1848, Lincoln labored manfully to turn his fellow Illinois delegates from Henry Clay's to Taylor's support. Taylor was nominated, without a platform, and he accepted without a statement of what he stood for. Clay and Daniel Webster, disappointed contenders themselves, naturally were not enthusiastic about the choice. Taylor was "a military man, and a military man merely," with "no training in civil affairs," Webster said. Such a nomination was "not fit to be made." The Democrats accused the Whigs of deserting their principles and riding on the coattails of a military hero.

Lincoln, campaigning for Taylor in and out of Congress, did not deny the coattail charge. He merely reminded the Democrats that, for many years, they had been using the coattail of another famous warrior, Andrew Jackson. "Like a horde of hungry ticks you have stuck to the tail of the Hermitage lion to the end of his life," Lincoln said memorably if inelegantly, "and you are still sticking to it, and drawing a loathsome sustenance from it, after he is dead." As for principles, Lincoln maintained that Taylor's views were no more obscure than those of the Democratic candidate. Taylor's views were not vague at all, he said. Had the general not made it clear already that on the public questions of the day he would respond to "the will of the people" as expressed in acts of Congress? Indeed, Taylor held to the best of principles—"the principle of allowing the people to do as they please with their own business."

While making the most of Taylor's military glory, Lincoln cleverly ridiculed the record of the Democratic candidate, Lewis

Cass, who had served competently in the War of 1812. It was on this occasion that Lincoln referred to his having been a "military hero," himself, in the Black Hawk War. "Speaking of Gen. Cass' career reminds me of my own," Lincoln joked in Congress. "If Gen. Cass went in advance of me in picking whortleberries, I guess I surpassed him in charges upon the wild onions. If he saw any live, fighting Indians, it was more than I did; but I had a good many bloody struggles with the mosquitoes. . . ."

Whortleberries, onions, and mosquitoes, coattails, hungry ticks, and a dead lion. No platform, no committed candidate, nothing but the will of the people, whatever it might turn out to be. Such was politics, such was statesmanship, as practiced by Congressman Lincoln in 1848. So far as the Presidential election was concerned, these tactics seemed to work. Taylor won.

But Lincoln lost. The Whig line, however effective it may have been in some parts of the country, destroyed the Whig majority in his own Congressional district. His distribution of his share of government jobs did little good, though he gave close attention to it. Barred by his taking-turns agreement, he did not seek reelection to Congress. The Whig whose turn it was, running perforce on Lincoln's record, was overwhelmingly defeated.

What was worse, Lincoln failed to get from the Taylor administration the government job (Commissioner of the General Land Office) which he desperately wanted and considered as no more than his just due. Prominent Whigs, including Webster and Clay, used their influence to aid a rival applicant. "It will now mortify me deeply if Gen. Taylors administration shall trample all my wishes in the dust merely to gratify these men," Lincoln confided to a friend. All his wishes were trampled in the dust, and he was deeply mortified.

At the age of forty—frustrated, despondent, seemingly at the end of his public career—he certainly appeared to be no natural-born genius in politics. Perhaps he had been, so far, unlucky. He had yet to grow in political skill as in other respects, and fortune was yet to favor him.

3

The events of the 1850s gave Lincoln his opportunity to get out of the woods and set foot again upon the path of politics. To help in his advancement, he now exploited to the utmost the magic in the names of two late, great politicians (or statesmen) of the Whig party, Webster and Clay.

Clay introduced in Congress the proposals that culminated in the Compromise of 1850, which supposedly put to rest the disturbing issues between North and South, including the question of slavery in the territories. Webster eloquently supported the Compromise with his argument that Congress need not act to keep slavery out of the West since God already had done so by creating geographical conditions unsuited to it there. Then Clay and Webster died, in 1852.

Two years later Lincoln's friend and rival Stephen A. Douglas maneuvered through Congress a bill for reopening the Louisiana Purchase to slavery and allowing the settlers of Kansas and Nebraska to decide for themselves whether to permit slaveholding in those territories.

Now, the Compromise of 1850, though unpopular in New England, where the abolitionists cursed Webster, was generally approved in Illinois and the old Northwest. Its most conspicuous sponsors, Webster and Clay, were famed in the prairie country as Union-savers. But, throughout the North, the Kansas-Nebraska Act provoked wild demonstrations of outrage which Douglas had failed to foresee. The Republican party rose out of the protest, and the Whig party, already disintegrating, was speeded on the way to extinction. In Illinois, as in other states, thousands of hesitating Whigs were left without a party home.

Douglas, with presidential as well as senatorial ambitions, faced the task of winning to the Democratic party as many of the homeless Whigs as he could. Lincoln, with ambitions of his own, set himself to heading off his most dangerous rival and steering the undecided Whigs into the Republican camp. Douglas tried to convince them that, in the Kansas-Nebraska business, he had but carried on in the spirit of their dead heroes, Webster and Clay. Lincoln undertook to contradict him. Thus Douglas the Democrat and Lincoln the Republican both sought votes by appealing to the memory of the departed Whig leaders, and each claimed to be their true and only disciple.

The argument had begun at least as early as the presidential campaign of 1852, when there was still a Whig party and Webster was still alive. At that time Lincoln accused Douglas of falsely crediting the Democrats with the Compromise of 1850 and brazenly stealing Clay's and Webster's ideas.

In 1854, after arousing opposition with his Kansas-Nebraska Act, Douglas emphasized the bipartisan nature of the Compromise of 1850, saying it had been the work both of Whigs like Clay and Webster and of Democrats like Lewis Cass. Then Lincoln protested: "The Judge [Douglas] invokes against me, the memory of Clay and Webster." He proceeded to ask: "For what is it, that their life-long enemy, shall now make profit, by assuming to defend them against their life-long friend?" And he answered his own query: "The truth is that some support from Whigs is now a necessity with the Judge, and for thus it is, that the names of Clay and Webster are now invoked."

Again, in 1856, when he was stumping for John C. Frémont, the first Republican presidential candidate, Lincoln countered Douglas by aligning himself on the side of the old Whigs. A Democratic newspaper reporter, dropping in on one of Lincoln's campaign talks, "heard him pronouncing, with thundering emphasis, a beautiful passage from Webster's compromise speech, and that too, *without the quotations.*"

This same contest for identification with Clay and Webster ran through the Lincoln-Douglas campaign of 1858. "It would be amusing, if it were not disgusting, to see how quick these compromise-breakers administer on the political effects of their dead adversaries, trumping up claims never before heard of, and dividing the assets among themselves," Lincoln exclaimed in a speech at Springfield before the formal debates began. Then in the first joint debate at Ottawa, Douglas came back at his opponent by asserting that not he but Lincoln was the compromise-breaker. "Lincoln went to work to dissolve the Old Line Whig party," Douglas resumed in the second debate at Freeport. "Clay was dead, and although the sod was not yet green on his grave, this man undertook to bring into disrepute those great compromise measures of 1850, with which Clay and Webster were identified." In appearances by himself at Tremont and Carlinville Lincoln denied Douglas's charges and repeated that he stood exactly where Clay and Webster had taken their stand. In the third joint debate at Jonesboro, Douglas returned to the attack and, in the fourth at Charleston, he elaborated by saying that "no sooner was the rose planted on the tomb of the Godlike Webster" than Lincoln and others tried to abolitionize the good old Whig party.

Neither Webster nor Clay had been, in fact, the sole authors of the Compromise of 1850. That was essentially a bipartisan achievement. Douglas himself, more than any other one man or two men, engineered the final passage of the compromise bills, and they were carried by the overwhelming vote of Democrats as well as Whigs. The roles of Clay and Webster were afterward so much exaggerated as to become almost mythological. The man who was mainly responsible for the Compromise was also largely responsible for the misconceptions regarding it. Manipulating the great Whig reputations in such a way as to attract former Whigs to the Democratic party, Douglas so minimized his own role in the events of 1850 that he distorted history and dimmed his own fame.

That is ironical enough, but the story has still more irony in it.

Lincoln, as well as Douglas, had been using the names of the two bygone politicians, reputed to be giants, in order to win votes. Not that Lincoln personally was lost in reverence for the departed great. He never quite forgave Clay and Webster for their part in frustrating his hopes for a government job. Possibly he still had his old disappointment in mind when, as President, he agreed in a Cabinet conversation that they had been "hard and selfish leaders." Nevertheless, in the rivalry with Douglas it had seemed important to Lincoln that he show a parallel between his policy and theirs.

In later generations, after his martyrdom, the name of Lincoln acquired a political magic incomparably more potent than ever had been the name of Clay or Webster or anyone else among the sainted dead. For decades after the Civil War the Republicans used the incantation of Lincoln's name to extremely good effect. At first they held a monopoly on the political remains of Honest Abe. Eventually the Democrats undertook to get their share of these assets, and they began to claim the soul of Lincoln as rightfully theirs. The Socialists, the Communists, the Prohibitionists, and others put in their exclusive claims. Today, politicians of all parties feel called upon, no matter what they advocate, to show they stand foursquare with The Rail Splitter from Illinois. All who seek the favor of the American electorate take pains to "get right" with him.

A hundred years ago the habits of politicians were essentially the same. Lincoln, for one, devoted a good deal of effort to getting right with Clay and Webster.

4

There is no need to question the sincerity of Lincoln in opposing Douglas and the Douglas program. As like as not, he really believed that Douglas's "popular sovereignty" would result in the fastening of slavery upon the territories, and was convinced that Congress had to prohibit the expansion of slavery, for the country's good.

His principles happened to coincide neatly with his ambition. But if he had been totally lacking in convictions and had been concerned with nothing but his political advancement, he still could have chosen no shrewder course than the one he actually followed.

By 1858 he was a far more careful, skillful politician than he had been in 1848. In a decade he learned much, and one of the things he learned was caution. His touch was far surer, as he drew every personal advantage he could from the political trends of the 1850s.

Douglas remained the most immediate, the most dangerous antagonist. He broke with his party head, President Buchanan, when Buchanan tried to force slavery upon Kansas, in violation of the popular-sovereignty principle of the Kansas-Nebraska Act. Some prominent Republicans in the East then hoped to win Douglas to the Republican fold—and with him his Democratic following of the Middle West. Horace Greeley, of the *New York Tribune,* took up the idea and played with it. "What does the New-York Tribune mean by its constant eulogizing, and admiring, and magnifying of Douglas?" Lincoln demanded of his friend, the Republican senator from Illinois, Lyman Trumbull. "Does it, in this, speak the sentiments of the Republicans at Washington? Have they concluded that the Republican cause, generally, can best be promoted by sacrificing us here in Illinois?" Lincoln would have none of it. He could have none of it if *he*—not Douglas—was to be the Republican leader of Illinois and the Midwest.

In his campaign to get Douglas's Senate seat, in 1858, Lincoln did his best to identify Douglas with slavery and thus to discredit him among Midwestern devotees of freedom and free soil. He even accused Douglas of conspiring with Buchanan to spread slavery and fix it permanently upon the nation. Actually, Buchanan at the moment was using the patronage of his administration to hinder Douglas and help Lincoln in the Illinois election. It would have been more apt to say that Lincoln was in league with Buchanan!

Lincoln lost in 1858—and yet he won. The Republicans got more votes than the Democrats did, and only the underrepresentation of the northern districts in the Legislature prevented the Republicans from controlling it and sending Lincoln to the United States Senate. He had compelled Douglas to state his popular-sovereignty views so forcefully that Douglas lost much of his following among Southerners who insisted that nobody, neither Congress nor the territorial governments, had the right to exclude slavery from the territories. Thus Lincoln weakened Douglas's chances for the Presidency in 1860. At the same time, he improved his own. At once, a few newspapers in Illinois and elsewhere began to mention him as a presidential possibility, and in the ensuing months the Lincoln-for-President talk steadily increased.

At what point Lincoln began to take his prospects seriously, he never said, and there is no way of knowing. No doubt every politician, however humble and obscure, has days when he thinks of the sudden rise of other undistinguished men and feels at least faint stirrings of hope within his own heart. Not every politician is fool enough to bray forth his aspiration the first time it occurs to him.

In December, 1858 Jesse W. Fell made a trip from Bloomington to Springfield and, in the cultured tones of the prosperous, well-educated man he was, told Lincoln he would make a formidable candidate. According to Fell's recollection, Lincoln replied casually: "Oh, Fell, what's the use of talking of me for the Presidency, whilst we have such men as Seward, Chase, and others, who are so much better known?" Fell urged: "What the Republican party wants, to insure success in 1860, is a man of popular origin, of acknowledged ability, committed against slavery aggressions, who has no record to defend, and no radicalism of an offensive character." Lincoln then said: "Fell, I admit the force of much that you say, and admit that I am ambitious, and would like to be President . . . but there is no such good luck in store for me as the Presidency."

The next April an enthusiastic Republican editor of Rock Island, Illinois, wrote to Springfield proposing a Lincoln-for-President movement. "I must, in candor, say I do not think myself fit for the Presidency," Lincoln wrote back. "I really think it best for our cause that no concerted effort, such as you suggest, should be made." As the months went by, Lincoln received other letters like the one from Rock Island, and he answered all of them in much the same spirit.

In December, 1859 he told Trumbull he "would rather have a full term in the Senate than in the Presidency." Soon he gave his friends the impression that he was, indeed, interested in being considered for the presidential nomination—but only to improve his chances for eventual election to the Senate. "I am not in a position where it would hurt much for me not to be nominated on the national ticket," he informed Norman B. Judd in February, 1860, "but I am where it would hurt some for me not to get the Illinois delegates." Finally, in April, when the national convention was only two months away, he began to admit to a few of his correspondents that he did have presidential hopes. To one, he said it must be remembered that "when a not very great man begins to be mentioned for a very great position, his head is very likely to be a little turned." To Trumbull he confessed: "The taste *is* in my mouth a little. . . ."

Whether or not Lincoln's coyness and hesitation reflected his modesty, he had been doing what any sensible aspirant would have done. Lincoln would have hurt his prospects if he had allowed a boom to get started prematurely. He would have made himself too conspicuous as a target for other contenders.

While Lincoln thus took care to keep himself from being knifed in the back, he was busy using the knife on his rivals for the nomination, and doing all he could to enhance his reputation as an outstanding Republican leader. During 1859 he was on the go much of the time, traveling a total of four thousand miles and speaking to twenty-three audiences, in such states as Ohio, Michigan, Wisconsin, and Kansas. In 1860 he spoke at Cooper Union in New York City, then toured New England to speak in several towns and cities. That same winter, he wrote out an autobiographical sketch and sent it to Jesse W. Fell for publication. He also had his eloquent debates with Douglas published. And all the while he kept up a ceaseless correspondence with Republicans in Illinois and throughout the country.

He was ready with a reply for those who asked how Illinois would react to the nomination of various preconvention favorites: William H. Seward, Salmon P. Chase, Edward Bates, or John McLean. As for Seward, he "is the very best candidate we could have for the north of Illinois, and the very *worst* for the south of it," Lincoln wrote. Chase "is neither better nor worse" than Seward, "except that he is a newer man." Chase appeared to be "right-minded; but still he may not be the most suitable." Bates "would be the best man for the south of our state, and the worst for the north of it." "I think neither Seward nor Bates can carry Illinois if Douglas shall be on the track; and that either of them can, if he shall not be." McLean "could carry it with D. on or off." In fact, McLean would be a good man if only he were ten or fifteen years younger. "I hear no objection to Mr. McLean, except his age; but that objection seems to occur to every one."

The conclusion was unexpressed, but it was plain enough between the lines. Illinois could be carried by only one man—Abraham Lincoln. Indeed, the implication was that, for the North as a whole, he was the only truly *available* man the Republicans could pick.

After the nominating convention at last had met in Chicago, in June of 1860, a majority of the delegates—on the third ballot—appeared to agree with the conclusion which Lincoln so assiduously had been hinting. No doubt his nomination was furthered by the claque of Illinoisans who raised a din in the convention hall, the Wigwam, whenever his name was mentioned. No doubt the victory was clinched by the patronage promises which his managers made. But Lincoln himself had laid the groundwork and had done it well.

Once he had been chosen as the Republican candidate, Lincoln put aside his law practice and gave his full time to the direction of his campaign. He continued to keep the silence which—except for the speeches he had made to denounce Douglas and demand free soil—he had observed before the convention. Now he had absolutely nothing more to say, in public. For a presidential candidate to stump in his own behalf was not yet accepted as the best political etiquette. Besides, for Lincoln to do so would have been most risky.

To win, he needed the votes of all kinds of dissident groups in the North. He needed the votes of former Whigs and former Democrats, of men sworn to destroy slavery and men indifferent or favorable to it, of German and Irish immigrants and of native Americans prejudiced against the foreign-born, of high-tariffites and low-tariffites, of tipplers and temperance men. The issue of the Catholic foreigner was especially delicate. In the previous Presidential election, in 1856, the Native American or Know-Nothing party, with its anti-Catholic, antiforeigner platform, had taken many votes that Republicans desired. Lincoln still thought of those nativist votes.

He was not a Know-Nothing and never had been. Once (in 1855) he had written, privately: "As a nation, we began by declaring that '*all men are created equal.*' We now practically read it 'all men are created equal, *except Negroes.*' When the Know-Nothings get control, it will read 'all men are created equal, except Negroes, *and foreigners, and Catholics.*' When it comes to this I should prefer emigrating to some country where they make no pretense of loving liberty—to Russia, for instance, where despotism can be taken pure, and without the base alloy of hypocrisy." Which was nobly said.

But Lincoln also observed (in 1855) that Know-Nothingism had "not yet entirely crumbled to pieces" and that it was important to "get the elements of this organization" for the Republican party. "I fear an open push by us now, may offend them, and prevent our ever getting them," he said, in confidence. "About us here, they are mostly my old political and personal friends; and I have hoped their organization would die out without the painful necessity of my taking an open stand against them."

He still refused, in 1860, to take an open stand against the Native Americans. When told that "Irishmen" were saying he had been seen coming out of a Know-Nothing lodge, he wrote a confidential letter stating that he had never been in such a place. "And now, a word of caution," he ended. "Our adversaries think they can gain a point, if they could force me to openly deny this charge, by which some degree of offence would be given to the Americans. For this reason, it must not publicly appear that I am paying any attention to the charge."

The candidate also declined to speak out on the tariff. He was an "old Henry Clay tariff Whig," he admitted confidentially. "Still, it is my opinion that, just now, the revival of that question will not advance the cause itself, or the man who revives it."

Though averring (in one of his many "Private & Confidential" letters) that he did not intend to serve liquor in the White House, he thought it "improper" for him to make a public statement in support of temperance.

He did not want to see the fugitive-slave law discussed. And of course he said nothing, publicly, in response to those who asked for some assurance about the future of slavery in the Southern states.

He was carrying out the strategy of avoidance which he had recommended for the party even before his nomination. His "main object" would be to "hedge against divisions in the Republican ranks," he had said. "The point of danger is the temptation in different localities to '*platform*' for something which will be popular just there, but which, nevertheless, will be a firebrand elsewhere," he had warned. "In a word, in every locality we should look beyond our noses; and at least say *nothing* on points where it is probable we shall disagree."

In the circumstances of 1860, with the Democratic opposition split, the Lincoln strategy worked. And Douglas, running as the candidate of the Northern Democrats, was at last brought down in defeat.

Afterward many a Republican was given credit as the Warwick of the victorious party. People assumed there must have been a President-maker behind the scenes. It was one of Lincoln's Illinois friends and managers—Norman Judd, or David Davis, or Jesse W. Fell, or Leonard Swett. It was Horace Greeley of the *New York Tribune* or Charles Ray of the *Chicago Tribune,* and about Ray a book eventually was written with the title *The Man Who Elected Lincoln.* It was perhaps Stephen A. Douglas, an unwitting Warwick. Or it was someone else.

The most likely choice has been overlooked. It is Abraham Lincoln.

5

President Lincoln repaid the political debts his managers had contracted at the Chicago convention. He appointed to his Cabinet the men who had been his rivals: Seward, Chase, Bates, and Cameron. He found other places for his Illinois backers, a diplomatic post abroad for Norman Judd, a position on the Supreme Court for David Davis, and so on. Rewarding foes as well as friends, Lincoln was both generous and judicious with the patronage. Unquestionably he did this in order to hold the Republican party together. When the Confederates chose to fire upon the flag at Fort Sumter, the patriotic response gave additional strength and unity to the organization.

But divisions soon reappeared. While there rose many personal and factional rivalries, these generally were overshadowed by the two-way conflict between Radicals and conservatives. Between the two groups the main difference was this: the Radicals demanded a war to abolish slavery and remake the South; the conservatives desired only (or primarily) the reestablishment of the Union. The country, the Congress, and the Cabinet were divided on war aims. Throughout his presidency Lincoln had to concern himself with the "main object" he had defined even before his nomination—to overcome divisions within the Republican ranks. He had to cope with the problem of keeping his party in one piece and keeping himself at the head of it.

The supreme test came with the election of 1864. Lincoln

craved a second term. "No man knows what *that gnawing* is till he has had it," he said, as if to apologize for his ambition, to Provost Marshal-General James B. Fry.

For a time, Lincoln's chances to satisfy that gnawing appeared to be slim indeed. Before his own renomination, a splinter group of Radicals held a separate convention and picked as their candidate the colorful, antislavery politician-general, John C. Frémont. After Lincoln's renomination, a number of prominent Republicans joined in a plot to set aside both Lincoln and Frémont and replace them with a single candidate upon whom the whole party presumably could unite. In August, with the election less than three months away, even the campaign manager, Henry J. Raymond, and the political wizard, Thurlow Weed, were convinced that the President could not be reelected.

Lincoln won, of course. Eventually the party was reunited behind him. He was able to win partly because of luck. The Democrats, while nominating the crowd-pleasing George B. McClellan, made the mistake of requiring their war hero to run on a peace platform. And news of Union victories, most notably of Sherman's victory at Atlanta, arrived just in time to refute the Democrats' plank declaring the war a hopeless failure. But, to bring about Lincoln's reelection, it took more than the errors of his opponents and the fortunes of the war. It took all his resourcefulness as an expert politician.

Just how he managed the election is in some respects not altogether clear. To this day, there remain at least two big puzzles. One of these has to do with his role in the nomination of Andrew Johnson as his running mate.

Alexander C. McClure released, some time after the fact, one very persuasive version of how Lincoln "chose" his Vice-president. Though Lincoln was sure of his own place on the ticket when the regular Republican convention met in Baltimore, he feared that his candidacy might be a rather empty honor unless, on election day, he and the party could get the votes of many nominal Democrats in addition to the votes of confirmed Republicans. The better to appeal to Democratic voters, the Republican party was calling itself the "Union" party. Lincoln wanted to do more than merely change the name. He wanted to create an unbeatable bipartisan and bisectional combination which would bring together Republicans and War Democrats, Northerners and (in principle at least) Southerners. The way to do this was to have the Republicans produce a kind of coalition ticket, giving the second place to a Democrat who supported the war effort, a Southerner who remained loyal to the Union. Such a man was available in the person of North Carolina-born Andrew Johnson, currently military governor of Tennessee.

Of course, the country already had a Vice-president, Lincoln's running mate of 1860, Hannibal Hamlin of Maine. Lincoln had nothing against Hamlin himself, though the two did not always see eye to eye on issues of national policy. But Hamlin was expendable, since Maine was safely Republican. The problem was to ease him out with no embarrassment to him, to Lincoln, to the party as a whole. It would not do for the President to cut his colleague's throat in public.

Therefore, during the sessions of the Baltimore convention, Lincoln pretended to leave the delegates entirely to their own devices. He even wrote a note to the effect that he would not interfere. Behind the scenes, however, he interfered indeed. To McClure and other trusted emissaries he gave the word for the insiders at Baltimore: Johnson is the man. And Johnson was nominated on the first ballot.

Such, in essence, is the story that McClure released in his *Philadelphia Times* after Hannibal Hamlin died (in 1891). But the story did not go unchallenged. Promptly Lincoln's former private secretary, John G. Nicolay, sent a telegram to the recently bereaved Mrs. Hamlin and gave it to the press. In the telegram he said that the McClure report was wholly erroneous. "Mr. Lincoln's personal feelings, on the contrary, were for Mr. Hamlin's renomination, as he confidentially expressed to me, but he persistently withheld any opinion calculated to influence the convention for or against any candidate, and I have written words to that effect." Nicolay referred the widow—and the public—to volume, chapter, and page of *Abraham Lincoln: A History,* the monumental work which he had written in collaboration with John Hay.

Those pages tell how Nicolay, in Baltimore, was asked to get a statement from Lincoln on the matter of the vice-presidency. Some of the delegates were puzzled because Lincoln's close friend Leonard Swett was urging the nomination of Joseph Holt, a War Democrat from Kentucky. Nicolay wrote to Hay in Washington and requested him to find out whether Swett was "all right" and whether Lincoln had any instructions, confidential or otherwise. In reply Lincoln endorsed Nicolay's letter with this message: "Swett is unquestionably all right. Mr. Holt is a good man, but I had not heard or thought of him for V. P. Wish not to interfere about V. P."

The wording of this message, McClure asserted in rebuttal, really upheld his own contention (Swett's support of Holt being, McClure said, only a stratagem to prepare the way for Johnson's nomination). He repeated his story that Lincoln had called him to the White House and earnestly explained how the nomination of a "well-known Southern man like Andrew Johnson" would "nationalize the Republican party" and save the Union. McClure dismissed Nicolay by saying he had been a mere clerk who knew nothing of the confidential councils of the President and was not trusted by him. Naturally Lincoln "did not proclaim himself a fool by giving Nicolay an opportunity to herald Lincoln's sacredly private convictions as to the Vice-Presidency."

Answering in kind, Nicolay cited the official proceedings of the convention to show that McClure himself had acted a very minor part at Baltimore. Did it stand to reason that the President had confided in McClure without confiding also in more important men? "You accuse President Lincoln of acting a low political deceit and with his own hand writing a deliberate lie," Nicolay expostulated. "That may be your conception of

Abraham Lincoln, but it is not mine. That may be your system of politics, but it was not his."

Later, to clinch his case, Nicolay obtained a statement from the chairman of the Illinois delegation of 1864. Not satisfied with Lincoln's note to Nicolay, this Illinoisan had gone personally to the White House. He found Lincoln "particularly anxious not to make known his preferences" yet somehow gathered that Lincoln did have a preference. "After my interview with him I was as positive that Hannibal Hamlin was his favorite as I am that I am alive to-day."

McClure, for his last rebuttal, contented himself with presenting the reminiscences he collected from several of Lincoln's old acquaintances, including Ward Hill Lamon. On the main point—that Lincoln had desired the nomination of Johnson and had used his influence to bring it about—these reminiscences sustained McClure.

There the Nicolay-McClure controversy rested. There it still rests, unfortunately without a definite decision for either side.

The second big puzzle regarding Lincoln's tactics in 1864 has to do with a rumored "deal" by which he got rid of Frémont as a rival Republican candidate and at the same time won the reluctant Radicals to his own support. Many Radicals, such as Henry Winter Davis and Benjamin F. Wade, who in June had issued the "Wade-Davis manifesto" denouncing Lincoln, sulkily refused to campaign for him as late as September, though they were not Frémont men. The plot to supersede Lincoln had collapsed, but some of the former plotters demanded, as the price of their assistance, that he reform his Cabinet by dismissing the member most obnoxious to them, namely, Postmaster General Montgomery Blair. Lincoln, in return for sacrificing Blair, is supposed to have required the withdrawal of Frémont from the Presidential race. On September 22 Frémont withdrew. The next day Blair resigned. After that, Wade, Davis, and the rest of the Radicals, including former Frémont men, joined heartily in the campaign to reelect the President.

Had Lincoln actually made a bargain with Frémont? According to the biographer of the Blair family, he had. "To prevent almost certain defeat, he entered into a bargain with the Frémont Radicals, they to support the Union National ticket in exchange for the decapitation of Postmaster-General Blair." But Frémont's biographer questions the bargain story, and one of Lincoln's biographers disposes of it as essentially "historical fiction."

The story first was told by Zachariah Chandler, a senator from Michigan, who was a fierce Radical and a friend of Wade, but who also was on good personal terms with Lincoln. According to his own account, Chandler undertook to heal the party breach. At the end of August he left his Michigan home to see Wade in Ohio and Lincoln and others in Washington. He found Wade willing to "give his earnest support" if Blair were removed. He found Lincoln willing to remove Blair "if harmony would follow." Then he proceeded to New York and "opened negotiations there with the managers of the Frémont movement." After putting him off for some time, they finally "agreed that, if Mr. Blair (whom General Frémont regarded as a bitter enemy) left the Cabinet," the general would withdraw.

In the light of other evidence, it seems uncertain whether Frémont himself entered into a bargain with Lincoln, no matter what Frémont's "managers" did. Frémont afterward denied that he had done so. Still, in his statement announcing his withdrawal, he hinted that he and his followers would show enthusiasm for Lincoln only if Lincoln reformed his administration.

On the other hand, it seems reasonably certain that Lincoln did agree to a bargain. There exist some scraps of contemporary correspondence which indicate as much. In letters of the time, Chandler is mentioned as seeing Lincoln to get his "ultimatum." Chandler himself writes that Lincoln "was most reluctant to come to terms *but came.*" Wade refers to Chandler's believing "it was essential that Frémont should withdraw." From such remarks as these, it seems safe to infer that Lincoln did promise to remove Blair if Frémont could be persuaded to quit. At least, Chandler so understood.

Whatever the truth about the Blair-Frémont deal—or about the choice of Andrew Johnson for the Union ticket—there can be no doubt that Lincoln himself was the chief strategist for his campaign in 1864, as he had been in 1860. He had advantages the second time that he did not have the first, and he made the most of them.

He did not always leave even the tactical details to his campaign manager or to the workers in the field. At times he took a hand in the management of the Republican speaker's bureau, selecting the men he thought most suitable for stumping in this area or that. He did not hesitate to step in to tell the state committees what to do when he felt they were functioning poorly.

Lincoln was especially active in hiring and firing government job-holders so as to meet the necessities of the campaign. At the New York Custom House he changed the top officials, removing men who were insufficiently enthusiastic themselves or incapable of arousing sufficient enthusiasm among New York voters. He approved the dismissal of Brooklyn Navy Yard workmen who would not swear they were loyal "Union" men.

As Commander in Chief of the Army and the Navy, Lincoln was in a position to ultilize Republican sentiment among the Boys in Blue. Most of the states allowed their soldiers and sailors to vote in the field or on deck, or by proxy at home. Some states allowed the men to vote only if they personally cast their ballots in their own precincts.

On the advice of Pennsylvania politicians, Lincoln asked Meade and Sheridan each to furlough five thousand of the state's troops so that these men could be home on election day. (Pennsylvanians could cast their ballots in the field, but Lincoln wanted to increase the "home vote," lest it appear that he was overly dependent on the Army.) At the urgent and excited request of the Indiana governor, Lincoln sent a note to Sherman suggesting that the general let some of his Hoosiers go home to vote. In response to an appeal from the chairman of the New York State committee, who desired "facilities for taking the votes of Seamen & Sailors," Lincoln sent a note to Navy Secretary Welles: "Please do all for him in this respect which you consistently can."

In Pennsylvania, Indiana, and New York, and in Illinois, Maryland, and Connecticut, the citizens in uniform may have made the difference between victory and defeat. One cannot be sure, since the total of the soldier ballots, as well as the proportion which was Republican, cannot be exactly known. It has been estimated that three-fourths or more were Republican. On the whole it seems likely that without the Army's help in the six crucial states Lincoln would have lost them—and the election.

6

"If Abraham Lincoln was not a master politician, I am entirely ignorant of the qualities which make up such a character," Alexander K. McClure declared in 1892. And McClure was not entirely ignorant of politics, or of Lincoln either. But he may not have been altogether accurate in his analysis of the qualities that made Lincoln a master.

Lincoln had a "peculiar faculty," McClure said, "of holding antagonistic elements to his own support, and maintaining close and apparently confidential relations with each without offense to the other."

He had a way with politicians. "You know I never was a contriver," McClure heard him say in his quaint, disarming manner to a group of Pennsylvanians he had summoned to the White House; "I don't know much about how things are done in politics, but I think you gentlemen understand the situation in your State, and I want to learn what may be done to insure the success we all desire." He proceeded to interrogate each man minutely about the campaign then in progress, about the weak points of the party and the strong points of the opposition, about the tactics to be used in this locality or that. Generalities, mere enthusiasm, did not interest him. He wanted facts. And he got them, along with the wholehearted cooperation of the gentlemen from Pennsylvania.

He understood the voters. "He had abiding faith in the people, in their intelligence and their patriotism," McClure thought; "and he estimated political results by ascertaining, as far as possible, the bearing of every vital question that was likely to arise, and he formed his conclusions by his keen intuitive perception as to how the people would be likely to deal with the issues."

Above all, he harnessed and used political power to get things done. "He was not a politician as the term is now commonly applied and understood," McClure believed; "he knew nothing about the countless methods which are employed in the details of political effort; but no man knew better—indeed, I think no man knew as well as he did—how to summon and dispose of political ability to attain great political results; and this work he performed with unfailing wisdom and discretion in every contest for himself and for the country."

Now, McClure undoubtedly was right in saying that Lincoln possessed a remarkable ability for holding together antagonistic elements. Undoubtedly, too, he had a knack of appealing to fellow politicians and talking to them in their own language.

But it is a little hard to see the kind of mystic partnership between Lincoln and the people which McClure believed existed. Direct, popular appeal does not appear to have been one of the strong points of Lincoln the political master. Rather, his strengths seem to have been those of a politician's politician, a manager of the party machine, a wire puller—in short, such a "contriver" as he professed not to be. Especially he relied upon the spoils system, spending a large proportion of his waking hours, down to the very day of his death, in the disposal of government jobs. Instead of appealing to the public for support on specific issues—as Andrew Jackson or Franklin D. Roosevelt did—Lincoln avoided issues as much as possible. He had a gift of noncommittalism.

And the statement that Lincoln knew how to "attain great political results" raises a question as to the meaning and measure of success in politics. Presumably this consists in gaining power, as a means, and using it toward some public end. If so, real success requires more than the mere winning of elections or the mere holding of elective office. It requires also the achievement of a set of governmental aims.

Of course, Lincoln was elected and reelected to the Presidency, yet he received no such popular majorities as a number of others have done—Dwight D. Eisenhower, Franklin D. Roosevelt, and Warren G. Harding, to name a few. In 1860 Lincoln was a minority winner, with only about 40 per cent of the total popular vote. In 1864, though he got a seemingly comfortable majority, approximately 55 per cent, the election was closer than that figure indicates. A shift of 2 per cent, or a little more than 80,000 votes, in certain areas, would have resulted in his defeat.

As President, how well did he succeed in realizing a positive program of his own? If his aim was simply to save the Union, the answer would seem to be clear enough, for the war was won and the Union saved during his presidency. And the answer is enough to justify his high reputation for statesmanship.

He succeeded, then, in his great political objective. But to do this—to hold the party together, keep himself in power, and preserve the nation—he apparently had to sacrifice some of his lesser aims. At the start of the war he was, or at least he is supposed to have been, a conservative. Before the end of it he had many a fight with the Radicals of his party—with the "Jacobins," as they were called by his secretary John Hay, who was familiar with the history of the French Revolution. These revolutionaries of the American Civil War sought to break up the social and political structure of the South. Lincoln presumably did not. Yet it seems that he gave in again and again to the Radicals.

"Against Lincoln and his conservative program the Jacobins waged a winning battle," T. Harry Williams contends. "The wily Lincoln surrendered to the conquering Jacobins in every controversy before they could publicly inflict upon him a damaging reverse. Like the fair Lucretia threatened with ravishment, he averted his fate by instant compliance."

And yet, perhaps, this seeming opposition between Lincoln and the Radicals did not really exist, or was in actuality much less sharp than it appears. Perhaps at heart he was a Radical himself in some respects, as earnest a friend of freedom as any of them. Perhaps he was only more understanding, more patient, more astute. Perhaps he only waited for the ideal moment when he could do most effectively what he had intended all along to do—that is, to free the slaves.

chapter 9

THE FRIEND OF FREEDOM

His hand trembled as he held the gold pen, ready to sign. He hesitated. Before him lay the broad sheet of paper on which was written the proclamation, complete except for his signature.

"Now, therefore I, Abraham Lincoln . . . on this first day of January, in the year of our Lord one thousand eight hundred and sixty-three . . . do order and declare that all persons held as slaves . . . are, and henceforward shall be free. . . ."

Finally, with several men about him in his office witnessing the act, he signed, writing out his full name (rather than the usual *A. Lincoln*). For all the care he took, his signature was noticeably uneven and infirm.

This, he insisted, was due to no hesitation or uncertainty about the policy he was proclaming. For three hours he had been shaking hands with the visitors who trooped into the White House from the mud and slush of a dismal, overcast New Year's Day. His hand was tired, swollen, hard to control.

Though, as he said, *he* had no doubt about the policy he was confirming, others since have disagreed as to what that policy actually was. Supposedly, of course, it was emancipation. Supposedly, with the trembling movement of his pen, he prepared the way for universal freedom even if he did not strike the shackles from the millions of bondsmen all at once. But possibly he was doing the opposite of what he seemed to do. Possibly he had adopted the idea of an Emancipation Proclamation as a stratagem to delay rather than to hasten the freeing of the slaves.

2

Some of the admirers of Lincoln, viewing the Emancipation Proclamation as the grand climax of his career, have thought of him as at heart an abolitionist, one who from early manhood had been awaiting his chance to put an end to slavery. This notion can be made to seem plausible enough if only a part of the record is revealed.

There is, for instance, the story of his second flatboat voyage down the Mississippi. He was then twenty-two. In New Orleans (the story goes) he with his companions attended a slave auction at which a "vigorous and comely" mulatto girl was being offered for sale. She was treated like a mare, the prospective bidders inspecting her up and down, pinching and feeling, and then watching while she was made to trot back and forth. To Lincoln the spectacle was so shameful it aroused in him at once an "unconquerable hate" toward the whole institution of slavery. "If I ever get a chance to hit that thing," he swore as he walked away, "I'll hit it hard."

Lincoln perhaps took a stand for freedom as a member of the Illinois Legislature in 1837, when resolutions were introduced in response to the mob murder of Elijah Lovejoy, the antislavery newspaperman of Alton. These resolutions, instead of denouncing lynch law, condemned abolitionist societies and upheld slavery within the Southern states as "sacred" by virtue of the Federal Constitution. Lincoln refused to vote for the resolutions. Not only that. Together with a fellow member he drew up a protest against them, declaring that slavery was "founded on both injustice and bad policy."

Interesting also are his reflections on his experience of 1841, when with his friend Joshua Speed he was returning from a Kentucky visit. He made part of the trip by steamboat down the Ohio. "You may remember, as I well do," he wrote to Speed fourteen years later, in 1855, "that from Louisville to the mouth of the Ohio there were, on board, ten or a dozen slaves, shackled together with irons. That sight was a continual torment to me; and I see something like it every time I touch the Ohio, or any other slave-border." Speed, having resettled in Kentucky, had come to differ with Lincoln on the slavery question, and Lincoln now was defending his own point of view. "It is hardly fair for you to assume," he wrote, "that I have no interest in a thing which has, and continually exercises, the power of making me miserable."

As a member of Congress, in 1850, Lincoln drafted and introduced a bill for the abolition of slavery in the District of Columbia.

During the 1850s, in his arguments with Stephen A. Douglas, Lincoln spoke often and with eloquence against slavery. On one occasion, in 1854, he said he hated Douglas's attitude of indifference toward the spread of slavery to new areas. "I hate it because of the monstrous injustice of slavery itself," he declared. "I hate it because it deprives our republican example of its just influence in the world—enables the enemies of free institutions, with plausibility, to taunt us as hypocrites. . . ." On another occasion Lincoln made his oft-quoted remark that the nation could not long endure half slave and half free. No wonder many Southerners considered him "all broke out" with abolitionism at the time he was elected President.

After he was in the White House, Lincoln continued to express himself eloquently for freedom. In a published reply to Horace Greeley, who was demanding action against slavery, he said (1862) it was his "oft-expressed *personal* wish that all men every where could be free." He confided in a private letter (1864): "I am naturally anti-slavery. If slavery is not wrong, nothing is wrong. I can not remember when I did not so think, and feel." And in a talk to Indiana soldiers (1865) he remarked: "Whenever I hear anyone arguing for slavery I feel a strong impulse to see it tried on him personally."

On the basis of these and other items from the record, Lincoln appears to have been a long-confirmed advocate of freedom, if not an outright abolitionist. But when the whole of the evidence is considered, the conclusion to be drawn is not so clear.

It is not even clear whether in fact Lincoln ever underwent the New Orleans experience which was supposed to have made him an eternal foe of slavery. John Hanks told the anecdote to Herndon in 1865. Hanks had been one of Lincoln's fellow voyagers on the flatboat, but did not go all the way with the others to New Orleans. So he could not have seen with his own eyes what happened at the slave auction he later described. Herndon said he also heard the story from Lincoln himself. In the account of the journey he gave in his autobiography of 1860, however, Lincoln made no mention of slaves or the slave trade (though of course he intended the autobiography for campaign purposes and could not have been so indiscreet as to emphasize any abolitionist convictions). In the autobiography he also spoke of a previous trip to New Orleans. With regard to this trip, he said nothing about slaves but did refer to Negroes, recalling that he and his one companion "were attacked by seven Negroes with intent to kill and rob them" and were "hurt some in the melee, but succeeded in driving the Negroes from the boat."

As for his stand against the 1837 resolutions of the Illinois Legislature, it is enough to point out that he actually took a position against *both sides* of the controversy. Slavery was bad, he held, but he also contended that "the promulgation of abolition doctrines tends rather to increase than to abate its evils."

Regarding the shackled slaves on the Ohio river boat, he gave at the time, in 1841, an account very different from the one he gave fourteen years afterward to Joshua Speed. Writing to Speed's sister Mary (September 27, 1841) he described the scene on board the boat quite philosophically as exemplifying "the effect of *condition* upon human happiness." Here were a dozen slaves, "strung together like so many fish upon a trot-line," who were being taken from their old Kentucky homes to be sold down the river, who were being separated from families and friends and carried off where slavery was reputed to be at its harshest. Yet, as Lincoln saw them, "they were the most cheerful and apparently happy creatures on board." He concluded that God "renders the worst of human conditions tolerable, while He permits the best, to be nothing better than tolerable."

The point is not that Lincoln was falsifying his emotions when, in the much later account to Speed, he wrote of the sight of those slaves in chains as having been a "continual torment" to him. Certainly he had not forgotten the scene, and very likely he had come to view it in retrospect with heightened feeling. His attitude toward slaves and slavery might well have changed with the passing years—especially the years after 1850, when the issue of slavery extension engrossed national politics.

As late as 1847 his torment apparently was not troublesome enough to deter him from accepting a slaveholder as a law client and arguing against a slave's claim to freedom. Though Illinois presumably was a free state, its laws still provided for Negro servitude of a sort. Under the laws slave labor could be used, provided the slaves were not kept permanently in the state. Slaves worked the Coles County farm of Robert Matson, who brought his blacks from Kentucky every spring and took them back to Kentucky every fall. One of them, Jane Bryant, aroused the ire of Matson's housekeeper and mistress, who demanded that she be sold and sent to the Deep South. Jane fled, enlisted the aid of antislavery people, was taken from them, and, lacking the required certificate of freedom, was held in accordance with the Illinois laws. Matson, claiming her as his property, appealed to Lincoln for legal aid. Lincoln took the case and lost.

In Congress, despite his bill for abolition in the District of Columbia, he took a yes-and-no attitude toward slavery. His bill was carefully hedged about, so as to offend no slaveholder. It provided for gradual emancipation, with payment to owners, and it was not to go into effect unless approved by the "free white citizens" of the District, in a referendum. The bill did not please abolitionists. One of them, Wendell Phillips, called Lincoln "the slave hound of Illinois."

As for his remarks on slavery during the 1850s, it should be borne in mind that Lincoln always was opposing the spread of the institution into the territories. He was not advocating its destruction in the Southern states. When he said the nation could not long remain half slave and half free, but must eventually become all one or the other, he doubtless was thinking of the real danger that the country might become *all slave*—if slavery were allowed to spread. He resisted the aggressive proslavery forces not only because of his concern for the sufferings of the black man, but also because of his concern for the welfare of the white man. Again and again he indicated that the civil liberties of every American, white as well as black, were at stake. He insisted upon "keeping the territories free for the settlement of free laborers." He was a free-soil man.

"You enquire where I now stand," he wrote in his letter of 1854 to Joshua Speed. "That is a disputed point. I think I am a Whig; but others say there are no Whigs, and that I am an abolitionist." And then he stated the limits of his antislavery zeal as precisely as he could: "I now do no more than oppose the *extension* of slavery." That was where he stood in 1854, and there is no convincing evidence that he had moved beyond that position by 1860 or 1861.

In fact, in the most widely read of his pre-nomination speeches, the one at Cooper Union in New York on February 27, 1860, Lincoln said he agreed with Thomas Jefferson and other founding fathers that slavery should be merely contained not directly attacked. *"This is all Republicans ask—all Republicans desire—in relation to slavery,"* he emphasized, underlining the words. *"As those fathers marked it, so let it be again marked, as an evil not to be extended, but to be tolerated and protected only because of and so far as its actual presence among us makes that toleration and protection a necessity."* Lincoln further said that emancipation should be most gradual and should be accompanied by deportation of the freed slaves. "In the language of Mr. Jefferson, uttered many years ago, 'It is still in our power to direct the process of emancipation, and deportation, peaceably, and in such slow degrees, as that the evil will wear off insensibly; and their places be, *pari passu*, filled up by free white laborers. If, on the contrary, it is left to force itself on, human nature must shudder at the prospect held up.' "

3

As President, even if he personally had desired immediate emancipation, Lincoln had reasons of policy for going slow with regard to slavery. At the outset of the war the border slave states—Maryland, Delaware, Missouri, and above all Kentucky—hung in the balance. It seemed to Lincoln essential that these states be kept loyal to the Union, and it also seemed to him that a forthright antislavery program might incline them toward the Confederacy.

Whatever the reasons, Lincoln in the beginning was most reluctant to use his Presidential powers against slavery. During his first year and more in office he lagged well behind the majority of his party in the cause of freedom. If, as he said, General McClellan had "the slows" when it came to advancing against the Confederate army, he himself had the same affliction when it was a matter of attacking the institution which Alexander H. Stephens called the cornerstone of the Confederacy.

Lincoln held back while Congress and some of his generals went ahead. General John C. Frémont proclaimed freedom for the slaves of disloyal masters in Missouri, and General David Hunter did the same for those in Georgia, South Carolina, and Florida. Lincoln revoked the proclamations of Frémont and Hunter, much to the disgust of all antislavery people, who were growing fast in numbers and in earnestness throughout the North. In the summer of 1861 Congress passed a confiscation act which freed such slaves as the foe put to military use. The next summer Congress passed a second confiscation act, which declared "forever free" all slaves whose owners were in rebellion, whether or not the slaves were being used for military purposes. Lincoln did not veto these laws, but neither did he see that they faithfully were carried out. He considered vetoing the second one, because in his judgment it amounted to an unconstitutional bill of attainder. He did not sign it until it had been amended, and even then he expressed to Congress his dissatisfaction with it.

While hesitating to enforce these laws, Lincoln responded in his own way to the rising sentiment in favor of emancipation. He came forth with a characteristically Lincolnian solution to the slavery problem. His plan contained five elements. First, the states themselves must emancipate the slaves, for in his opinion slavery was a "domestic" institution, the concern of the states alone. Second, slaveowners must be paid for the chattels of which they were to be deprived. Third, the Federal government must share the financial burden by providing Federal bonds as grants-in-aid to the states. Fourth, the actual freeing of the slaves must not be hurried; the states must be given plenty of time, delaying final freedom until as late as 1900 if they wished. Fifth, the freed Negroes must be shipped out of the country and colonized abroad, but they must be persuaded to go willingly. State action, compensation, Federal aid, gradual emancipation, and voluntary colonization—these were the indispensable features of the Lincoln plan.

To carry out this plan he had to gain the approval of Congress, the border slave states, and the leaders of the Negro race. Congress responded affirmatively but without enthusiasm, indicating its willingness to vote the necessary funds. None of the border politicians were won over to the scheme, however, and very few Negroes could be persuaded to leave their native land, the United States.

Three times in the spring of 1862 Lincoln appealed to the border-state congressmen. He told them that, if their states would only act, the war soon would be over, for the Confederacy lived upon the hope of winning the border states, and, once these had declared for freedom, that hope would be gone. He warned the congressmen that, if their states refused to act, slavery in time would disappear anyhow. It would be destroyed "by mere friction and abrasion—by the mere incidents of war." The border states, he eloquently said, had before them the grand opportunity of saving the Union. But he made no headway whatsoever; again and again they turned the opportunity down.

Meanwhile he did not let up in his efforts to talk the free Negroes into leaving the country. Some of their own leaders advocated starting life anew in the Negro republic of Liberia or Haiti. Lincoln preferred Central America as their new home. In his eagerness he was taken in by a group of land speculators who offered to sell the Chiriqui territory on the Isthmus of Panama. They pictured Chiriqui as a land rich in coal, among other things, but eventually became so effusive in their praises of this tropical paradise it became clear that their title was dubious and the resources nonexistent.

He was nevertheless loath to give up the colonization idea itself. He invited to the White House a group of five prominent Negroes—the first of their race a President ever so honored—and he honored them further by saying frankly that there was no place for them and their people in the United States. Though they might be treated better in the North than in the South, they would suffer discrimination everywhere so long as they remained in this country. "The ban," he said, "is still upon you." From Negroes who heard of this interview, the response was most unfavorable. One wrote to Lincoln: "Pray tell us is our right to a home in this country less than your own?"

If, in the summer of 1862, Lincoln had had his way, the later history of this country would have been radically changed. For instance, if the states had adopted his plan, there would probably be few Negroes left in the country, North or South. By 1900 the slaves of the border states would have been set free and sent abroad. The slaves of the Confederate states, if these states too had chosen to adopt the Lincoln plan, would have enjoyed the same fortune or suffered the same fate.

If, on the other hand, the war had come to an early end, as Lincoln hoped, the slaves of the Confederate states could have been left in bondage indefinitely, or at least until they were freed by some hand other than his. Even in the border states, after emancipation, slavery might have been reestablished by action of the states. What these states had done, they could undo, according to Lincoln's conception of State rights. Indeed, in order to discourage this contingency, he drafted an emancipation bill containing the proviso that, if any state should abolish and then reintroduce the institution, it would have to return to the Federal government the Federal funds it had received as a grant-in-aid!

4

President Lincoln did not behave like a great emancipator during the first year-and-a-half of his term of office. The question is, did he change his mind and his policy after that? More particularly, did he intend—with the preliminary proclamation of September 21, 1862, and the final one of January 1, 1863—to free the slaves?

According to most accounts, he did. Despite his campaign

pledges and the constraints of the Constitution, argue supporters of this position, he decided that he must strike at slavery for reasons of military necessity. He came to this conclusion, and drafted a fitting proclamation, in July of 1862. When he read this draft to his Cabinet, Seward advised him to withhold the announcement till the Union armies had won a victory on the battlefield. Otherwise, Seward cautioned, the proclamation might sound like a confession of military failure, like "the last *shriek* on our retreat." So Lincoln stalled, awaiting the hoped-for victory. When a delegation of Chicago churchmen appealed to him, he asked them whether a proclamation would do any good, whether it would not be as futile as the Pope's legendary bull against the comet. Before they left, he assured them that he had not decided against a proclamation, but held the matter under advisement. When Horace Greeley in the *New York Tribune* called upon him to make freedom a reality, he patiently replied (August 22, 1862): "My paramount object in this struggle *is* to save the Union, and is *not* either to save or to destroy slavery. If I could save the Union without freeing *any* slave I would do it, and if I could save it by freeing *all* the slaves I would do it; and if I could do it by freeing some and leaving others alone I would also do that." At last McClellan's checking of Lee at Antietam gave Lincoln at least a substitute for victory, and a few days later he accordingly issued the document he long since had decided upon.

This is a familiar story, and there is a certain amount of evidence to give it historical substance. There is, for example, the record Welles made of a conversation Lincoln had with him and Seward on Sunday, July 13, while on a carriage ride to a funeral. "It was on this occasion and on this ride that he first mentioned to Mr. Seward and myself the subject of emancipating the slaves by proclamation in case the Rebels did not cease to persist in their war on the Government and the Union, of which he saw no evidence," Welles wrote afterward. "He dwelt earnestly on the gravity, importance, and delicacy of the movement, said he had given it much thought and had about come to the conclusion that it was a military necessity absolutely essential for the salvation of the Union, that we must free the slaves or be ourselves subdued, etc., etc." Welles added this comment: "It was a new departure for the President, for until this time, in all our previous interviews, whenever the question of emancipation or the mitigation of slavery had been in any way alluded to, he had been prompt and emphatic in denouncing any interference by the General Government with the subject."

Welles may have remembered accurately what the President said on that Sunday, though the record of the conversation is not a regular diary entry but a reminiscence that the diarist put down after the lapse of considerable time. And Lincoln, if Welles summarized his sentiments accurately, may have meant what he said. Yet in the ensuing weeks others who saw Lincoln reported him as saying things that seemed to belie his determination to proclaim freedom for the slaves. When Greeley visited the White House to repeat the plea of his *Tribune* editorial, Lincoln protested that he dared not antagonize Kentuckians and impel them to desert to the rebel side. He expressed this same concern to others, including the Chicago religious group. If he really had made his decision and only was waiting for the auspicious moment to proclaim it, he might have put off his tormenters by frankly telling them so. As it was, he left even some of his official advisers to wonder whether he ever would issue the proclamation he had read to the cabinet.

These inconsistencies of his have led to the suspicion that, till after the battle of Antietam, he made no irrevocable commitment, even to himself. Here and there he dropped hints that he might issue the proclamation—and then again might not. Apparently his purpose was to prepare his hearers for the possibility that he might call the whole thing off. He was waiting for a decisive victory, but if that kind of victory had come, he might have forgotten about the proclamation. Some historians claim that he dusted it off and gave it to the world only when he learned the true proportions of Antietam. McClellan, though he turned Lee back, had let him get away. If McClellan had administered a crushing defeat, the proclamation might have stayed in its pigeonhole.

This theory depends on the supposition that Lincoln at the time was not so much concerned about military necessity as about political necessity. He had to contend with a strong bloc of Republicans in Congress, headed by Thaddeus Stevens in the House and Charles Sumner and Henry Wilson in the Senate, backed by a majority of the party, who had become Radicals on the slave question. They were demanding that the President carry out the laws, the confiscation acts, the act for the enrolment of Negro troops. They held the firm conviction that, to win the war, the government must free the slaves and use them against their former masters. As their strongest argument, the Radicals cited the succession of Union defeats on the Virginia front. The way the war was being fought, it was not being won, and it therefore must be fought another way. There was even the possibility that they might try to stop the flow of money and supplies if Lincoln did not give in. Only a conclusive victory, only a dramatic refutation of the Radical argument, would restore his freedom of action. He prayed for such a victory, and then came the disappointing news of Antietam.

To pursue this argument to its logical conclusion, Lincoln then pulled out the proclamation as his trump. In issuing it he did not really yield to the Radicals. Rather, he outfoxed them. At first they hailed the document as a triumph for them and their cause, but soon they were disillusioned, since the proclamation had as its purpose and effect the checking of the Radical program. Having announced in September that he would make a final proclamation the first of the following year, Lincoln had an excuse for disregarding the laws about confiscation and Negro troops throughout the intervening months. He also had a policy with which to frustrate Stevens's drive for legislation to make soldiers and freemen out of slaves from the border states. During the months of delay he hoped at last to gain approval for his own plan, the familiar plan of gradual emancipation by the states themselves, with Federal funds to pay to slaveowners and to rid the country of the freed slaves.

There is testimony, from some of the men who knew Lincoln, to give credence to this view. There is, for instance, the testimony of Edward Stanly, a proslavery, State-rights, Unionist North Carolinian whom Lincoln had appointed as military governor of the occupied North Carolina coast. Stanly had taken the job with the understanding that Lincoln would not interfere with slavery in the states. Once the proclamation had been issued, Stanly went to Washington intending to resign. After several talks with Lincoln, however, Stanly was satisfied. He returned to his job, but first he called at the office of James C. Welling, editor of the *National Intelligencer*. Welling wrote in his diary: "Mr. Stanly said that the President had stated to him that the proclamation had become a civil necessity to prevent the Radicals from openly embarrassing the government in the conduct of the war."

Quite apart from testimony such as this, a fairly strong inference of Lincoln's delaying tactics can be drawn from the text of the proclamation. The preliminary announcement said that after January 1, 1863, the slaves in states then still in rebellion would be considered free. The final proclamation excluded from the area of freedom not only the loyal border states but all the Confederate states and parts of states that the Union forces had occupied. As cynics pointed out at the time, Lincoln was leaving the slaves untouched in places where he had the ability to free them, and he was offering liberty only to those he had no power to reach. Congress already had enabled him to do more than this. The second confiscation act provided for the liberation of all slaves belonging to disloyal masters, regardless of the masters' residence. Instead of issuing the kind of proclamation that he did, Lincoln needed only to proclaim that he was enforcing the second confiscation act, and then he could have proceeded to order the seizure of enemy-owned slaves in every place where the Union armies got control—if his object truly had been to weaken the enemy by making inroads into his Negro manpower.

Lincoln himself gave indisputable proof that, after the preliminary proclamation, he remained as passionately devoted as ever to his own gradual-emancipation scheme. In his message to Congress of December 1, 1862, just one month before the final proclamation, he had little to say about that forthcoming pronouncement and much to say about his favored plan. He proposed a constitutional amendment to put the plan into effect. On this subject he reached one of the peaks of his eloquence. "Fellow-citizens, *we* cannot escape history," he said. "We of this Congress and this administration, will be remembered in spite of ourselves. The fiery trial through which we pass, will light us down, in honor or dishonor, to the latest generation." These words are justly famous. What is often forgotten is the fact that they were conceived as part of a plea for deporting American-born Negroes from America. Lincoln in this message actually used the word *deportation,* as if he had in the back of his mind the thought of resorting, if necessary, to the compulsion which that word implies.

No inspired phrases were to be found in the paper that Lincoln signed with the gold pen, in the quavering hand, on January 1, 1863. In itself this proclamation was a dull and prosaic document—no ringing call to freedom. The proclamation had some effect in attracting slaves out of rebeldom and into the Union lines, where they were set free, but the existing laws of Congress provided for that much and more. After two years, when the war was ending, Lincoln estimated that some 200,000 slaves had gained their liberty under his edict. That was only about one in twenty of the total number of slaves, which amounted to nearly four million. And even that minority had no sure hold on freedom. Lincoln himself doubted the constitutionality of his step, except as a temporary war measure. After the war the freedmen would have risked reenslavement, had nothing else been done to confirm their liberty.

All this does not necessarily disprove the commonly accepted story of what Lincoln did or tried to do in signing his famous proclamation. Maybe he meant to hasten freedom, maybe to delay it. Nobody knows.

5

Actual freedom for the Negroes—or at least the end of chattel slavery—came in consequence of the Thirteenth Amendment. President Lincoln played a part in bringing about this constitutional change, yet he was slow to take an out-and-out antislavery stand, and indeed he gave some indications that his conversion never was complete.

He did not claim to have originated the idea of such an amendment, though the abolitionists did. At Cleveland in May 1864 a group of these extreme Republicans nominated John C. Frémont for the Presidency and adopted a platform with a Thirteenth Amendment as the key plank.

When the regular Republicans met in convention the following month, Lincoln was aware of the need for winning the dissidents back to the party fold. He called to the White House the chairman of the Republican National Committee, Senator E. D. Morgan, and gave him instructions for his speech opening the convention. "Senator Morgan," he is reported to have said, "I want you to mention in your speech when you call the convention to order, as its keynote, and to put into the platform as the keystone, the amendment of the Constitution abolishing and prohibiting slavery forever." Senator Morgan did as the President wished. That platform included a plank stating that slavery was the cause of the rebellion, that the President's proclamations had aimed "a death blow at this gigantic evil," and that a constitutional amendment was necessary to "terminate and forever prohibit" it. Undoubtedly the delegates would have adopted such a plank whether or not Lincoln, through Senator Morgan, had urged it.

When Lincoln was reelected on this platform, and the Republican majority in Congress was increased, he was justified in feeling, as he apparently did, that he had a mandate from the people for the Thirteenth Amendment. The newly chosen Congress, with its overwhelming Republican majority, would not meet until after the Lame Duck Session of the old Congress during the winter of 1864–1865. But Lincoln did not wait. Using all his resources of patronage and persuasion on certain of the Democrats, he managed to get the necessary two-thirds vote before the session's end. He rejoiced as the amendment went out to the states for ratification, and he rejoiced again and again as his own Illinois led off and other states followed one by one in acting favorably upon it. He did not live to rejoice in its ultimate adoption.

Yet, for all he did to see that freedom finally was written into the fundamental law, Lincoln to the last seemed to have a lingering preference for another kind of amendment, another kind of plan. He still clung to his old ideas of postponing final emancipation, compensating slaveholders, and colonizing freedmen. Or so it would appear. As late as March of 1865, if the somewhat dubious Ben Butler is to be believed, Lincoln summoned him to the White House to discuss with him the feasibility of removing the colored population of the United States.

6

Lincoln is a paradoxical hero. His name has been lighted down from generation to generation as a synonym for liberty and equality. His name also has been made to symbolize the opposite doctrine of white supremacy and black oppression.

Lincoln the friend of freedom is well and widely known. For most liberals, he occupies a place beside that of Thomas Jefferson. For many Negroes, he long has held a lone position as a kind of folk god.

His exaltation dates back to January 1, 1863, when throughout the North and the conquered areas of the South the colored people held proclamation meetings to celebrate his deed in their behalf. At a Washington meeting, which began on New Year's Eve, a pastor told each member of his flock to "get down on *both knees* to thank Almighty God for his freedom and President Lincoln too." To people such as these the proclamation, whatever its inward meaning, was the outward sign of an answer to their prayers.

Most of the abolitionists joined in honoring Lincoln at the time of his emancipation edict, but some of them qualified their praise, still doubting his sincerity. At last, when he had won Congressional approval for the Thirteenth Amendment, almost all the lingering doubts were dispelled and almost all the doubters satisfied. Even William Lloyd Garrison no longer could contain himself. To a Boston meeting of celebrators Garrison said: "And to whom is the country more immediately indebted for this vital and saving amendment of the Constitution than, perhaps, to any other man? I believe I may confidently answer—to the humble rail splitter of Illinois—to the Presidential chainbreaker for millions of the oppressed—to Abraham Lincoln!"

Less well known than Lincoln the slaves' chainbreaker is Lincoln the hero of Negro-baiters and white supremacists. Yet he has been that kind of image also. Few Negroes or friends of the Negro ever admired him more or praised him oftener than did a certain Mississippi advocate of white supremacy, James K. Vardaman.

In the early 1900s this long-haired, dramatic Great White Chief of Mississippi stood out as the most rabid racialist in the most racist-dominated Southern state. When Theodore Roosevelt dined with the Negro educator Booker T. Washington in the White House, Vardaman sneered at the President as a "wild broncho buster and coon-flavored miscegenationist." In his campaign for the governorship Vardaman said that if he were in office, he would do what he could to protect a captured Negro "fiend" from a lynching mob. "But if I were a private citizen I would head the mob to string the brute up, and I haven't much respect for a white man who wouldn't." As governor, he opposed what he called "this policy of spoiling young Negroes by educating them." In the United States

Senate during the first World War, he took every opportunity to expound his belief in a white man's country. Do not draft Negroes into the Army, he advised his fellow senators, for it is dangerous to give them a sense of citizenship and a training in the use of guns. Repeal the Fifteenth Amendment so that Negroes cannot even pretend to have the right to vote. Enforce segregation and do not let the races mix, for the Negro is by nature morally inferior and must never be allowed to corrupt the pure blood of the heaven-favored white. Such were the aims and the convictions to which Vardaman devoted his real eloquence.

This Mississippian once made a pilgrimage to his hero's home town, to Springfield, Illinois. The year was 1909, the centennial of Lincoln's birth. The previous year had been a disgraceful one for Springfield. Municipal leaders were looking ahead to anniversary celebrations when, on a summer night, thousands of the townspeople suddenly went wild with hate. They set out to lynch a Negro who (though innocent) was being held on the charge of raping a white woman, and when the sheriff frustrated them by spiriting the man away, they turned their vengeance upon the whole colored community. It took four thousand state troopers all of a week to quiet the city and end the so-called "race riot." (This incident, by the way, and not some crisis in the South, gave rise to the National Association for the Advancement of Colored People.) When Vardaman visited Springfield the feeling among local Negrophobes still ran high, and a huge crowd came out to applaud his lecture on the inherent virtue of the white race.

Vardaman never tired of praising "the immortal Lincoln," never tired of quoting "the wise words of this wondrous man." He insisted that he and Lincoln saw eye to eye. "I have made a very careful study of Mr. Lincoln's ideas on this question," he declared in a Senate speech, "and I have said often, and I repeat here, that my views and his on the race question are substantially identical." Next to Thomas Jefferson, he thought, Lincoln understood the Negro problem better than anyone else of former days. To prove his point, Vardaman cited Lincoln's advocacy of Negro colonization. He explained the Lincoln policy thus:

"Up to the very time of Mr. Lincoln's death he told the Negroes who came to see him here in Washington, 'You will not be permitted to share in the government of this country, and I am not prepared to say that you ought to be, if I had the power to give you that right.'

"He said further: 'The shackles of slavery will be stricken from your arms. You, the educated and more fortunate members of your race, take the others and go to some country'—his idea was the same that Jefferson's was—'and there work out your own salvation.' I do not pretend to quote Mr. Lincoln literally. The great desire of his patriotic heart was that the friction might be avoided by deportation."

The words of Lincoln that Vardaman repeated oftenest, the words he knew almost by heart, came from the debate with Douglas at Charleston, Illinois, on September 18, 1858. These words formed for Vardaman a sort of golden text. Here they are, exactly as Lincoln uttered them:

"I will say then that I am not, nor ever have been in favor of bringing about in any way the social and political equality of the white and black races, [applause]—that I am not nor ever have been in favor of making voters or jurors of Negroes, nor of qualifying them to hold office, nor to intermarry with white people; and I will say in addition to this that there is a physical difference between the white and black races which I believe will forever forbid the two races living together on terms of social and political equality. And inasmuch as they cannot so live, while they do remain together there must be the position of superior and inferior, and I as much as any other man am in favor of having the superior position assigned to the white race."

7

Yet, despite these contradictions, Lincoln does deserve his reputation as emancipator. True, his claim to the honor is supported very uncertainly, if at all, by the proclamation itself.

The honor has a better basis in the support he gave to the Thirteenth Amendment. It is well founded also in his greatness as the war leader, who carried the nation safely through the four-year struggle that brought freedom in its train. But the best reason for his reputation is, perhaps, to be discovered in something else. Consider the example he set his fellow Americans by treating all men as human beings, regardless of the pigment of their skin.

The real and final emancipation of the Negro may depend more upon attitudes than upon laws. The laws, the constitutional amendments, are important, even indispensable. But, as the abolitionist Henry Wilson observed, many of those who voted for the Thirteenth Amendment and other antislavery measures did so without conversion or conviction. Many acted from a desire to hurt the slaveholder rather than to help the slave. Within their hearts still lurked the "foul spirit of caste," the spirit of race prejudice. Until this prejudice was overcome, the Negroes, though no longer the slaves of individual masters, would continue to be in a sense the slaves of the community as a whole.

Now, Lincoln himself was one of those who veered to an actively antislavery line for reasons of wartime expediency. He did not pretend to do otherwise. And he was well aware of race prejudice as an existing fact in the United States. Hence his pathetic eagerness to find new homes for freedmen in foreign lands. Yet he had the capacity to rise above prejudice, and he grandly rose above it. Again and again, during the last two years of his life, he made the White House a scene of practical demonstrations of respect for human worth and dignity. He proved that whites and Negroes, without the master-servant tie, could get along together happily in his own official home, no matter what the antagonisms that might trouble the nation at large. A kindly, unself-conscious host, he greeted Negro visitors as no President had done before.

The distinguished former slave Frederick Douglass called upon Lincoln several times at his summer cottage at the

Soldiers' Home. Douglass made at least three visits to the White House. On the final occasion, when he tried to enter as an invited guest at the inaugural reception in 1865, policemen manhandled him and forced him out. Making his way in again, he managed to catch Lincoln's eye. "Here comes my friend Douglass," the President exclaimed, and, leaving the circle of guests he had been conversing with, he took Douglass by the hand and began to chat with him. Years later Douglass wrote: "In all my interviews with Mr. Lincoln I was impressed with his entire freedom from popular prejudice against the colored race. He was the first great man that I talked with in the United States freely, who in no single instance reminded me of the difference between himself and myself, of the difference of color, and I thought that all the more remarkable because he came from a state where there were black laws."

There were black laws in Illinois indeed—laws that denied the Negro the vote and deprived him of other rights. Illinois in those days was a Jim Crow state. That was where Lincoln had spent most of the years of his manhood, among people who had migrated from slave country farther south, as he himself had done. Naturally he had shared some of the Negrophobic feeling of his neighbors in Kentucky, in southern Indiana, in central Illinois. That was where, in geography and in sentiment, he came from.

But he did not stay there. The most remarkable thing about him was his tremendous power of growth. He grew in sympathy, in the breadth of his humaneness, as he grew in other aspects of the mind and spirit. In more ways than one he succeeded in breaking through the narrow bounds of his early environment.

This helps to explain and to reconcile those conflicting images of Lincoln—on the one hand, the racist; on the other, the champion of the common man, black as well as white. The one view reflects the position he started from, the other the position he was moving toward. There is confusion regarding particular phases of his Presidential career because nobody knows for sure just what point he had reached at any given moment. But there should be little question as to which way he was going.

To see Lincoln in this light is to make him more than ever relevant, more than ever inspiring, for us in the stormy present, in the fiery trial through which we too must pass. Lincoln, as a symbol of man's ability to outgrow his prejudices, still serves the cause of human freedom. He will go on serving so long as boundaries of color hem in and hinder any man, any woman, any child.

chapter 10

THE PEACE-MAKER

On Capitol Hill, cannon boomed that January afternoon. The House of Representatives adjourned for the day, and Republican congressmen celebrated like boys let out of school. With several of his and Lincoln's friends, Representative Isaac N. Arnold of Illinois hurried the mile down Pennsylvania Avenue to the Executive Mansion, to tell the President. The Thirteenth Amendment, abolishing slavery, had been approved and was going out to the states for ratification. When Lincoln heard the news, Arnold reported, it "filled his heart with joy."

During this, the fourth January of the war, Lincoln also had other news to cheer him. At last the Confederacy was tottering. Some of its most prominent men were reported to be anxious for peace. Jefferson Davis himself had appointed peace commissioners, and these men now were coming through the Union lines, to confer either with Lincoln or with anyone he might send to talk with them. Lincoln had little reason to expect these emissaries could or would bind the Confederacy to his terms. Yet his position was strong and theirs weak. Their mission in itself was a sign of defeat, a sign that the end of the rebellion could not be very far away.

On the same day that the Thirteenth Amendment passed Congress, Lincoln had occasion to write out his peace terms once again. He had stated them often before, but never twice in the same form.

At the start his war aims had been simple enough. They were contained in the one word—*union.* The war would end as soon as the Union could be restored. And the Union would be restored as soon as the war ended.

Such was also the prevailing mood of Congress and the Northern people, in the beginning. On the very day after the July 1861 Bull Run defeat, which indicated that the war would be both long and hard, Congress resolved that the struggle was to be carried on for nothing but the restoration of the Union.

But Congress soon moved beyond that stand. With the first and second confiscation acts, opening the way to freedom for the enemy's slaves, Congress hinted strongly that the nation, once reunited, would not be quite the same as it had been before. Meanwhile, in Congress and the country, there rose a cry for the President to enforce the confiscation acts and avow emancipation as frankly and officially a war aim.

But Lincoln was slow to change, if indeed he ever changed his own main objectives. Had the war ended after one year of fighting, there is little question what his peace terms would have been. He showed his hand in his dealings with Louisiana, a state already conquered by the summer of 1862. The people of Louisiana, he then said, had only to set up a government acknowledging Federal authority and conforming to the Federal Constitution. While doing this, they could have the protection of the United States Army. "The army will be withdrawn so soon as such state government can dispense with its presence; and the people of the state can then upon the old constitutional terms, govern themselves to their own liking. This is very simple and easy." Simple and easy it would have been indeed, if the Louisianans had acted on the President's advice—and if Congress had been willing to go along with his policy.

He appeared to change, to enlarge, his war aims when he issued his famous Emancipation Proclamation. Yet it is doubtful whether he actually did change, whether he made freedom for *all* slaves an indispensable condition of peace.

True, when he announced his "ten per cent plan" of reconstruction, in December 1863, he added to the requirements for setting up new states in Louisiana and certain other conquered areas (in Tennessee and Arkansas, for instance). Now the task for the Louisianans was not to be so simple and easy as it would have been a year and a half earlier. Now, when ten per cent of the voting population had taken an oath of future loyalty to the United States, they could start the state-making process. Before they were done, they would have to abolish slavery. (Of course what was done by state action could be undone by state action: once readmitted to the Union, Tennessee, Louisiana, and Arkansas could have reestablished slavery if nothing were done to prevent them.)

Mere abolition was not enough to suit the Radicals in Congress. They opposed the prompt readmission of seceded states on any terms. In the Wade-Davis Bill they required that a majority of the voting population swear to *past* loyalty before a state could be remade and readmitted. Such a majority (of white men) would have been hard to find in any Southern state. Unwilling to sign this obstructionist measure, Lincoln pocket-vetoed it (July 1864), though he announced that any state wishing to do so could try the Congressional plan. He intimated that reconstruction procedures might properly differ according to variations of time and place.

As will appear, he probably would not have insisted upon

emancipation as an absolutely necessary step in *all* the rebel states, if peace without complete emancipation could have been had in the summer or fall of 1864.

At that time, peace talk was much in the news. The Confederacy was pressing a peace offensive, to take advantage of the growing war-weariness in the North. Horace Greeley and other well-meaning citizens caught at the Confederate peace offers, irregular and often insincere though these were. The effect was to put Lincoln on the spot. Unless he accepted the offers, which were illusory, he would seem to stand in the way of what everybody North and South desired—peace. To deal with this dilemma he addressed a note (July 18, 1864) "To Whom it may concern:

"Any proposition which embraces the restoration of peace, the integrity of the whole Union, and the abandonment of slavery, and which comes by and with an authority that can control the armies now at war against the United States, will be received and considered by the Executive government of the United States, and will be met by liberal terms on other substantial and collateral points. . . ."

Peace, union, *and the abandonment of slavery*. No Confederate agent was authorized to accept or even to consider more than the first of these three terms. And many Northerners were unwilling to go on fighting for the third one, abolition. Conservatives pulled back while the Radicals pushed ahead on the slavery issue. Some of the conservatives protested to Lincoln against his implication that the North must continue the war to free the slaves, even after reunion was won.

In reply, Lincoln took back the offending part of what he had said in his message "To Whom it may concern." Or, at least, he explained it away. "To me it seems plain," he wrote, "that saying reunion and abandonment of slavery would be considered, if offered, is not saying that nothing *else* or *less* would be considered, if offered." Rather, he still held the position he had taken in his Greeley letter two years earlier: his purpose was to save the Union, and he would save it without freeing any of the slaves if he could. But he could not, he said. To bring the colored people over from the rebel to the Union side, he had had to tempt them with the promise of freedom. "And the promise, being made, must be kept." That is, it must be kept in dealing with those Negroes who actually had come over to the Union side—with those former slaves *already freed* under the emancipation policy. Some 150,000 of them were serving the United States as soldiers, seamen, or laborers. Those thousands of people must not be reenslaved, Lincoln insisted. But there were more than three million others who still lived in bondage, and he was not necessarily demanding that the war go on until these millions also were free. "If Jefferson Davis wishes, for himself, or for the benefit of his friends at the North, to know what I would do if he were to offer peace and reunion, saying nothing about slavery, let him try me," Lincoln wrote. Davis did not try him.

As the peace agitation reached a climax, the presidential contest of 1864 was getting under way. The Democratic platform called for an armistice, a peace convention, and the restoration of the Union as it had been—without the abolition of slavery. The Republican platform endorsed the pending antislavery amendment to the Constitution and gave no sanction to a truce without reunion first. Republicans accused the Democrats of favoring peace at any price, even at the price of disunion. Democrats accused the Republicans of opposing peace until abolition could also be gained.

In fact, however, the issues were not so clearly and broadly drawn between Candidate Lincoln and Candidate McClellan. A War Democrat, McClellan stood for fighting on till the rebellion was crushed, while leaving slavery alone. Even the Peace Democrats—the "Copperheads"—did not favor peace without reunion: they assumed that reunion would be the consequence of negotiations during an armistice. On the other hand, while the Radical Republicans were unequivocal on both union and freedom, Lincoln himself carefully qualified his views on slavery. In his correspondence and conversations (as in 1860, he made no campaign speeches) he reiterated his opposition to *re*enslaving those Negroes who were *already free.* He argued that this policy made him the true Union candidate and the only one. "The party who could elect a President on a war & slavery restoration platform," he explained, "would, of necessity, lose the colored force; and that force being lost, would be as powerless to save the Union as any other impossible thing." Emancipation, so far as it already had gone, must not be reversed, though it need not go any farther, he was saying. Only to this degree did he commit himself as more devoted to abolition than McClellan.

After his reelection, in his annual message of December 6, 1864, Lincoln still refrained from saying the rebels must agree to complete emancipation before he would end the war. He did say he took back nothing he previously had said regarding slavery. "I repeat the declaration made a year ago, that 'while I remain in my present position I shall not attempt to retract or modify the Emancipation Proclamation, nor shall I return to slavery any person who is free by the terms of that proclamation, or by any of the acts of Congress.' "

And he added: "In stating a single condition of peace, I mean simply to say that the war will cease on the part of the government, whenever it shall have ceased on the part of those who began it."

There Lincoln stood at the end of 1864. The next month (January 31, 1865) the House of Representatives passed the resolution for a Thirteenth Amendment, which the Senate earlier had approved. And Lincoln wrote out instructions for his Secretary of State to confer informally with the Confederate commissioners.

"You will make known to them that three things are indispensable," the President directed. These three things, his minimum terms, usually have been summarized as union, emancipation, and a final end to hostilities (with no armistice). Yet, as before, Lincoln seemingly did not insist upon complete emancipation. He put his second point thus: "No receding, by the Executive of the United States, on the Slavery question, from the position assumed thereon, in the late Annual Message to Congress, and in preceding documents." As before, what he apparently meant by "no receding" was no return to slavery for those already emancipated in fact.

During the next ten weeks, the last weeks of the war and of his life, how far was Lincoln willing to go toward making a quick and easy peace? Was he willing to leave the great majority of slaves in bondage? Was he willing to recognize certain of the rebel state governments as lawful authorities in their respective states?

2

The breeze blew cold and the water was a little rough on the morning of February 3, 1865, as Lincoln waited on the *River Queen,* which was anchored off Fortress Monroe, in Hampton Roads. He had decided to join Seward in talking with the Confederate peace men. A rowboat was bringing these men to the Presidential steamer.

Whatever its prospects for producing a reunion of the country, the meeting ahead would be, for Lincoln, a welcome personal reunion. Alexander H. Stephens, Vice-president of the Confederacy, headed the rebel commissioners, and Stephens once had been a close friend. Lincoln had deeply admired the sickly, shriveled, brilliant Georgian when the two were Whig colleagues in Congress, working together to make Zach Taylor President.

The Confederates were already aboard and in the *River Queen's* saloon when Lincoln entered it. Stephens was taking off his gray wool overcoat, a long, coarse-woven, bulky thing of Southern wartime manufacture. He unwound several scarves he wore to help protect himself against the February wind. Lincoln said later, in gentle amusement, that he had never seen such a small nubbin come out of such a big shuck.

With Stephens were the Alabaman John A. Campbell and the Virginian R. M. T. Hunter. Though assistant secretary of war in the Richmond government, Campbell was suspect among many of his fellow Southerners. They were not sure his heart was in the cause. They were slow to forgive him for what seemed to them an ambiguous role in 1861, when as a justice of the United States Supreme Court he had acted as go-between for Seward in promising Jefferson Davis's agents that Fort Sumter was to be given up. Hunter, an active man for all his fat, was president pro tem of the Confederate Senate. All three were factional foes of Davis and far more ready to consider peace than he was.

Lincoln and Seward shook hands with them, and a four-hour conversation began, during which a servant now and then brought in refreshments. Stephens and Lincoln did most of the talking. At first they reminisced of the old days. Soon Stephens got around to the subject that had brought them together again.

What was said cannot be known for sure. No minutes were kept and no records made, at the time. Afterward Lincoln and Seward gave only sparse, noncommittal reports. All three of the Confederates left more extensive accounts, but only Stephens put down his recollections in much detail. We have to take the word of Stephens and his colleagues for most of our knowledge of the Hampton Roads conference. We have to take their word with such reservations and doubts as may seem appropriate in the case of testimony recorded after the event, by interested participants.

According to Stephens's story, Lincoln promptly made plain that he could consider no armistice and no treaty or agreement of any sort, with the Confederacy or with its separate states, until the question of reunion first had been disposed of. Any formal arrangement would amount to at least a quasi recognition of Confederate independence, he said, and he could never consent to that. But he did not rule out the possibility of negotiations with the separate states once they had ceased hostilities and agreed to rejoin the Union. Stephens and his colleagues were not empowered to discuss peace on any basis ther than independence for the Confederacy. Yet the conversation went on.

Campbell asked the hypothetical question how the Union was to be restored—supposing the Confederate States were willing to accept reunion. Lincoln said they should disband their armies and allow the Federal government to resume its functions in the South. Seward quoted from the President's December message; "... the war will cease on the part of the government, whenever it shall have ceased on the part of those who began it." But, Campbell persisted, there were difficult matters that would have to be settled—such matters as the property seized under the confiscation acts. Seward explained that these things would be left to Congress and the courts to decide. He was sure the policy would be liberal. Confiscated property would be returned or paid for "after the excitement of the times had passed off."

Stephens asked about the Emancipation Proclamation. What effect would it have on the slaves? "Would it be held to emancipate the whole, or only those who had, at the time the war ended, become actually free under it?" Lincoln replied that this was a judicial question. "His own opinion was, that as the Proclamation was a *war measure,* and would have effect only from its being an exercise of the war power, as soon as the war ceased, it would be inoperative for the future. It would be held to apply only to such slaves as had come under its operation while it was in active exercise."

Seward broke the news that, only a few days before, Congress at last had passed the resolution for a Thirteenth Amendment to abolish slavery throughout the United States. He said this too was a war measure. If the war should end very soon, the amendment probably would not be ratified by the requisite number of states. In saying this, Seward seemed pointedly to hint that the Southern states themselves, if they would quit the war and rejoin the Union, could defeat the amendment and extend the life of slavery. Lincoln said nothing to remove the impression that Seward left.

After a long pause, however, Lincoln spoke up: "Stephens . . if I were in your place, I would go home and get the Governor of the State [Georgia] to call the Legislature together, and get them to recall all the State troops from the war; elect Senators and Members to Congress, and ratify this Constitutional Amendment *prospectively,* so as to take effect—say in five years." Slavery was doomed, he said. "It cannot last long in any event and the best course, it seems to me, for your public men to pursue, would be to adopt such a policy as will avoid, as far as possible, the evils of immediate emancipation."

Stephens wanted to know if the Southern states would be given representation in Congress, once they had abandoned the war. Lincoln answered that, as for himself, he thought the states should and would be "immediately restored to their practical relations to the Union." Again and again he used this phrase—"their practical relations to the Union"—and always spoke of the prompt restoration of such relations as the main object. But he refused to enter into any definite agreement on this or any other point; he would not negotiate with "parties in arms against the Government."

Hunter exclaimed: "No treaty, no stipulation, no agreement, either with the Confederate States jointly, or with them separately, as to their future position or security!" He protested that this meant nothing but unconditional surrender for the Confederacy and its people. Seward observed that there had been no mention of unconditional surrender or any equivalent phrase. The United States, he said, was not assuming the role of conqueror. All the government required was obedience to the laws. The Constitution would protect the rights of the Southern people. "But," Hunter pointed out, "you make no agreement that these rights will be so held and secured!"

Lincoln stepped in to say that, with respect to the confiscation acts and other penal laws, their enforcement was up to him as President, and he was willing to give his word: he would exercise his powers "with the utmost liberality." He went on to add that he, personally, would be willing to be taxed to remunerate slaveowners for their slaves, if the Southern states would end hostilities and abolish slavery. Again, however, he refused to enter into any definite agreement.

Campbell took lightly the prospect of future punishments. He remarked (as he reported to a Richmond colleague two days after the conference) that "he had never regarded his neck as in danger. Lincoln replied that there were a good many oak trees about the place where he [Campbell] lived, the limbs of which afforded many convenient points from which he might have dangled." Lincoln said this in anger. It was his only show of temper or harshness throughout the conference.

If the reports of Stephens and his colleagues are to be trusted, Lincoln, as of February 3, 1865, would have undertaken a peace of reconciliation, a peace of almost unbelievable generosity. The Southerners needed only to lay down their arms and acknowledge and obey the Federal laws. They would then be pardoned, their rights and property restored (with few exceptions). Their states promptly would be put back into the old "practical relations" with the Union. Slaveowners could even keep their slaves, at least for a time.

To the Confederate commissioners, and still more to Jefferson Davis, these were the terms of a ruthless conquerer. Or, rather, these were no terms at all. This was unconditional surrender!

To the Radical Republicans in the North, these would have seemed the terms of a soft-headed sentimentalist, if they had been made public. The Cabinet and the Congress undoubtedly would have prevented peacemaking on such terms—even if Davis had been eager to accept them.

3

Though it was still March by the calendar—March 28—the morning was soft and mild. Yet Lincoln had on his black winter overcoat, as well as his black silk hat, when he followed General Grant out of the log hut and started down the plank walk in Grant's headquarters camp, at City Point, near Richmond.

Next to emerge from the hut was a red-haired, rather slightly built man in a slouch hat and a battle-worn uniform of faded blue. He seemed to explode with nervous energy, talking fast, with quick gesticulations.

This was William Tecumseh Sherman. He had arrived the previous afternoon from his own camp at Goldsboro, North Carolina. That was his latest stop on the famous march from Atlanta to the sea and then from Savannah northward. His mission at City Point was to confer with Grant about the final moves of the war. Finding the President there, Sherman had seized the opportunity to talk with him too. Already, since arriving, Sherman had spent some time with Lincoln at the latter's floating residence, the *River Queen,* which was tied up at the wharf on the James.

Again, this second day, Sherman went aboard with Lincoln and talked—and listened. During most of the two-day conversation Grant was present, and during part of it Admiral David D. Porter also. Lincoln put nothing in writing. Grant had little to say either at the time or afterward. Porter made some notes, but not immediately. Sherman eventually had occasion to recall the meetings with great positiveness. In the main, Porter then corroborated Sherman's memory of the President's remarks. Yet these City Point discussions remain mysterious—even more so than the earlier Hampton Roads conference.

As Sherman recalled the scene on board the river boat, Lincoln when at rest or listening sat with his arms hanging as if lifeless, his face dull and lined with care. Then, whenever he began to talk, his figure took on new life and his face lighted up. Sherman was sure he did not mistake Lincoln's spirit toward the South—his kindliness, his magnanimity, his desire to get the war over with and the Union restored with as little suffering as possible. According to Sherman, both he and Grant let Lincoln know they expected one last bloody battle before the enemy gave up. "Mr. Lincoln exclaimed, more than once, that there had been enough blood shed, and asked us if another battle could be avoided."

Sherman (by his own account) asked the President if he was ready for the end of the war, if he had plans for the disposal of the rebel armies after their defeat, if he had any ideas as to what should be done with the Confederate leaders, Jefferson Davis in particular. Lincoln was quite definite in his reply. "He said he was all ready; all he wanted of us was to defeat the opposing armies, and to get the men composing the Confederate armies back to their homes, at work on their farms and in their shops." As for Jeff Davis, he should be allowed to clear out, to "escape the country," though Lincoln observed that it would not do for him to say this publicly. He was prepared for the "civil reorganization of affairs at the South as soon as the war was over."

Admiral Porter, in his subsequent narrative, indicated the same general impression of the attitude of Lincoln. "He wanted peace on almost any terms, and there is no knowing what proposals he might have been willing to listen to," Porter recalled. "His heart was tenderness throughout, and, as long as the rebels laid down their arms, he did not care how it was done."

Sherman afterward insisted that Lincoln had been both clear and specific on what was to become the most controversial point. Did Lincoln intend to recognize, even temporarily, any of the existing rebel governments in the Southern states? Sherman wrote:

"He distinctly authorized me to assure Governor Vance and the people of North Carolina that, as soon as the rebel armies laid down their arms, and resumed their civil pursuits, they would at once be guaranteed all their rights as citizens of a common country; and that to avoid anarchy the State governments then in existence, with their civil functionaries, would be recognized by him as the government *de facto* till Congress could provide others."

At noon on March 28 Sherman went ashore, and Lincoln bade him good-by at the gangplank. Aboard his own fast steamer, the *Bat,* Sherman headed down-river for the Carolina coast and ultimately Goldsboro. With him went his brother John, United States Senator from Ohio. Years later the Senator was to recall that, on this trip, the general discussed Lincoln's generous peace views and fully agreed with them. The Senator himself preferred a sterner policy.

Soon after General Sherman's return to North Carolina, a reporter for the Philadelphia *Public Ledger* heard him say that, if the victors were humane once they had the victory in their grasp, "the State would be the first to wheel into the line of the old Union."

4

Smoke and the smell of burning were in the air on the warm afternoon of April 4. Parts of Richmond still smoldered from the fires that had raged the day before.

A boat rowed by a dozen blue-clad sailors pulled alongside a landing on the James. Six marines with carbines in hand stepped out, and then the President of the United States with his son Tad, a few army and navy officers, and six more marines.

A tall black hat stood out above the group as they walked up a street toward Richmond's Capitol Hill. At every step the procession grew, a crowd of Negroes and whites collecting and following along. The Negroes shouted, sang, jumped up and down, clapped their hands, and blessed the Lord and Massa Lincoln. When the perspiring President stopped to rest, at the foot of the hill, the mob of admirers closed in. A cavalry escort was sent for; it cleared the way, and the climb began.

On the hill stood a large, handsome, more or less cube-shaped mansion, with a plot of thick, green grass around it. This house was now the headquarters of Major General Godfrey Weitzel, commander of the Union occupation troops. It had been the Confederate "White House," the official residence of Jefferson Davis, until he suddenly vacated it, only a couple of days before Lincoln's arrival. Wearily Lincoln made his way up the steps and inside, where he settled into a chair at a desk—the same chair that Davis used to sit in when he wrote.

While in the Davis house, Lincoln received important callers. One of these was John Campbell, with whom he had conferred aboard the *River Queen* at Hampton Roads just two months previously. Campbell was the only high-ranking Confederate official who stayed in Richmond after the withdrawal of Lee's army, which now was somewhere to the west of the city, with Grant's army in hot pursuit. For all that anybody in Richmond knew, a climactic and bloody battle was yet to be fought.

Lincoln and Campbell had this much in common: they hoped to save lives and expedite the return of peace. But it was afterward to appear that they were far apart in their assumptions as to what peace meant and how it was to be achieved. Apparently, while seeming to agree, they badly misunderstood one another.

That April afternoon the two men talked while General Weitzel listened. Campbell thought that the leading politicians of Virginia, if allowed to get together in Richmond, might take steps to remove the state and her soldiers from the war, then prepare for political reconstruction and reunion. Lincoln was interested. He asked Campbell to bring some of the Virginia leaders to see him the following day.

Leaving the Davis house, Lincoln toured the city in an open carriage and viewed the blackened ruins. Then, with his party, he was rowed back to the gunboat *Malvern,* in the James.

On the morning of April 5 Campbell appeared on board the *Malvern* with the one member of the Virginia Legislature he could find. General Weitzel again was present.

Lincoln now gave Campbell a written statement of peace terms. These included the three indispensable conditions already familiar to Campbell—reunion, no receding as to slavery, no armistice. "If there be any who are ready for those indispensable terms, on any conditions whatever," Lincoln had added, "let them say so, and state their conditions. . . ." And then a threat and a promise: if war should be "further persisted in," property would be confiscated to pay for at least the additional cost; but confiscations, with a few exceptions, would be "remitted to the people of any State" which should promptly withdraw its "troops and other support" from resistance to the Federal government.

In the conversation on the *Malvern,* as Campbell afterward remembered it, Lincoln said he was considering the idea of letting the rebel Legislature meet in Richmond. He said this very same body, which had acted as a member of the Confederacy in opposition to the Union, ought to recognize the authority of the Union and disavow that of the Confederacy. "It was in the situation of a tenant between two contesting landlords, who was called to attorn to the one who had shown the better title, was his remark."

Lincoln let Campbell know he would later hear more definitely from him. Campbell and the other visitors left the gunboat. It then took Lincoln back to City Point.

After parting with the President, General Weitzel spoke to Charles A. Dana, Lincoln's assistant secretary of war, who was in Richmond. Dana telegraphed to his superior, Secretary Stanton, to report that Campbell had talked with the President "to consider how Virginia can be brought back to the Union." The Virginians did not demand much. "All they ask is an amnesty and a military convention, to cover appearances. Slavery they admit to be defunct." They "were sure if amnesty could be offered the rebel army would dissolve and all the States return." The President "did not promise the amnesty, but told them he had the pardoning power, and would save any repentent sinner from hanging."

At City Point the next day Lincoln composed a letter for General Weitzel. "It has been intimated to me," Lincoln wrote, "that the gentlemen who have acted as the Legislature of Virginia, in support of the rebellion, may now desire to assemble at Richmond, to take measures to withdraw the Virginia troops, and other support from resistance to the General government. If they attempt it, give them permission and protection. . . . Allow Judge Campbell to see this, but do not make it public."

Lincoln also wrote to tell Grant about having authorized the "rebel Legislature" to meet. "I do not think it very probable that anything will come of this," he said. "From your recent dispatches it seems that you are pretty effectually withdrawing the Virginia troops from opposition to the government."

In Richmond, after seeing Lincoln's letter to Weitzel, Campbell met with five members of the Legislature to make plans for its assembling as soon as possible. He recommended to Weitzel that the South Carolina Legislature also be convened and that it be "invited to send commissioners to adjust the questions that are supposed to require adjustment." He urged an armistice and said it would lead to the "disbanding" of the Confederate armies.

Obviously Campbell was thinking of a series of peace negotiations between the Federal government and the separate rebel states. And why not? He had received from Lincoln a pledge of pardon for Confederate leaders, a request that the Confederates put forth their own collateral terms (while accepting the three minimum demands), and a permission for the Confederate Legislature of Virginia to assemble. Lincoln's attitude must have seemed to Campbell like an invitation to diplomatic bargaining.

But did Lincoln have anything like that in mind? Or was he thinking merely of allowing the "gentlemen" who had acted as the rebel Legislature to act just once more for withdrawing the Virginia troops?

5

Late in the afternoon of April 9 the *River Queen* steamed up the Potomac, and Lincoln stepped ashore at the Washington wharf. He had been called back from City Point by word that Secretary Seward had been badly injured in a carriage accident.

On that same April 9, at Appomattox Court House, about ninety miles west of Richmond, Lee surrendered to Grant. The terms were generous. Grant paroled Lee, his officers, and his men, thus in effect amnestying them. In doing so, Grant went somewhat beyond Lincoln's orders. These forbade him to make political arrangements, and an amnesty was a political as well as a military matter. But Lincoln did not repudiate the terms.

Next day Federal employees were given a holiday, and the capital like the rest of the North rejoiced at the surrender news. A celebrating crowd jammed the White House yard and called for the President, while a brass band struck up "Hail to the Chief" and followed with "Yankee Doodle" and "America." Lincoln came out, promised to make a speech some other time, and suggested that the band play "Dixie." That song had been appropriated by the "adversaries over the way" but was now a lawful prize of war, he said. So the band played "Dixie," and then he went back to his business.

He was in the midst of a Cabinet meeting. His permission for the assembling of the Virginia Legislature still stood. If his only object in the arrangement with Campbell had been to get the Virginia soldiers out of the war, he surely would have revoked that permission by now, since Lee's army no longer existed. By revoking it, he could have avoided a most unpleasant issue with his Cabinet. All the members present, Radicals and conservatives alike, disapproved his action in regard to the Virginia Legislature. (Seward was absent, in bed with his injuries.) They still disapproved when the Cabinet met again on April 11. Some of them went to him individually to protest.

These men did not desire a quick and easy restoration of the Southern states. Those states must first be drastically remade. The slaves must all be freed and protected in their freedom. They must be given the right to vote, some Radicals were saying. And the former ruling class of whites must be deprived of political power. The rebels, in Thaddeus Stevens's words, must be made to "eat the fruits of foul rebellion." Otherwise the Negro would be reenslaved and, incidentally Southern and Northern Democrats would rejoin to rule the nation.

The conservative Gideon Welles, Secretary of the Navy, in his diary and in a later magazine article, told of Lincoln's speaking to him about the Cabinet opposition. The President "said Stanton and others were dissatisfied" and asked Welles's candid judgment. Welles replied that he questioned the wisdom of convening rebel legislators: they might embarrass the administration by making extreme demands. But Lincoln thought the Southerners were too thoroughly beaten to cause much trouble. "His idea was, that the members of the legislature, comprising the prominent and influential men of their respective counties, had better come together and undo their own work." In the difficult transition from war to peace it was essential to have in existence a temporary authority which could command the obedience of the people. "Civil government must be re-established, he said, as soon as possible; there must be courts, and law, and order, or society would be broken up, the disbanded armies would turn into robber bands and guerillas, which we must strive to prevent. These were the reasons why he wished prominent Virginians who had the confidence of the people to come together and turn themselves and their neighbors into good Union men." So far as Welles's record of this conversation goes, Lincoln did not even mention the withdrawal of the Virginia troops as a reason for his having consented to the assembling of the Legislature in the first place.

On the night of April 11, standing at an upstairs window in the White House, Lincoln made the speech he had promised—his last public address. (In Richmond, that same day, a group of prominent citizens, with the approval of General Weitzel, issued a call for the assembling of the Legislature.)

"We all agree," Lincoln told his Washington audience, "that the seceded states, so-called, are out of their proper practical relation with the Union; and that the sole object of the government, civil and military, in regard to those states is to again get them into that proper practical relation." And he repeatedly asked: "Can Louisiana be brought into proper practical relation with the Union *sooner* by *sustaining*, or by *discarding* her new state government?" Thus he pled for the acceptance of his "ten per cent plan" in Louisiana.

But he did not insist upon the very same plan for the whole of the South. "What has been said of Louisiana will apply generally to other states," he observed. That is, it was urgent to get the others also into the proper relationship as soon as possible. "And yet so great peculiarities pertain to each state; and such important and sudden changes occur in the same state; and, withal, so new and unprecedented is the whole case, that no exclusive, and inflexible plan can safely be prescribed as to details and collaterals." On the other hand, "Important principles may, and must, be inflexible."

What he considered important and inflexible principles is uncertain. Perhaps they were the ones embodied in his minimum peace terms as stated in his annual message of 1864, his instructions to Seward for the Hampton Roads conference, and his memorandum to Campbell at the first Richmond interview. The familiar three points—reunion, no reenslavement of Negroes emancipated during the war, and peace without armistice—are all that can be stated with any degree of certainty as representing Lincoln's objectives.

Before concluding his last speech, Lincoln enigmatically remarked: "In the present *'situation'* as the phrase goes, it may be my duty to make some new announcement to the people of the South. I am considering, and shall not fail to act, when satisfied that action will be proper." What new announcement, what new action, he had in mind, no one knows.

The following day he sent a telegram to General Weitzel in Richmond. On account of it, he was afterward to be accused of quibbling out of his agreement with Campbell. The telegram read:

"I have just seen Judge Campbell's letter to you of the 7th. He assumes as appears to me that I have called the insurgent Legislature of Virginia together, as the rightful Legislature of the State, to settle all differences with the United States. I have done no such thing. I spoke of them not as a Legislature, but as 'the gentlemen who have *acted* as the Legislature of Virginia in support of the rebellion.' I did this on purpose to exclude the assumption that I was recognizing them as a *rightful* body.

I dealt with them as men having power *de facto* to do a specific thing, to wit, 'to withdraw the Virginia troops, and other support from resistance to the General Government,' for which in the paper handed Judge Campbell I promised a specific equivalent, to wit, a remission to the people of the State, except in certain cases, the confiscation of their property. I meant this and no more. In as much however as Judge Campbell misconstrues this, and is still pressing for an armistice, contrary to the explicit statement of the paper I gave him; and particularly as Gen. Grant has since captured the Virginia troops, so that giving a consideration for their withdrawal is no longer applicable, let my letter to you, and the paper to Judge Campbell both be withdrawn or, countermanded, and he be notified of it. Do not allow them to assemble. . . ."

On the morning of April 14 the President held another Cabinet meeting—the one at which he told his dream of being in an indescribable vessel and moving rapidly toward an indistinct shore. Stanton now proposed a period of military occupation for the South. His plan would have combined Virginia and North Carolina in a single military district. Welles objected to this detail, on the grounds that it might destroy the individuality of the separate states. Lincoln, though upholding Welles's objection, did not overrule the Stanton plan as a whole. On the contrary, he asked Stanton to revise it, treating Virginia and North Carolina separately, and to have copies of the revised plan for the next meeting of the cabinet. One of the Radicals, Attorney General James Speed (brother of Lincoln's old-time friend Joshua), inferred that Lincoln was coming over to the Radical side. "He never seemed so near our views," Speed believed. "At the meeting he said he thought [he] had made a mistake at Richmond in sanctioning the assembling of the Virginia Legislature and had perhaps been too fast in his desires for early reconstruction."

That night a telegram from Richmond was delivered at the White House. Campbell begged for a chance to see the President again. But the President was out for the evening. He had gone to the theater.

6

Not long after Lincoln's assassination, Campbell was arrested, carried away from Richmond, and confined at Fort Pulaski in Georgia. The charge against him was that he had "abused the confidence of Mr. Lincoln, misrepresented his views and promises, and by perversion, misled Gen. Weitzel into grave errors of official misconduct." More specifically, he had "violated and concealed the explicit conditions laid down by Mr. Lincoln that the public men of Virginia were to meet only as individuals called together for consultation and to promote order."

Campbell vigorously denied this charge. He admitted that he had urged upon the President a liberal and magnanimous policy. He said he himself had recommended that the President call together, at Richmond, a group of prominent Virginians to get their counsel and cooperation in the reconstruction of the state. "But," he insisted, "the calling together of the political body, the 'rebel legislature,' was the suggestion of Mr. Lincoln's own mind."

"It never entered into my imagination to conceive that he used the word 'Legislature' to express a convention of individuals having no public significance or relations," Campbell declared. He was positive he had neither misunderstood Lincoln nor misled Weitzel. After all, Weitzel had been present at both of the Campbell-Lincoln conferences in Richmond. *"He heard every word that Mr. Lincoln spoke to me, and Mr. Lincoln wrote to him, not to myself."* In Lincoln's original letter to Weitzel there had been no explicit condition that "the public men of Virginia were to meet only as individuals." Such a condition would not have made sense, in the context. "The pledge was that if any State would abandon the contest and withdraw its troops, that confiscations would be discharged. How was a State to comply except through its authorities? Mr. Lincoln wanted prompt, efficient action to terminate a ruinous war, and we must infer that he expected the usual means for the purpose, but besides this he designated the Legislature as the appropriate instrument to be employed."

Campbell did not blame Lincoln. "I have not complained of Mr. Lincoln's alteration of his policy, nor of the order revoking the call of the Virginia Legislature." Events had moved rapidly during those April days and had made a change in the whole aspect of things. "This change was great and Mr. Lincoln had contracted no debt to me, by any promise or declaration to me which forbade a change in his policy."

Latter-day Confederates were to be less charitable to Lincoln than Campbell was. They were to say that the President had committed himself to dealing with the existing state governments in the South as "legitimate authorities." Then he ran against the violent opposition of his Cabinet members. "In the face of such determined resistance from his advisers, Lincoln renounced his liberal policy and the next day withdrew his permission for the assembling of the State government, attempting to quibble out of his original sanction," one Southern historian writes. "Thus Lincoln broke faith with the Virginians."

"This view," a dissenting historian maintains, "leaves out of consideration both the care with which Lincoln worded his original letter to Weitzel, so that it might not be misconstrued precisely as it nevertheless was misconstrued; and the fact that in the interim Lee's army had surrendered, for all practical purposes taking Virginia out of the war."

Did Campbell misconstrue Lincoln? Or did Lincoln break faith with Campbell?

To both questions, the best answer seems to be yes—and no. The facts apparently are these: Lincoln's main concern originally was to get Lee out of the war. But he also had in mind the prospect of using the going governments in the South, at least the one in Virginia, as a means of preserving order and preventing guerilla warfare during the transition from war to peace. That is, he had two objects. The first of them was eliminated by Lee's surrender. The second was frustrated by opposition in the North, if not also by Campbell's misunderstanding

Lincoln, and interpreting too broadly the role he had intended for the rebel governments.

7

On the morning of April 17 General Sherman was about to take a train out of Raleigh, North Carolina, when a cipher telegram arrived from Washington. Decoded, the message revealed that Lincoln had been assassinated. Sherman kept the news quiet, for fear it might infuriate his men and provoke trouble in Raleigh. He proceeded with his train trip.

At Durham station he left the train and continued on horseback until he found the man he had arranged to meet. This was the gray-clad, gray-bearded Joseph E. Johnston, commander of what was left of the Confederate army in North Carolina. The two generals found a tiny weather-beaten house and borrowed it from the owner, a farmer named Bennett. Sherman revealed to Johnston the contents of the recent telegram. Johnston, beads of sweat appearing on his forehead, remarked that the assassination was a calamity for the South. Then the generals talked of peace.

A couple of days before, Sherman had telegraphed to Secretary Stanton that he would "accept the same terms as General Grant gave General Lee and be careful not to complicate any points of civil policy." Now, at Bennett's farmhouse, Sherman offered those terms. Johnston, according to his later narrative, countered that his situation was too different from Lee's to justify him in such a surrender. Lee's army had dwindled to almost nothing and had been trapped; Johnston's still could put up a fight. Johnston proposed to Sherman that they make a broad, inclusive settlement bringing peace to the whole country and disposing of all the armies "to the Rio Grande." He reminded Sherman that other great generals in history, Napoleon for instance, had risen to the challenge and the glory of assuming the peacemaker's role. "General Sherman replied, with heightened color, that he appreciated such a sentiment, and that to put an end to further devastation and bloodshed, and restore the Union, and with it the prosperity of the country, were to him objects of ambition." As the former foemen talked, they grew increasingly cordial. The sun was setting when they finally parted, to meet again the following day.

When Sherman reappeared at the Bennett farmhouse, he brought with him some "medical stores" and invited Johnston and a companion—John C. Breckinridge, who had run against Lincoln for President in 1860—to share the bottle before they got down to work. There ensued some discussion and disagreement between Sherman and the other two as they sat at a table. He began to write. Suddenly he rose, took another drink of whisky, and looked thoughtfully out of the window at the sunny Carolina countryside. Then he returned to the table and, without a pause, finished writing out what amounted practically to a treaty of peace. Johnston read it and was satisfied. He signed. So did Sherman. They parted again, and Sherman returned to Raleigh.

Among the terms of this Sherman-Johnston convention (April 18, 1865) were the following: 1. "The recognition, by the Executive of the United States, of the several State governments, on their officers and Legislatures taking the oaths prescribed by the Constitution of the United States, and, where conflicting State governments have resulted from the war, the legitimacy of all shall be submitted to the Supreme Court of the United States." 2. "The people and inhabitants of all the States to be guaranteed, so far as the Executive can, their political rights and franchises, as well as their rights of person and property, as defined by the Constitution of the United States and of the States respectively."

While dispatching a copy of the agreement to the authorities in Washington, Sherman also sent a copy to Grant and with it a message rather proudly explaining what he had done. The agreement, he wrote, "is an absolute submission of the enemy to the lawful authority of the United States, and disperses his armies absolutely; and the point to which I attach most importance is, that the dispersion and disbandment of these armies is done in such a manner as to prevent their breaking up into guerilla bands." Nothing about slavery had been included, but General Johnston had "admitted that slavery was dead," and, said Sherman, "I could not insist on embracing it in such a paper, because it can be made with the States in detail." His arrangement, he concluded, echoing the words of Johnston, would "produce peace from the Potomac to the Rio Grande."

Sherman naturally felt hurt when the higher-ups in Washington—President Johnson, Secretary Stanton, General Grant—repudiated his work. And he was infuriated when Stanton gave to the press a potpourri of documents and statements which made it appear that he had flouted his orders and had virtually turned traitor to the Union cause. Radicals in the North denounced him as either criminal or insane.

After the storm of denunciation had broken over his head, Sherman wrote defensively to Grant (April 28): "I had seen General Weitzel's invitation to the Virginia legislature, made in Mr. Lincoln's very presence, and had failed to discover any other official hint of a plan of reconstruction." A few weeks later (May 21) he wrote to an army friend in New York: "I am about to go before the war investigating committee, when for the first time, I will be at liberty to tell my story in public." He hinted at the story he presumably would tell: "Stanton and Halleck . . . sought the opportunity to ruin me by means of the excitement naturally arising from the assassination of the President . . . whose views and policy I was strictly, literally following." Yet, the next day, testifying before the Congressional committee on the conduct of the war, in Washington, Sherman did not contend that he had been strictly, literally following Lincoln's views and policy. He did mention his conferences with Lincoln at City Point on March 27 and 28. He was asked if any arrangements with regard to peace were made at that time. And he replied: "Nothing definite; it was simply a matter of general conversation, nothing specific and definite." On other occasions in the spring of 1865 he referred to the controversial Johnston convention without stating or implying that Lincoln was the real author of its terms. Sherman entangled himself in a record of self-contradictions.

One biographer has attempted to explain these away by saying he kept quiet about Lincoln's role because he desired to spare the name of the late President from the odium of what had turned out to be a most unpopular arrangement. Even if that were true of Sherman's public statements, it would hardly apply to a confidential letter to his good friend Grant—such as the letter in which he said he had "failed to discover any other official hint of a plan of reconstruction" besides the news of Lincoln's permission for the calling of the Virginia Legislature.

Ten years afterward, in his *Memoirs,* Sherman wrote that Lincoln in his conversations at City Point had been "full and frank," had indicated clearly his willingness to use extraordinary means to disband the rebel armies and get the soldiers home, and had authorized specifically the temporary recognition of rebel state governments. Sherman insisted he had but carried out the President's instructions. He included in his *Memoirs* a narrative of Admiral Porter which appeared to confirm his own story. "Mr. Lincoln did, in fact, arrange the (so considered) liberal terms offered General Jos. Johnston, and . . . I feel sure that he [Sherman] yielded to the wishes of the President in every respect." Lincoln, if alive, would have approved what Sherman did. So Porter maintained, and he had been present during at least a part of the conversations at City Point.

Still later (in 1892) Senator John Sherman recalled the trip he had taken with his brother from Grant's headquarters to North Carolina in March of 1865. Senator Sherman said he then had been "fully advised" by General Sherman of the latter's recent conversations with Lincoln. And the Senator declared that "at the meeting with Johnston General Sherman acted . . . in exact accordance with what he understood were the instructions of Mr. Lincoln."

Most historians have accepted, as substantially true, the Sherman-Porter version of the events. But, upon examination, this version appears to be somewhat less than convincing.

The testimony of Sherman's brother is of dubious value. It was given more than a quarter of a century after the events. By that time the Senator probably remembered little of what his brother actually had told him on their trip to North Carolina. Indeed, the Senator did not even remember that the conversations had been held at City Point. He said he had been "fully advised by General Sherman of the conference between Lincoln, Grant, Porter, and himself at *Hampton Roads.*"

Though Porter was an eyewitness and recorded his recollections within a year or so, his account is not much if any more reliable than John Sherman's. Porter was vague. He never mentioned the actual terms of the controversial Sherman-Johnston convention, and he gave no sign that he even knew exactly what these were. Rather, he unwittingly proved that he *did not know* exactly what they were. He referred to "the very course Grant, Sherman, and others pursued, in granting liberal terms to defeated rebels." Apparently he was under the delusion that Sherman, in dealing with Johnston, followed the "very course" Grant had pursued in dealing with Lee.

As for Sherman's own recollections, they do not harmonize with all the things he had been saying at the time, in April and May of 1865. Nor do all these things harmonize with one another, or with Johnston's narrative of his meetings with Sherman.

The probable truth is that Lincoln, when talking with Sherman at City Point, spoke in general language of his desire for an early and generous peace, but did not mention specific terms. After returning to North Carolina, Sherman heard of Lincoln's authorizing the call for the rebel Legislature of Virginia but did not hear (till later) of Lincoln's revocation of the call. Sherman assumed that the Virginia arrangement was a concrete example of what Lincoln must have meant by his generalities about a generous peace. Sherman also learned of Grant's terms to Lee. He intended to offer, and did offer, the same terms to Johnston. Then, when Johnston urged a wider settlement, Sherman reconsidered. Among other things, he proposed for North Carolina and the rest of the Confederate states the same privileges he supposed Lincoln had been contemplating for Virginia. Afterward Sherman convinced himself he had not been merely guessing about Lincoln's intentions but had received and carried out definite instructions from the President.

Assuming the opposite for the sake of argument—assuming that Sherman did what Lincoln actually had told him to do—there remains the question whether Lincoln, if alive, would have approved the Sherman-Johnston convention. And the correct answer probably is that he would *not.*

Throughout the war, Lincoln had shifted his peace policy from time to time, in response to political pressures. At first, his objective was simply the restoration of the Union. Then, beset by Radical agitation, he added emancipation as at least a partial and subsidiary aim. When conservatives protested, during the election campaign of 1864, he qualified and narrowed his emancipation stand. In his peace talks of 1865 he did not appear to insist upon immediate and unconditional freedom for all slaves. He seemed to take for granted that, no matter what was done, slavery would prove to be a casualty of war. For a time he was willing to let rebel Legislatures—one of them, at least—meet and act as interim state governments. Then he ran into a Radical uproar and yielded to it. On the last day of his life he evidently went so far as to consent to the principle of military reconstruction in the South. If he had lived a week longer he most likely would have done precisely what his successor, President Johnson, did. Whether or not he earlier had authorized such terms as Sherman eventually gave the foe, Lincoln would have overruled them when the showdown came.

chapter 11

THE MARTYR AND THE MYTH

1· CHAPTER FROM A LOST HISTORY

On July 3, 1881, having lived somewhat beyond his allotted threescore years and ten, Abraham Lincoln died quietly in his sleep, after a brief illness, at his home in Springfield, Illinois.

The previous day, in Washington, an assassin had shot President James A. Garfield. This news continued to fill the headlines. The report from Illinois was not neglected, however; obituaries of Lincoln were carried in all the papers. While editors wondered about the prospects for Garfield and the nation—whether he would live or die, and what would be the consequences of his death—they also recalled the past and speculated upon one of the might-have-beens of history. Suppose the bullet from Booth's gun had reached Lincoln that April evening in 1865....

Then Andrew Johnson would have become President. Johnson in 1865 had the reputation of a Radical, yet he was a Southerner and a Democrat. He was strong-willed and stubborn—not a supple, subtle politician. Unless he saw eye to eye with the most extreme group of Republicans, he probably would have got into serious difficulty with the party that had elected him to the vice-presidency. He might even have been impeached. Certainly he would not have handled politics and policies with the skill that Lincoln demonstrated throughout his second as well as his first term in office.

Of course, Lincoln had his troubles during the second term. He was saved by his sure instinct for dealing with politicians, his deep concern about the Republican party and its preservation, his willingness to compromise. These traits of his could be read between the lines, in 1881, as newspapers reviewed the high spots of Lincolnian reconstruction from 1865 to 1869.

At the end of the Civil War, Lincoln's policy for the postwar South was not entirely clear in its details. He possessed no fixed and uniform program for the region as a whole. As he said in his speech of April 11, 1865, "so great peculiarities" pertained to each state, and "such important and sudden changes" occurred in the same state, and "so new and unprecedented" was the whole problem, that "no exclusive and inflexible plan" could "safely be prescribed." With respect to states like Louisiana and Tennessee, he continued to urge acceptance of new governments set up under his "ten per cent plan" during the war. With respect to states like Virginia and North Carolina, he seemed willing, near the war's end, to use the old rebel governments temporarily as a means of transition from war to peace. He was on record as opposing the appointment of "strangers" (carpetbaggers) to govern the South. He also opposed the vote for Negroes, except the "very intelligent" and those who had served the Union cause as soldiers.

In spirit and in general outline, Lincoln's intentions with

regard to reconstruction, early in 1865, seemed clear enough. He favored a rather quick and easy restoration of the Southern states to their "practical relations" with the Union. But the Radicals of his party disagreed with him. They and he appeared to be farther apart than a year before, when he pocket-vetoed the Wade-Davis bill and was denounced in the Wade-Davis manifesto.

At the time of the assassination attempt, in April 1865, Lincoln already had begun to modify his stand and narrow the gap between himself and the Radicals. He recalled the permission he had given for the assembling of the rebel Legislature in Virginia, and he approved in principle War Secretary Stanton's plan for the military occupation of the South. The Radicals in his official family felt that he was coming over to their side after the Cabinet meeting on the morning of April 14.

That evening occurred the incident in Ford's Theater. The mad actor, John Wilkes Booth, fired point-blank at the President from only a few feet away and yet, in his excitement, failed to make a direct hit, the bullet only grazing Lincoln's head. The same night, the convalescing Seward was badly mauled in an assassination attempt at his home, and Vice-president Johnson escaped without injury only because of the irresolution of the conspirator assigned to murder him.

It was a night of terror—terror which spread throughout the North with the spread of the news. Stanton spoke darkly of a Confederate plot, and most Northerners believed him. They became more nearly unanimous than ever in their conviction that rebels must suffer and the South be remade. Public opinion caught up with the position the Radicals already had reached.

The terror was still at its height, and the would-be assassin Booth still at large, when the news came that General Sherman had made what amounted practically to a treaty, and a very generous one, with the Confederate Johnston in North Carolina. Lincoln promptly and firmly overruled the Sherman-Johnston agreement. At the same time he issued a statement freeing Sherman of all censure. Sherman had been out of touch with recent events, Lincoln charitably explained.

Not long after that, the President made the "new announcement to the people of the South" which, in his speech of April 11, he had said might be forthcoming. In this new announcement he was rather cautious with words. Radical Republicans professed to find much comfort in the phrasing, but so did conservative Republicans and many Democrats, Southern as well as Northern. What Lincoln proposed was temporary military government for the South. This was the way, he explained, to bring about safe transition from war to peace, from rebellion to reunion. An army was needed to prevent outbreaks of guerilla warfare, to protect the freedmen in their new-found liberty, and to reassure the Southern whites who feared Negro uprisings.

Within a year Lincoln and the Radicals had drifted apart again. Some of them denounced him because of his vetoes and his pardons. He vetoed a couple of reconstruction bills, including one for giving civil rights immediately to Southern Negroes. He pardoned former rebel leaders, right and left. He even pardoned a couple of convicted assassination conspirators—Mrs. Mary Surratt, who had been condemned to death, and Dr. Samuel Mudd, who had been sentenced to prison on the Dry Tortugas—and he commuted to life imprisonment the death sentences of the other three consigned to the gallows (Booth himself was killed resisting capture). The vetoes and pardons led a few extremist congressmen to speak openly of impeachment

As the Congressional elections of 1866 approached, a crisis brewed within the Republican party. A faction of Radicals in Congress were about organize in opposition to what they called the party of the President's friends. They denounced the Seward influence and demanded Seward's removal as Secretary of State. Lincoln responded in his characteristic way. On the one hand, he appeased the Radicals by procuring Seward's resignation. On the other hand, he defied and disciplined the more extreme of the Radicals by his manipulation of patronage. He removed a number of government job holders who were friends of the extremists. Some of these job holders he did not immediately replace with new men. He left the jobs empty as a kind of bait. By these tactics he held his party together and kept himself at the head of it, in fact as well as name. The returns on election day foretold a greatly increased Republican majority for the next Congress.

Meanwhile, at the end of the last session of the existing Congress, in March of 1867, Lincoln killed a Radical reconstruction measure by withholding his signature. He sent in a message explaining his objections to one of the bill's features—the "ironclad oath," which required a Southerner to swear he *never* had willingly supported the rebellion, before he could take any part in statemaking or in politics. Lincoln still believed, as he had all along, that the oath should look ahead and not back, that a man should swear to future and not to past loyalty.

Without waiting a call from the President, the newly elected Congress met immediately after the final adjournment of the previous one. Many congressmen seemed determined to pass the same sort of reconstruction bill as before, ironclad oath and all. But Lincoln blunted a good deal of opposition, talking with Republican leaders, both conservative and Radical, and even with Democrats. He made some further changes in the Federal payroll, removing a few more office holders and appointing new men to their places and to the other places he previously had left vacant. Most of the Radicals in the Senate and the House calmed down. Congress passed a modified bill, and the President signed it.

This Reconstruction Act of 1867 was something of a hybrid. It was not exactly what either Lincoln or the Radicals desired. They would have preferred the ironclad oath, to keep most Southern whites from voting or holding office, but on this point Lincoln was unmovable. On the other hand he would have preferred only a limited suffrage for freedmen, yet all adult males among the Negroes were given the right to vote.

In most of the reconstructed Southern states, this right to vote proved illusory in practice. States like Mississippi and South Carolina were almost solidly Democratic from the start. Negroes were allowed to go to the polls only if they followed the advice of their white neighbors and voted as Democrats. But in North Carolina and a few other states a two-party system quickly reappeared. In these states, many Negroes exercised the right of suffrage, and did so with considerable freedom. There sprang into being a sizable party of conservative Republicans —or Conservative Unionists, as they usually preferred to call themselves. This party was made up largely of old Whigs, of men with whom Lincoln and many of his friends had co-operated in the years before the Republican party was born.

Radicals continued to criticize Lincoln. Some of them accused him of cultivating the friendship of former rebels so as to build a personal machine in the South. Others accused him of throwing the freedmen to the wolves, of leaving them to the tender mercies of their former masters. But these critics could do little more than grumble. They took up Ulysses S. Grant as a conquering hero with a future in politics no less than in war. Lincoln, with his genius for holding the support of opposites, stayed on good terms with Grant as well as those former Confederate generals who had turned Republican.

Such, in essence, was the story which the Lincoln obituaries recalled in 1881. On the whole, the editors both Republican and Democratic adjudged Lincoln a worthy statesman, one of the very greatest in the history of the republic. Some of the newspapers noted that, by the record of his first term alone, to say nothing of his second term, he deserved to be compared favorably with the long-dead and long-honored George Washington. Indeed, one paper reprinted a selection of comments made in 1863, 1864, and the first months of 1865, to show that Lincoln's greatness had been appreciated even that early.

In the summer of 1863 the *Washington Chronicle* had found a resemblance between Abraham Lincoln and George Washington in their "sure judgment," "perfect balance of thoroughly sound faculties," and "great calmness of temper, great firmness of purpose, supreme moral principle, and intense patriotism." About a year later the *Buffalo Express* referred to Lincoln's "remarkable moderation and freedom from passionate bitterness," then added: "We do not believe that Washington himself was less indifferent to the exercise of power for power's sake." Similar comparisons occurred to English journalists. In March 1865 the *Spectator* of London observed that, while Lincoln faced a task not quite so heavy as Washington's, he required as great or greater personal resources, for he was compelled to perform the task without the benefit of education or experience comparable to Washington's.

In the midst of the war another English journal, the *Liverpool Post,* suggested that "no leader in a great contest ever stood so little chance of being the subject of hero worship as Abraham Lincoln," if one were to judge only by the way he looked. His long arms and legs, his grotesque figure, made him too easy to caricature and ridicule. "Yet," the newspaper concluded, "a worshiper of human heroes might possibly travel a great deal farther and fare much worse for an idol than selecting this same lanky American." His inner qualities—his faithfulness, honesty, resolution, insight, humor, and courage—would "go a long way to make up a hero," whatever the man's personal appearance.

Such estimates of Lincoln were widely reechoed after his death in 1881. The consensus was that he deserved to be remembered as a national hero, for he had served the nation well, reuniting it after four years of war and then holding it together through four years of troubled peace.

2

The foregoing is, of course, hypothesis after April 14, 1865. It is history as it conceivably might have been written if Lincoln had lived to finish his second term.

If Booth *had* missed, our knowledge of Lincoln undoubtedly would be much clearer than it is, much less clouded by mystery and myth. The awful fact of the assassination falls between us and the man. It is like a garish, bloodstained glass, in which all perspectives are distorted, and the over-all view dimmed. Lincoln's whole life tends to become obscured by the circumstances of his death.

In the assassination itself, posterity has been prone to see little but the unearthly, incredible, and weird. Considering the legends that have since arisen, the bare facts are distinctly anticlimactic.

John Wilkes Booth, Maryland-born, a member of a famous thespian family and himself an actor of some note, developed a psychopathic vanity and a mad attachment to the Southern cause. Craving to strike a spectacular blow for himself and for the South, he plotted at first to kidnap President Lincoln and later to kill him, along with other high officials of the government. On the night of April 14, 1865, in Ford's Theater, he succeeded in mortally wounding the President. The rest of his plan went awry, though one of his accomplices horribly mauled the Secretary of State. Booth managed, despite a broken leg, to make his way into Virginia. There he was trapped in a tobacco barn and was shot to death. After a military trial three men and a woman were hanged as fellow conspirators, and four men were sent to prison.

That is a fair summary of the events, but such a dry recital was not enough for a people emotionally upset by four years of war, nor has it sufficed for later generations of Americans. From the moment that Booth pulled the trigger, the myth makers got busy, and since then the implausible often has seemed more satisfying than the plausible, the unreal more convincing that the real.

It has seemed somehow appropriate, for example, to believe that Booth was *not* killed in the Virginia tobacco barn. The victim must have been somebody else. The real Booth got away. Reports of the exhumation of the body, and of inconsistencies and disagreements among those who undertook to identify it, had the effect of confirming doubts whether the right man had been caught. It had been said, for instance, that certain of

Booth's neck vertebrae, bullet-shattered when he was shot, had been removed. But the exhumed corpse lacked no vetebrae. "Under such circumstances," an authority on *Myths after Lincoln* observes, "it is no wonder that, before long, various dark-haired, pallid men who walked with a limp, began to be pointed out as J. Wilkes Booth." A Virginia preacher was taken for him. A Texas saloon-keeper claimed to be the real Booth. And, year after year, other suspects or pretenders arose.

Whether or not Booth made his escape, similar myths aver, he must have had high-placed abettors in the assassination scheme. He could hardly have conceived it all by himself. To discover the mastermind, the archplotter, one has but to look for a motive and a person capable of acting upon it. At least three such villains have been nominated.

To the war-worn and assassination-shocked people of the North in 1865, Jefferson Davis was a most likely suspect. As President of the Confederacy he had authorized irregular methods of warfare while hostilities were on. His spies and agents in the North had undertaken to sabotage railroads, set fire to hotels and other buildings, free rebel prisoners, and stir up sedition. As the devil of Union propaganda for four years, Davis now seemed equal to anything, no matter how foul or fiendish. When he was captured in flight, after the fall of Richmond, he was held on charges which included complicity in Lincoln's murder.

To some Radical Republicans it appeared, once the conflict between their representatives in Congress and the stubborn new President had come to a head, that Andrew Johnson might be the guilty man. He, after all, had had much to gain from Lincoln's death—the Presidency itself. Moreover, though in earlier times a foe of Jefferson Davis, he had become in a sense the successor of Davis rather than of Lincoln, for was he not the champion of the rebels in their resistance to Radical reconstruction?

To at least one student of the assassination, there was a less obvious but more likely suspect than either Johnson or Davis.

This—believe it or not—was none other than a member of Lincoln's own official family. It was the man who is credited with having said so simply and fittingly, as Lincoln breathed his last: "Now he belongs to the ages." It was the Secretary of War, Edwin M. Stanton.

Stanton took charge of pursuit and punishment after the assassination. He raised the hue and cry for Jefferson Davis and gave official confirmation to the idea that the whole thing had been a Confederate plot. Could it be that he was trying cleverly to divert suspicion from himself? Supposedly he profited from Lincoln's death. He might have been frustrated in his policies of vengeance upon the South, and he might even have lost his position in the Cabinet if Lincoln had lived. And Stanton—heartless, two-faced, unprincipled—had a personality which might well have qualified him for even the most unthinkable of crimes.

The evidence against him is at best circumstantial. Besides throwing off suspicion upon Davis and the South, he did other things that can be made to seem incriminating. He was grossly negligent, to say the least, in the provisions he made for Lincoln's safety on the fateful night of April 14. He bungled the chase after Booth in such a way that, had it not been for the broken leg, the assassin surely would have got away. Stanton reserved for his own "trusted lieutenants" the actual capture, and it happened—or did it merely happen?—that the fugitive was not returned alive, to talk. Extraordinary measures were taken to silence Booth's associates before their trial, and then to stop their mouths forever by peremptory convictions and execution or banishment. As for Stanton's contacts with Booth, President Johnson could have been the go-between. Johnson is said to have been acquainted with Booth, and Stanton is said to have had a "singular hold" over Johnson.

Of course, Stanton's latter-day accusers must concede, all this is guesswork; against Stanton there is no evidence that would hold up in court. And so the accused is left without a charge to be answered, but with innuendo which evades reply.

Now, Stanton had his repulsive traits, but it remains to be proved that he could, or did, contrive Lincoln's murder. More than that, it remains preposterous, and his trial-by-innuendo results in a gross libel upon his name. The same is true of the charges against Davis and Johnson. Indeed, no legal case could be made against Davis, and he was never brought to trial.

Whatever help Booth had, the crazy actor surely was the prime mover of his crazy plot. Its shape reveals the workings of his diseased mind. The deed must be done in a theater, before the eyes of a crowd, because the actor had to have an audience. The theater was not a logical place, or would not have been for an assassin whose sole concern was to kill and flee.

There were plenty of other opportunities to pick off the President, opportunities that would better have enabled the assassin to make sure of his escape. Lincoln, though not wholly unprotected, was not efficiently guarded, especially during the first two or three years of the war. Generally he had an escort of some kind, but often he did not. Even at night he would go out on foot, on horseback, or in his carriage, unguarded and at times alone. If he stayed home he was scarcely safer, for the White House doors were far from proof against intruders. On one occasion a representative of the United States Sanitary Commission, amazed at having walked unchallenged into Lincoln's presence, ventured to protest to him against the absence of proper security arrangements.

Lincoln was aware of danger. He could not help being aware of it. From time to time assassination threats came to him in crank letters, one of which informed him: "You shall be a dead man in six months from date Dec. 31st, 1863." Other assassination threats were made openly, in the newspapers, as in the LaCrosse, Wisconsin, *Democrat,* which proclaimed during the electoral campaign of 1864: "If Abraham Lincoln should be re-elected for another term of four years of such wretched administration, *we hope that a bold hand will be found to plunge the dagger into the Tyrant's heart for the public welfare.*" One night, according to one of Lincoln's bodyguards, Ward Hill Lamon, a shot was fired at the President as he rode alone toward his summer cottage at the Soldiers' Home. His tall hat was knocked off, with a bullet hole through it.

In referring to the danger, Lincoln sometimes discounted it, assuring his friends that he was less apprehensive than they about his life. At other time, in gloomier moods, he seemed to think he had little chance of surviving the presidency. There was solace for him in his fatalistic philosophy, though there was little in it to thwart a plotter against his life.

So, to much of the mystery-making about the assassination, a common-sense reply would seem to be something like this: there is comparatively little mystery in the fact that Lincoln finally was shot. The mystery, if any, lies in the fact that he was not assassinated sooner than he was.

3

Nevertheless, the assassination story does have its moot points, its unresolved dilemmas. Were all the accused and convicted conspirators actually guilty? Was Mrs. Mary E. Surratt? Was Dr. Samuel A. Mudd? Did she deserve the gallows, and did he deserve confinement at hard labor on a remote and barren island?

Until his arrest, the well-bred, well-educated Mudd practiced medicine and farmed, in Southern Maryland. Like many of his neighbors he sympathized with the rebellion, at least for a time, but he changed his attitude and in 1864 voted for Lincoln's reelection, or said he did. That November, at his home, he casually met a strikingly handsome and graceful young man with dark eyes, black mustache, and olive skin, who was introduced as the well-known actor John Wilkes Booth. The young man said he was looking for a farm, and Dr. Mudd apparently had land to sell. Booth stayed overnight at the doctor's house.

Booth's talk of real estate was only a subterfuge. Actually, he was hatching plans for a desperate stroke by which to save his beloved Confederacy. He aimed to kidnap the President of the United States and hold him for ransom. The price was to be high. It would include the cessation of hostilities and the recognition of Southern independence.

Through Dr. Mudd, Booth made the acquaintance of John H. Surratt and, through John, his widowed mother. Mrs. Surratt, about forty-five, was personable or plain, according to the conflicting descriptions of her. She appears to have been captivated by the charming Booth, and perhaps she developed romantic daydreams about him, though this cannot be proved. Certain it is she shared his love for the South, his hatred for the North. And she held a pious conviction that the Lord would punish Northerners for their wickedness and pride. She readily fell in with Booth's abduction scheme. He found her a most valuable recruit, for on H Street in Washington she ran a cheap boardinghouse which he could use as headquarters and hide-out.

At the Surratt house from time to time the little band of hot secessionists whom Booth gathered around himself met to plot. These included the muscular Lewis Powell, alias Payne, a former Confederate soldier from Florida; the stupid and shiftless George Atzerodt, a coachman and Confederate spy; the feckless David E. Herold, a youthful druggist's clerk; and Mrs. Surratt and her son. Booth matured his kidnaping plot and outlined the part each was to play. They accumulated the necessary supplies—guns, ammunition, whisky, ropes, and what not—and left them under Mrs. Surratt's care.

Richmond fell and the Confederacy collapsed before Booth got around to his rescue work. His thoughts then turned to vengeance. He decided to murder Lincoln and, for good measure, to have Seward and Johnson murdered also. But it is not clear just when he came to this decision, or how many of his late associates were informed of the new plan. To Atzerodt he assigned the killing of Johnson and to Payne the killing of Seward. To Herold he gave the task of assisting the getaway from Ford's Theater, while he reserved the highest honor for himself. Whether he told Mrs. Surratt of his altered enterprise or allowed her any share in it is not altogether certain.

On Friday, April 14, 1865, she asked one of her boarders, a twenty-three-year-old government employee named Louis J. Weichmann, to drive her the thirteen miles to Surrattsville, in southern Maryland, where she owned a tavern. This she leased to John M. Lloyd. As a tavernkeeper, Lloyd was hardly an ideal choice, since with his prodigious capacity for liquor he must have drunk up most of the profit. In a rented buggy Mrs. Surratt and Weichmann made the trip to Surrattsville and back during the afternoon. For her, it was a fateful journey. What she said en route and at the tavern was, of course, not recorded at the time. She was to hang because of what Weichmann and Lloyd afterward testified about her remarks that day, and because of a lie she told a few days later.

On Monday night the military police descended upon her house, looking for her son. He had fled, but the police came upon other quarry. While they were at Mrs. Surratt's, they answered a knock on the door, to find a bewildered man with a pickax on his shoulder. He explained that he had been hired to do some work for Mrs. Surratt and had come to inquire when he could begin. The police asked her about him. Raising her right hand, as if she were in the witness box, she solemnly declared (according to later testimony): "Before God, I do not know him, never saw him, and never hired him." But she had seen him and did know him. He had been one of the kidnap-plotters who met at her house. He was Powell, or Payne, and he recently had attempted to kill the Secretary of State.

On Friday night, Booth and Herold stopped briefly at the Surrattsville tavern, then rode on through the moonlight. Before dawn, they reached the house of Dr. Mudd. Booth needed a physician to treat his broken leg. Mudd helped Herold bring Booth into the house, then put him on a sofa, slit his left boot to remove it (inside was the name "J. Wilkes"), set the bone, applied an improvised splint, and assisted the cripple upstairs and to bed. After Booth woke in the afternoon, Mudd talked with him, fashioned a homemade crutch, then sent the two riders on their way.

When detectives got to Mudd, he at first denied that he had received or treated a visitor of Booth's description. The doctor's prevarications weakened his case, as Mrs. Surratt's did hers.

At his trial, Dr. Mudd insisted he did not recognize Booth at the time he treated him. "I did not see his face at all," Mudd testified. He said Booth covered his head with a shawl or cloak while on the sofa, turned his face away while being assisted up the stairs, and shaved off his mustache before the afternoon chat. Now, it seems hard to believe that neither Mudd nor his wife remembered so unforgettable a man as Booth, who only a few months previously had been their guest. The judges of the military commission did not believe it. Yet the doctor may have told the truth at his trial, though he had lied to the detectives who first questioned him. Perhaps he had panicked upon learning the identity of his mysterious patient.

Against Mrs. Surratt the most telling witnesses were her boarder Weichmann and her tavernkeeper Lloyd. Weichmann testified that, on the buggy ride to Surrattsville, she had taken along a couple of packages which she said were "things of Booth's." (It was alleged that this was why Booth on his flight paused at the Surrattsville tavern!) Weichmann testified, further, that on the return to Washington she said that the rejoicing in the city soon would be turned to sadness, also that Booth was an instrument of the Almighty to punish the sinful and the proud. And, to cap his testimony, Weichmann recalled hearing things which indicated that Booth had visited the Surratt house an hour before the assassination. The other damning witness, Lloyd, maintained that Mrs. Surratt, while at the tavern, gave instructions to have shooting irons ready in the evening.

Lloyd was an alcoholic and an unreliable witness. Weichmann, himself suspected of complicity, may have made up testimony so as to save his own neck. One of the official reporters for the military commission, after listening to the trial day after day, concluded that Mrs. Surratt was innocent of the assassination plot. And the members of the commission themselves, whether because of mere chivalry or because of lurking doubts, addressed to President Johnson a plea for mercy in her case.

But there was no mercy. On July 7, 1865, as the sun beat down in the Washington prison yard, the widow was hanged along with Powell and Adzerodt and Herold. Then she and they were buried at the foot of the gallows.

Nearly three years later, when President Johnson was impeached, he was formally accused of an assortment of high crimes and misdemeanors, and he was informally accused of other things, including gross cruelty in rejecting the petition of the judges for mercy to Mrs. Surratt. Johnson protested that no such petition ever had been brought to him, and he charged War Secretary Stanton and Judge Advocate General Joseph Holt with deliberately keeping the matter from him.

Before leaving office in 1869, President Johnson pardoned Dr. Mudd, who by then had spent the better part of four years in a military prison on the Dry Tortugas, a Godforsaken islet a hundred miles off the Florida coast.

The doctor's guilt is especially open to question. Most probably he was guilty of nothing more serious than indiscretion in expressing rebel sympathies during the war, and then poor judgment in trying to cover up his visit from a patient who proved to have been the President's assassin. Mudd was unlucky. Had Booth not had the accident with his leg, he surely would not have gone near Mudd's house a second time. The house was some distance off the route Booth had planned for his original kidnaping venture, and it seems unlikely that Mudd was even a party to that earlier plot.

Mrs. Surratt unquestionably was a member, and a willing one, of the abduction conspiracy. But that was not the charge which brought her to the gallows. She was tried for complicity in the assassination. Of this, she probably was innocent. She probably was a victim of the irresponsibility of overimaginative witnesses, and a sacrifice prepared by Stanton to feed the popular hatred of the South.

4

Lincoln, dead, was deified at once. Of course it was to have been expected that his opponents—they were numerous—should promptly desist from calumny, at least for a while, if not to honor the man, then to honor the principle of speaking no ill of the dead. They did more than cease. They turned to praise—almost to worship. Even in the South, though some took malicious satisfaction in the death of Lincoln, many mourned him as no ordinary mortal. In the North the fiery girl orator, America's "Joan of Arc," Anna E. Dickinson, who had been mimicking and making fun of him on the platform, talked on in tones of reverence as if she always had done so. In England the comic magazine *Punch,* more candid than many an American contemporary, confessed the error of its former ways.

To foes of slavery it seemed plain that the murdered Lincoln was a martyr to the crusade for human liberty. "O God, Thou hast Thy martyr for Thy cause, assert that cause until slavery be rooted out from all the borders of our land," the abolitionist Phillips Brooks prayed at a Philadelphia mass meeting. "Our President has fallen in the prime of his energy and usefulness, another martyr to the demon—Slavery," the *Chicago Tribune* declared. "Abraham Lincoln has joined the noble army of Freedom's Martyrs. 'Christ died to make men holy; he died to make men free!' " said *Leslie's Illustrated Weekly.* And many another commentator agreed. Lincoln the Christlike martyr—this concept arose from no single mind. It was everywhere at once, spontaneous, like an obvious truth.

The assassination had occurred on Good Friday, and on the Sunday memorable as "Black Easter" hundreds of preachers found a sermon in the event. Some of them saw more than mere chance in the fact that assassination day was also crucifixion day. "Yes, it was meet that the martyrdon should occur on

Good Friday," a Baptist preacher told his Hartford flock. "It is no blasphemy against the Son of God and the Saviour of men that we declare the fitness of the slaying of the second Father of our Republic on the anniversary of the day on which He was slain. Jesus Christ died for the world, Abraham Lincoln died for his country."

A few ministers of the gospel, dissenting from their fellows, feared that the deification of the late President already had gone too far. "I have frequently seen the statement in our papers," one of the dissenters said, "and I have often heard it remarked, that Lincoln was the idol of the people. I fear this declaration was founded in truth. The people of this country are inclined to hero-worship. There is a tendency in the human heart to exalt the creature to the throne of the Creator and render him that homage which is alone due to God."

Yet, in most pulpits, the idea of partnership between God and Lincoln prevailed. Lincoln in life had been an instrument of the Almighty; he also served God's purposes in death. His removal cleared the way for sterner men to deal with the traitors of the South. Effected as it was, by means of a treacherous plot, the horrible deed stirred the Northern people to the performance of their divinely appointed task. Now, without question, they would support the government in the thoroughgoing policy which was required to make the freedmen absolutely free. Preachers called upon the Lord to scourge the wicked and had little doubt that wickedness was pretty much a sectional monopoly.

Radical politicians paraphrased the pulpit when, among themselves, they talked of Lincoln's elimination as a "godsend" to them. They made the most of the nation's grief. Stanton, their leader in the cabinet, took charge of the funeral train, sending it on a roundabout itinerary with frequent stops to enable the largest possible numbers to look upon the sad-faced, coffined figure. The spectacle was "half circus, half heartbreak." The more the people grieved for Lincoln and the more they raged over his murder, the more they would become convinced that the Radicals were right (and, though this side of it was overlooked, that Lincoln therefore had been largely wrong) in the matter of reconstructing the South. Thus Lincoln, in his coffin and in his grave, was made to further policies he had resisted in the Presidency.

From the outset, Republican politicians worked hard to manufacture a party saint, and they continued to labor at the task for years without end. They succeeded well. Throughout more than three decades, from Grant to McKinley, the name of Lincoln, with its connotations of freedom and union, was one of the party's most valuable vote-getting assets.

Lincoln's saintly reputation, however, is not a mere by-product of politics, not a mere deposit left by the oratory of power seekers pursuing their cynical vocation. As has been seen, his apotheosis was quick, effected overnight and with considerable spontaneity. The politicians encouraged, directed and capitalized upon a movement that was far bigger than they.

The preachers, more than the politicians, gave impetus to the idea of a kind of sainthood in Lincoln, and the preachers continued to keep the idea fresh, while taking care not to overstep the shadowy line between hero worship and blasphemy. The analogy between Lincoln and Christ was not allowed to expire with the passing of the general hysteria his death occasioned. As late as 1922, in an analysis of Lincoln's greatness, the dean of the Yale Divinity School drew a parallel, "with the utmost reverence," between the life of "the greatest man of the Nineteenth Century" and the life of "the Greatest of all the Centuries."

Both were humbly born, the one in a log cabin, the other in the manger of a stable, according to the Yale dean. Their fathers were carpenters. Jesus, in speaking at the Nazareth synagogue, used words that would have fit well in Lincoln's first inaugural when He said that God had sent Him "to bind up the broken-hearted, to preach deliverance to the captives, and to set at liberty them that are bruised." Lincoln, like Jesus, spoke in parables and homely sayings. Each in his own fashion had to contend with the bigoted on the one hand and the morally dull and slow on the other. Of Lincoln's looks it might have been said as it was said of the promised Messiah: "There is no form nor comeliness in him that we should desire him." The characteristic sadness of the wartime President is a reminder of the One who was called "A Man of Sorrows and acquainted with grief."

As if these similarities were not enough, there is that final and conclusive parallel, the one so widely noted on the Black Easter of 1865. Lincoln went to his fatal rendezvous on the anniversary of the day that Christ had gone to the cross. In the nineteenth century as in the first, it seemed to the dean, there could be no remission of sin without shedding of the most precious blood.

Finally, it would seem no mere coincidence that, in the middle of the twentieth century, an author should write a best seller with the title *The Day Lincoln Was Shot* and then produce a sequel with the title *The Day Christ Died.*

Plainly Lincoln's reputation has been shaped not only by the achievements of his life but also by the timing and the circumstances of his death. In a sense, perhaps, he was more fortunate than some of his rivals for historical fame, such as George Washington, who a dozen years after leaving the presidency died prosaically of what would now be called a "strep throat."

5

Lincoln is both man and myth, sixteenth President and national folk hero. Either way, he is superlative.

The historical Lincoln appeals because of the grand if not entirely glorious events in which he had a central part. He appeals because of the subtleties of his personality, the reechoing vibrations of which still have the power to stir a resonance in all but the most unresponsive. He appeals because of the very elements in his history that make him in so many ways unknown, if not unknowable.

Lincoln the legend may be studied as an entity in itself, apart from Lincoln the man, though it is not always possible to separate the unreal from the real. The two images, the legendary and the historical, overlap.

The legendary is to be sought in imaginative literature and in folklore—in poems, plays, novels, anecdotes, and the like. But it also is to be found in ostensibly factual productions, including footnoted biographies and history books.

The legendary Lincoln has grown into a protean god who can assume a shape to please almost any worshiper. He symbolizes democracy and at the same time a more than regal splendor, as a person who from humble birth soared to "a majesty higher than kings." He is an uncommon common man. In the ode of Richard Henry Stoddard (1865) he is

One of the People! Born to be
Their curious epitome
To share yet rise above
Their shifting hate and love.

He embodies the virtues of the middle class, as Ralph Waldo Emerson has said. As others point out, he combines the virtues of all levels of society. He is Old Abe—and a natural gentleman. He is also Honest Abe and a being of superhuman shrewdness and cunning. He is Father Abraham, the wielder of authority, support of the weak. He also is an equal and a friend. "And he was my neighbor, anybody's neighbor," as Witter Bynner writes.

He is a product of his prairie days in the West, of his birth and parentage in the South, of his Yankee ancestry in the East. He belongs to every section, is confined to none, is uniquely the symbol of Americanism: "New birth of our new soil, the first American." He is more than that. Rising beyond the limitations of a national hero, he symbolizes for all the world (the English playwright John Drinkwater declares) the universal values of the spiritual, the moral, the intellectual, the democratic—and the values of Anglo-American unity besides.

A myth is a mirror that reflects much of the inward as well as the outward traits of a people. In our conceptions of the mythical Lincoln, we Americans reveal many of our own aspirations and ideals. Some of the representations are tawdry and tedious. Some are self-interested, designed to sell a product or advance an irrelevant cause. Some are fraudulent. Yet, on the whole, we need not be ashamed of what we have made of Lincoln. In honoring him we honor ourselves.

BIBLIOGRAPHICAL ESSAY

This essay does not mention all the books and articles relevant to the subjects discussed in the preceding chapters, nor does it include all the materials examined in the preparation of those chapters. It does intend to direct the reader to the outstanding expressions of diverse points of view on Lincoln questions. Most of the items listed are available in the larger university and public libraries.

Chapter 1: THE MOST SHUT-MOUTHED MAN

Reprints of all the known photographs of Lincoln, together with quotations describing him and an interesting discussion of his physical appearance, are to be found in Frederick H. Meserve and Carl Sandburg's *The Photographs of Abraham*

Lincoln (1944). Meserve is the outstanding collector of Lincoln photographs, and all students of Lincolniana are profoundly indebted to him. In *Lincoln: A Picture Story of His Life* (1952), Stefan Lorant reproduces the photographs and respectfully differs with Meserve about their number. Meserve classifies 124 different poses. Lorant shows that some of these actually are one and the same picture. He concludes that the number of distinct and separate Lincoln photographs totals only 99.

A number of the Lincoln issues are surveyed by Roy P. Basler in *The Lincoln Legend: A Study in Changing Conceptions* (1935), which emphasizes interpretations in imaginative literature; by James G. Randall in "Moot Points in the Lincoln Story," reprinted in his *Lincoln the Liberal Statesman* (1947); in Paul M. Angle's "The Changing Lincoln," in *The John H. Hauberg Historical Essays,* edited by O. Fritiof Ander (1954); and in David Donald's *Lincoln Reconsidered: Essays on the Civil War Era* (1956).

The Lincoln biographers are appraised and analyzed in a summary treatment by Basler in *The Lincoln Legend* and at considerable length by Benjamin P. Thomas in *Portrait for Posterity: Lincoln and His Biographers* (1947). On William H. Herndon, David Donald's *Lincoln's Herndon* (1948) is indispensable.

The earliest of the classic biographies is Josiah G. Holland's *The Life of Abraham Lincoln* (1866). Ward Hill Lamon used Herndon's materials and a ghost writer, Chauncey F. Black, to produce *The Life of Abraham Lincoln* (1872). In collaboration with Jesse W. Weik, Herndon wrote *Herndon's Lincoln: The True Story of a Great Life* (3 vols., 1889), a second edition of which was published as *Abraham Lincoln: The True Story of a Great Life* (2 vols., 1892). Still another edition, for the general reader the best, with notes and corrections by Paul M. Angle, bears the title *Herndon's Life of Lincoln* (1930). The great work of John G. Nicolay and John Hay, after appearing serially in the *Century Magazine,* was republished as *Abraham*

Lincoln: A History (10 vols., 1890). Ida M. Tarbell, after publishing a series of Lincoln articles in *McClure's Magazine,* wrote *The Early Life of Abraham Lincoln* (1896) and *The Life of Abraham Lincoln* (2 vols., 1900). A couple of widely read one-volume lives are Lord Charnwood's *Abraham Lincoln* (1917) and Nathaniel W. Stephenson's *Lincoln: An Account of His Personal Life, Especially of Its Springs of Action as Revealed and Deepened by the Ordeal of War* (1922). Thomas, in *Portrait for Posterity,* does not deign to discuss the Stephenson book, but Basler gives it considerable attention in *The Lincoln Legend,* concluding: "Sandburg combined with Stephenson may be recognized as the best version of the private Lincoln; Charnwood, perhaps, has the best of the public Lincoln." Basler was referring to Carl Sandburg's *Abraham Lincoln: The Prairie Years* (2 vols., 1926). These volumes were followed by Sandburg's *Abraham Lincoln: The War Years* (4 vols., 1939). Albert J. Beveridge died before he had completed more than his *Abraham Lincoln, 1809–1858* (2 vols., 1928). James G. Randall was near the end of his *Lincoln the President* (4 vols., 1945–1955) when he died. Benjamin P. Thomas's *Abraham Lincoln* (1952) supersedes Charnwood, Stephenson, and all other one-volume Lincoln biographies.

The character of the Robert Todd Lincoln collection of Lincoln correspondence, open to scholars in the Library of Congress since 1947, is indicated, with a generous sampling, by David C. Mearns in *The Lincoln Papers* (2 vols., 1948). Practically all Lincoln's known writings are available in *The Collected Works of Abraham Lincoln,* edited by Roy P. Basler (9 vols., 1953–1956). A judicious selection from these volumes is reprinted in *The Living Lincoln,* edited by Paul M. Angle and Earl S. Miers (1955). Contemporary newspapers accounts of Lincoln are collected in *Lincoln as They Saw Him,* edited by Herbert Mitgang (1956).

In Jay Monaghan's *Lincoln Bibliography, 1839–1939* (1943) the abundance and diversity of a century of writing on Lincoln is set forth. The most usable and valuable guide for the general reader is Paul M. Angle's *A Shelf of Lincoln Books* (1946).

Chapter 2: THE SON, LOVER, HUSBAND

In addition to what is embodied in Herndon's life of Lincoln, Herndon materials on Lincoln's home and love life are to be found in Jesse W. Weik's *The Real Lincoln* (1922) and Emanuel Hertz's *The Hidden Lincoln, from the Letters and Papers of William H. Herndon* (1938). Leonard Swett's recollections are in *Reminiscences of Abraham Lincoln by Distinguished Men of His Time,* edited by Allen T. Rice (1885).

Among the more noteworthy studies of Lincoln's ancestry and parentage are the following: Caroline Hanks Hitchcock, *Nancy Hanks: The Story of Abraham Lincoln's Mother* (1899); William E. Barton, *The Paternity of Abraham Lincoln* (1920); Ida M. Tarbell, *In the Footsteps of the Lincolns* (1924); J. G. De Roulhac Hamilton, "The Many-Sired Lincoln," in the *American Mercury* (1925); Louis A. Warren, *Lincoln's Parentage and Childhood* (1928); and William E. Barton, *The Lineage of Lincoln* (1929).

On Lincoln and women, see Julien Gordon's "Abraham Lincoln in His Relations to Women," in *Cosmopolitan* (1894), and William E. Barton's *The Women Lincoln Loved* (1927). In *Lincoln's Other Mary* (1946) Olive Carruthers relates the Mary Owens affair in fiction closely based on fact, and R. Gerald McMurtry gives a thorough historical account, with the relevant documents, in the same book. Carl Sandburg and Paul M. Angle, in *Mary Lincoln, Wife and Widow* (1932), dispose of the Sarah Rickard case. The Ann Rutledge story is considered by Angle in the *Lincoln Centennial Association Bulletin* (1928), by Jay Monaghan in the *Abraham Lincoln Quarterly* (1944), and by James G. Randall in the second volume of his *Lincoln the President* (1945). Randall, in his very nearly exhaustive study of the matter, concludes that the Rutledge story is in its more colorful features disproved, in its barest essentials unproved. In *The Courtship of Mr. Lincoln* (1957) Ruth

Painter Randall dismisses the idea that Ann and Lincoln ever were in love, but Angle considers it a real possibility.

As early as the 1890s Ida M. Tarbell disproved the Herndon version of the breakup between Lincoln and Mary Todd. A generation later Miss Tarbell noted ruefully that, despite her efforts, the story of Lincoln's failure to appear at his own wedding was still flourishing on every hand. In *Mary Lincoln: Biography of a Marriage* (1953) Ruth Painter Randall gives evidence and argument which should spike the story for all time. Mrs. Randall, attacking Herndon all along the line, presents the most thorough and best documented account of Mrs. Lincoln and the Lincoln marriage. In a sequel, *Lincoln's Sons* (1955), Mrs. Randall treats with sympathy and rare perception the relationship between Lincoln and all his boys, especially Robert. On Lincoln as a father, the little book of reminiscences by Julia Taft Bayne, *Tad Lincoln's Father* (1931), gives a few rewarding insights.

Chapter 3: THE INSTRUMENT OF GOD

"The Genesis of the Lincoln Religious Controversy" is succinctly presented by Albert V. House, Jr., in the *Proceedings of the Middle States Association of History and Social Science Teachers* (1938). It is fully and absorbingly treated in David Donald's *Lincoln's Herndon* (1948). See also Herndon's life of Lincoln.

The case for Lincoln's orthodoxy is made by the following, among others of his contemporaries and acquaintances: Josiah Holland, *Life of Abraham Lincoln* (1865); Noah Brooks, "Personal Recollections of Abraham Lincoln," *Harper's Magazine* (1865), "Personal Reminiscences of Lincoln," *Scribner's Monthly* (1878), and *Washington in Lincoln's Time* (1895); Francis B. Carpenter, *Six Months at the White House with Abraham Lincoln* (1866; republished as *The Inner Life of Abraham Lincoln* in 1883); and James A. Reed, "The Later Life and Religious Sentiments of Abraham Lincoln," *Scribner's Monthly* (1873).

Lincoln's spiritualist acquaintances claim him as a spiritualist in Warren Case's *Forty Years on the Spiritual Rostrum* (1888), and Nettie Colburn Maynard's *Was Lincoln a Spiritualist?* (1891). "Was Lincoln Really a Spiritualist?" Jay Monaghan inquires in the *Journal of the Illinois State Historical Society* (1941); after a careful review of the available evidence, Monaghan concludes that Lincoln was not. Nevertheless, spiritualists continue to raise the question and to answer it affirmatively, as in Paul Miller's "Was Abraham Lincoln a Spiritualist?" in the *Psychic Observer* (1945). Ruth Painter Randall, in *Mary Lincoln* (1953), shows the disillusionment of both the Lincolns with spiritualism. But Harriet M. Shelton, in *Abraham Lincoln Returns* (1957), renews the argument on behalf of the spiritualists and tells of Lincoln's messages to and through her and his materialization in her presence.

Good, inclusive accounts of Lincoln's religion are William E. Barton's *The Soul of Abraham Lincoln* (1920), and Harlan Hoyt Horner's *The Growth of Lincoln's Faith* (1939). A perceptive, brief interpretation is Ruth Painter Randall's "Lincoln's Faith Was Born of Anguish," in the *New York Times Magazine,* February 7, 1954. See also James G. Randall and Richard N. Current's *Lincoln the President: Last Full Measure* (1955).

Chapter 4: THE MAN WHO SAID NO

The literature on the coming of the Civil War is so voluminous as to be almost unmanageable. An invaluable introduction to the whole subject is Thomas J. Pressly's *Americans Interpret Their Civil War* (1954). Also extremely valuable, though briefer, is the essay by Howard K. Beale, "What Historians Have Said about the Causes of the Civil War," in *Theory and Practice in Historical Study,* edited by Merle Curti (1946). The main issues are brilliantly set forth by Kenneth M. Stampp in "What Caused the Civil War?" in *Problems in American History,* edited by Richard W. Leopold and Arthur S. Link (1952; rev. ed., 1957). Certain of the issues are presented at somewhat greater length in *Slavery as a Cause of the Civil War,* edited by Edwin C. Rozwenc (1949), a volume in the Amherst College *Problems in American Civilization* series.

Among the leading "revisionist" interpretations are the following: Charles W. Ramsdell, "The Natural Limits of Slavery Expansion," in the *Mississippi Valley Historical Review* (1929), and "The Changing Interpretation of the Civil War," in the *Journal of Southern History* (1937); George Fort Milton, *The Eve of Conflict: Stephen A. Douglas and the Needless War* (1934); Avery O. Craven, *The Repressible Conflict* (1939) and *The Coming of the Civil War* (1942); James G. Randall, "The Civil War Restudied," in the *Journal of Southern History* (1940), revised and reprinted as "A Blundering Generation," in Randall's *Lincoln the Liberal Statesman* (1947). A revisionist point of view also underlies Randall's masterly synthesis, *The Civil War and Reconstruction* (1937).

The sharpest attacks upon revisionism have come from Bernard DeVoto, in his review essay on the first two volumes of Randall's *Lincoln the President,* in *Harper's Magazine* (1946); Louis M. Hacker, in *Fortune Magazine* (1947); Arthur M. Schlesinger, Jr., "The Causes of the Civil War: A Note on Historical Sentimentalism," in *Partisan Review* (1949), an article putting forth the "log jam" theory; and Peter Geyl (a professor of American history at the University of Utrecht, in the Netherlands), "The American Civil War and the Problem of Inevitability," in *The New England Quarterly* (1951).

Ulrich B. Phillips, in *American Negro Slavery* (1918), argues that slavery on the whole was unprofitable—"It was less a business than a life; it made fewer fortunes than it made men." Kenneth M. Stampp, in *The Peculiar Institution: Slavery in the Ante-Bellum South* (1956), concludes that slaveholders in general made money and that "there was no evidence in 1860 that bondage was a 'decrepit institution tottering toward a decline.'"

James Ford Rhodes, in *History of the United States from . . . 1850 to . . . 1877* (vol. 3, 1895), says "it seems almost certain" that the Crittenden Compromise would have passed if it had had Lincoln's endorsement. Rhodes concludes: "No fact is clearer than that the Republicans in December [1860] defeated the Crittenden compromise; few historic probabilities have better evidence to support them than the one which asserts that the adoption of this measure would have prevented the secession of the cotton states, other than South Carolina, and the beginning of the civil war in 1861." Clinton E. Knox, in "The Possibilities for Compromise in the Senate Committee of Thirteen and the Responsibility for Its Failure," in the *Journal of Negro History* (1932), questions Rhodes's view and argues that a majority of the Republicans on the committee probably would not have approved the compromise even if Lincoln had favored it. David M. Potter, in *Lincoln and His Party in the Secession Crisis* (1942), emphasizes the possibilities for peace with reunion if Lincoln had strengthened the hand of Southern Unionists by coming out for compromise. Kenneth M. Stampp, in *And the War Came: The North and the Secession Crisis, 1860–1861* (1950), doubts the sincerity of many of the compromisers and suggests that, in the circumstances, compromise was a lost cause from the start.

Mary Scrugham's *The Peaceable Americans of 1860–1861* (1921) is valuable because of its extensive quotations from the correspondence of Republican politicians. *Lincoln on the Eve of '61: A Journalist's Story by Henry Villard,* edited by Harold G. and Oswald Garrison Villard (1941), gives a firsthand, day-to-day picture of the president-elect at Springfield and on the way to Washington during the secession winter.

Chapter 5: THE BRINGER OF WAR

Soon after the fall of Fort Sumter, Jefferson Davis described Lincoln's Sumter policy as a "manoeuvre," in a speech quoted in Davis's *The Rise and Fall of the Confederate Government* (2 vols., 1881). Many other contemporary Southerners branded Lincoln as the aggressor and accused him of contriving to put the blame for hostilities upon the South. See, for example:

Edward A. Pollard, *Southern History of the War* (1862); Alexander H. Stephens, *A Constitutional View of the Late War between the States* (2 vols., 1868–1870); and "Papers of Hon. John A. Campbell—1861–1865," in the *Southern Historical Society Papers* (1917). From time to time Southern writers have repeated and elaborated upon the charge, among them Mary Scrugham in *The Peaceable Americans of 1860–1861* (1921), and Archibald Rutledge in "Abraham Lincoln Fights the Battle of Fort Sumter," in the *South Atlantic Quarterly* (1935). The most thorough and best-documented presentation of the Southern case, however, is that of Charles W. Ramsdell in "Lincoln and Fort Sumter," in the *Journal of Southern History* (1937), an essay that has become the *locus classicus* for the maneuver theory. John S. Tilley, in *Lincoln Takes Command* (1941), carries the thesis beyond the bounds of reason and makes glaring errors. E. Merle Coulter, in *The Confederate States of America, 1861–1865* (1950), blames Lincoln for the start of the war but leaves open the question whether Lincoln was a "bungler" or a "cunning villain." David R. Barbee, in "Line of the Blood—Lincoln and the Coming of the War," in the *Tennessee Historical Quarterly* (1957), continues the arraignment of Lincoln.

Not all Lincoln's champions have denied the maneuver charge. Nicolay and Hay, in their ten-volume history, praised the President (vol. IV) for pretty much the same policy that Southern critics condemned him for. By means of the Sumter expedition, dispatched as it was after due delay, Lincoln succeeded in "gaining a coveted 'choice of position' and allowing the rebels to attack and thus consolidate the North. When he finally gave the order that the fleet should sail he was master of the situation . . . master if the rebels hesitated or repented, because they would thereby forfeit their prestige with the South; master if they persisted, for he would then command a united North. . . . No act of his will gain him greater credit than this kindly forbearance and patient wisdom. . . ." Such was the judgment of Nicolay and Hay.

Disagreeing with them as well as with Ramsdell, Randall

presents a cogent case for Lincoln and for his Sumter policy as peaceful in intent. See Randall's "When War Came in 1861," in the *Abraham Lincoln Quarterly* (1940), or essentially the same article rewritten and reprinted as "Lincoln's Sumter Dilemma" in *Lincoln the Liberal Statesman* (1947). See also *Lincoln the President,* vol. I. David M. Potter powerfully reinforces the refutation of the maneuver thesis in his independent study of *Lincoln and His Party in the Secession Crisis* (1942).

Kenneth M. Stampp contends that Lincoln intended and expected neither war nor peace as such but pursued a policy of "calculated risk" to preserve the Union. See Stampp's "Lincoln and the Strategy of Defense in the Crisis of 1861," in the *Journal of Southern History* (1945); also *And the War Came: The North and the Secession Crisis, 1860–1861* (1950). In my opinion, Stampp provides much the most perceptive and convincing account of Lincoln's Sumter policy.

On Lincoln's dealings with Virginia Unionists, *The Secession Movement in Virginia, 1847–1861,* by Henry T. Shanks (1934), is highly informative, though not conclusive. Benjamin P. Thomas, in *Abraham Lincoln* (1952), says: "Whether or not Lincoln promised to abandon Fort Sumter if the Virginia secession convention would adjourn, which has long been a point of controversy, is settled by two letters in the Robert Todd Lincoln Collection." In these two letters, of January 9 and 10, 1863, Lincoln repeated a statement earlier attributed to him, to the effect that he had made such a promise in 1861. These letters, it seems to me, by no means settle the controversy.

My chapter on the Sumter question is based in part on unpublished materials from the Robert Todd Lincoln collection.

Chapter 6: THE MILITARY GENIUS

The English military expert, G. F. R. Henderson, expresses a very low opinion of Lincoln as a war director in *Stonewall Jackson and the American Civil War* (2 vols., 1898). John C. Ropes, in *The Story of the Civil War* (2 vols., 1898–1899), also is critical of Lincoln.

Nicolay and Hay in their *Abraham Lincoln: A History*

praised Lincoln for his management of the war as for everything else. Francis V. Greene, Major General, U. S. Volunteers, wrote "Lincoln as Commander-in-Chief," in *Scribner's Magazine* (1909), to "show the accuracy of Lincoln's judgment on purely military questions." Sir Frederick Maurice, in "Lincoln as a Strategist," in *Forum* (1926), defends Lincoln as a war leader of a democracy rather than a "strategist" in a strictly military sense. See also Maurice's *Statesmen and Soldiers of the Civil War* (1926). The thesis of Colin R. Ballard's *The Military Genius of Abraham Lincoln* (1926; republished, with a preface by Fletcher Pratt, 1952) is sufficiently indicated by the title and is strongly argued in the text. Ballard assumes, however, that Lincoln ceased to be an active "military genius" and turned the whole responsibility over to Grant upon the latter's elevation to supreme command. T. Harry Williams, in *Lincoln and His Generals* (1952), supports a more thoroughgoing thesis than does Ballard. Williams argues that Lincoln was the real genius of the war to the very end. Williams's case for Lincoln is much the most solidly grounded, the most skillfully reasoned, and the most effectively written of all.

In *McClellan's Own Story* (1887), the hapless general presents his vindication in such a way as, unwittingly, to do himself perhaps as much harm as good with posterity. The strongest and best-sustained argument against McClellan is to be found in Peter S. Michie's *General McClellan* (1901). In *Lincoln and the Radicals* (1941) T. Harry Williams depicts in crackling prose the political intrigue to break McClellan down. The most recent and the most solid defense of McClellan is *General George B. McClellan, Shield of the Union* (1957), by Warren W. Hassler, Jr.

Kenneth P. Williams, in *Lincoln Finds a General: A Military Study of the Civil War* (4 vols., 1950—), tears down McClellan in order the more dramatically to build up Grant. Undoubtedly this elaborate and detailed work deserves the acclaim it has received. Nevertheless, the author is so prejudiced against McClellan that he uses any and every possible source as a club to hit the general with. Grant also is exalted in *The Generalship of Ulysses S. Grant* (1929) and *Grant & Lee: A Study in Personality and Generalship* (1933) by J. F. C. Fuller, who is at pains to correct "the conventional point of view that Grant was a butcher and Lee one of the greatest generals the world has ever seen." Grant, while writing with the appearance of modesty, exalts himself in his *Personal Memoirs* (2 vols., 1885–1886).

David Donald's *Lincoln Reconsidered* (1956) contains a stimulating essay on the Napoleonic theory of warfare and its effect upon Civil War strategy.

Chapter 7: THE TENDERHEARTED

Stories of Lincoln's kindheartedness are retold in *Lincoln Talks: A Biography in Anecdote,* edited by Emanuel Hertz (1939). Instances of Lincoln's pardoning proclivities are given at great length in Carl Sandburg's *Abraham Lincoln: The War Years,* vol. IV. The outstanding authority on the Presidential pardon policies as they affected Southerners is Jonathan T. Dorris, author of *Pardon and Amnesty under Lincoln and Johnson: The Restoration of the Confederates to Their Rights and Privileges* (1953). Also relevant and revealing, though its main emphasis is on the role of oaths in the North, is Harold M. Hyman's *Era of the Oath: Northern Loyalty Tests during the Civil War and Reconstruction* (1954). A cynical view of Lincoln's clemency is given by Donn Piatt in *Reminiscences of Abraham Lincoln by Distinguished Men of His Time,* edited by Allen T. Rice (1885).

Two books on Lincoln's interest in weapons are J. O. Buckeridge's *Lincoln's Choice* (1956), and Robert V. Bruce's *Lincoln and the Tools of War* (1956). Buckeridge deals particularly with the Spencer rifle and Lincoln's role in the adoption of that gun. Bruce makes a more inclusive study, giving attention to all kinds of weapons in which Lincoln was interested. I am much indebted to Bruce's work, though he should not be held responsible for my inferences or conclusions.

Chapter 8: THE MASTER POLITICIAN

On Lincoln as a statesman, see Allan Nevins's *The Statesmanship of the Civil War* (1953). On Lincoln as a politician, see Alexander K. McClure's *Abraham Lincoln and Men of War-Times* (1892) and *Lincoln as a Politician* (1916); Harry J. Carman and Reinhard H. Luthin's *Lincoln and the Patronage* (1943); Richard Hofstadter's *The American Political Tradition* (1948); and David Donald's *Lincoln Reconsidered* (1956).

Donald maintains that the central thesis of T. Harry Williams, in *Lincoln and the Radicals* (1941), is untenable. Williams describes a sharp alignment of the Radicals against Lincoln, who was forced to give in to them on major points, who indeed surrendered to them. Donald holds that, until the fight with Johnson over reconstruction, the so-called Radicals were not a coherent, consistent group, nor were all of them hostile to Lincoln.

William B. Hesseltine describes a political victory for the President in *Lincoln and the War Governors* (1948). James G. Randall throws light on Presidential public relations in "The Unpopular Mr. Lincoln," a chapter in *Lincoln the Liberal Statesman* (1947). Indeed, information and insights on Lincoln the politician are scattered throughout Randall's writings.

For the Nicolay-McClure controversy regarding Lincoln's role in the nomination of Johnson for Vice-president, see McClure's *Abraham Lincoln and Men of War-Times,* which has an appendix containing the correspondence between McClure and Nicolay. James F. Glonek, in "Lincoln, Johnson, and the Baltimore Ticket" in the *Abraham Lincoln Quarterly* (1951), "disproves Lincoln's alleged participation in the nomination of Andrew Johnson for Vice President"—at least to the satisfaction of Benjamin P. Thomas, who adopts the Glonek version in his biography of Lincoln. But William F. Zornow, in *Lincoln and the Party Divided* (1954), rejects Glonek's conclusions on this point and agrees in the main with McClure.

On the question of the Lincoln-Frémont-Blair "deal," see the following: *Zachariah Chandler: An Outline Sketch of His Life and Public Services* (1880); Allan Nevins, *Frémont, the West's Greatest Adventurer* (2 vols., 1928, revised as *Frémont, Pathmarker of the West,* 1939); William E. Smith, *The Francis Preston Blair Family in Politics* (2 vols., 1933); Winfred A. Harbison, "Zachariah Chandler's Part in the Reelection of Abraham Lincoln," in the *Mississippi Valley Historical Review* (1935); and Charles R. Wilson, "New Light on the Lincoln-Blair-Frémont 'Bargain' of 1864," in the *American Historical Review* (1936).

Lincoln's efforts to "get right" with Clay and Webster are described by Richard N. Current, "Lincoln and Daniel Webster," in the *Journal of the Illinois State Historical Society* (1955). Lincoln's "politicking" during his career as a congressman may be traced in Beveridge's *Lincoln,* vol. I. A much more thorough and more critical account, which corrects Beveridge at several points, is Donald W. Riddle's *Congressman Abraham Lincoln* (1957).

Don C. Seitz's *Lincoln the Politician* (1931) does not live up to the expectations aroused by its title. But an excellent treatment of Lincoln as a politician, with regard to his nomination in 1860, is provided by William E. Baringer in *Lincoln's Rise to Power* (1937).

Chapter 9: THE FRIEND OF FREEDOM

All the biographers, of course, treat with comparative fullness the subject of Lincoln and slavery. A basic work, by a wartime Illinois congressman who knew the President, and who stressed the antislavery theme in his career, is Isaac N. Arnold's *The History of Abraham Lincoln and the Overthrow of American Slavery* (1866). A later work by Arnold, again emphasizing this theme, is *The Life of Abraham Lincoln* (1885). Another useful work by a contemporary antislavery politician is Henry Wilson's *History of the Rise and Fall of the Slave Power in America* (3 vols., 1872–1877). Probably the best exposition of Lincoln's own, preferred emancipation plan is to be found in the second volume of Randall's *Lincoln the President.*

A recent and forthright statement of the view that Lincoln used his famous proclamation as a dodge to delay actual freedom is presented by Ralph Korngold in *Thaddeus Stevens* (1955). See especially chapter VII, "The Truth about the Emancipation Proclamation." Some contemporary impressions of Lincoln's slow and incomplete conversion to the antislavery cause are recorded in *Reminiscences of Abraham Lincoln,* edited by Allen T. Rice (1885). On Lincoln's relationships with Negroes, see Frederick Douglass's recollections in the Rice volume; Benjamin Quarles's *The Negro in the Civil War* (1953); and Warren A. Beck's "Lincoln and Negro Colonization in Central America," in the *Abraham Lincoln Quarterly* (1950).

James K. Vardaman's views on Lincoln and the Negro are repeated and elaborated in a number of his Senate speeches, two of which have been noted in particular, those of February 6, 1914, and August 16, 1917, in the *Congressional Record.* There is a sketch of Vardaman in the *Dictionary of American Biography,* and there are several contemporary magazine articles concerning him, but no full-length study of the man has yet been published.

Chapter 10: THE PEACEMAKER

On Lincoln's peace-planning his own words, as contained in the *Collected Works,* comprise the best source and one that has been strangely neglected or misread. *The Diary of Gideon Welles* (3 vols., 1911) contains the observations on the matter by Lincoln's sympathetic Secretary of the Navy. Welles retold and elaborated upon his diary materials in "Lincoln and Johnson: Their Plan of Reconstruction and the Resumption of National Authority," which was published in *Galaxy* magazine (1872). An old but still useful study is Charles H. McCarthy's *Lincoln's Plan of Reconstruction* (1901).

For the Hampton Roads conference, the most circumstantial account is that of Alexander H. Stephens in his *War between the States,* vol. II. Stephens's story is confirmed at certain points by John A. Campbell's narrative in the *Southern Historical Society Papers* (1917). Some of the common elements of these two accounts are still more strongly confirmed by a contemporary, informal report of Campbell as recorded in a Confederate official's diary, only recently published: *Inside the Confederate Government: The Diary of Robert Garlick Hill Kean,* edited by Edward Younger (1957). According to Kean's diary, Campbell related, only a few days after the conference at Hampton Roads, that Lincoln had said the slavery question would have to be handled by the courts. Jefferson Davis was not satisfied with his commissioners' official report and "wanted them to add that Lincoln and Seward insisted on abolition." Campbell and his colleagues refused thus to doctor their report.

An important source for the question of the calling of the Virginia Legislature, in addition to the correspondence in the *Collected Works,* is the narrative of John A. Campbell, cited above. William M. Robinson, Jr., in *Justice in Grey: A History of the Judicial System of the Confederate States of America* (1941), renews the charge that Lincoln "broke faith" with the Virginians. A recollection of Lincoln's remarks on the Virginia matter is given in Charles H. Ambler's *Francis H. Pierpont: Union Governor of Virginia and Father of West Virginia* (1937).

The view that Sherman's terms to Johnston were really Lincoln's terms is presented by Sherman himself in the *Memoirs of William T. Sherman* (2 vols., 1875), in which he includes Admiral Porter's narrative. Joseph E. Johnston's *Narrative of Military Operations* (1874) does not quite jibe with Sherman's recollection. Lloyd Lewis, in *Sherman, Fighting Prophet* (1932), restates and elaborates upon Sherman's case, contending that the general refrained from exposing Lincoln's authorship, as long as he did, in order to spare the name of the dead President from the obloquy the Sherman-Johnston convention aroused in the North. Randall and a number of other historians follow the Sherman-Porter-Lewis thesis.

This view is forcefully challenged by Raoul S. Naroll in "Lincoln and the Sherman Peace Fiasco—Another Fable?" in the *Journal of Southern History* (1954). Certainly Naroll makes it difficult to believe that Sherman could have been acting under any *specific* instructions from Lincoln. On the other hand, Naroll overstates his case as a result of his assumption that Lincoln, as of late March 1865, was committed to immediate, complete, irrevocable emancipation—an assumption I question.

Chapter 11: THE MARTYR AND THE MYTH

Otto Eisenschiml, in *Why Was Lincoln Murdered?* (1937), points the finger of suspicion at Stanton. The most readable account of the assassination and its aftermath is Lloyd Lewis's *Myths after Lincoln* (1929). George S. Bryan's *The Great American Myth* (1940), which disagrees with Lewis in some respects, is more detailed at certain points and probably more reliable on the whole.

Roy P. Basler's *The Lincoln Legend* is still the basic work on its subject. See also David Donald's analysis of "The Folklore Lincoln" in *Lincoln Reconsidered*. Much Lincoln mythology is exemplified in Emanuel Hertz's collection of anecdotes, *Lincoln Talks*. Charles R. Brown, in *Lincoln the Greatest Man of the Nineteenth Century* (1922), compares Lincoln and Jesus. For Lincoln in comparison with other American heroes, see Dixon Wecter's *The Hero in America*.

INDEX